Hidden from History

Hidden

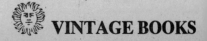

Sheila Rowbotham

from History:
Rediscovering Women in History
From the 17th Century to the Present

A Division of Random House, New York

VINTAGE BOOKS EDITION, February 1976

Library of Congress Cataloging in Publication Data

Rowbotham, Sheila.
Hidden from history.

1. Women—History. 2. Women—Great Britain—History
I. Title.
[HQ1597.R68 1976]   301.41′2′0941   75-28146
ISBN 0-394-71621-3

Contents

List of Abbreviations Used

ILP	East London Federation of the Suffragettes
ELFS	Independent Labour Party
SDF	Social Democratic Federation
WSPU	Socialist Labour Party
SLP	Women's Social and Political Union

Acknowledgements

For ideas, information and help I would like to thank:

Joan Smith whose paper on women's production and the family at the International Socialists' day school on the family in spring 1972 forced me to re-examine my own ideas historically.

Keith Thomas for sending me his articles on the double standard of sexual morality and women in the puritan sects.

Christopher Hill for his talk to the Ruskin History Workshop in 1972 on the family and his talk on 'Sex and Sects' at a meeting of London Workers Education Association history tutors in January 1973.

Hermione Harris, whose interest in spirit possession, prophecy and witchcraft and the relationship of myths and magic to social reality has helped me to think about these subjects.

Edward Thompson for sending me his article on the moral economy of the eighteenth century crowd, Mary Collier's poem and Tom Mann's article on co-operative households and both him and Dorothy Thompson for their criticisms of *Women, Resistance and Revolution* and for letting me read Alf Mattison's letter book and their copies of *Commonweal*.

Gay Webber for lending me her paper on the background to nineteenth century anthropology.

Suzy Fleming for help on the Women's Labour League.

Gloden Dallas for long conversations about socialism and feminism in Leeds before 1914.

Anna Davin for telling me about the conditions of women's work in London in the late nineteenth century.

Florence Exten-Hann and Maurice Hann for giving me their time in remembering socialism, feminism and the trade union movement in Bristol and Southampton in the early 1900s.

Bill Fishman for introducing me to East End anarchism in the same period.

Barbara Winslow for lending me her thesis on Sylvia Pankhurst and the East London Federation of the Suffragettes.

Wilhelmina Schroeder and the Institute of Social History in Amsterdam for allowing me to consult the Sylvia Pankhurst papers.

Sheffield Public Library for letting me use the Carpenter collection.

Julian Harber and Chris Goodey for help on the shop steward movement during World War I.

Jean Gardiner for the use of her unpublished paper on the effect of the 1914-18 war on women's position in the economy.

Stanmore and West Wickham WEA classes for their accounts of their experiences which range from childhood in the 1900s, dilution and war work to feminism and nursery education in the twenties and the situation of women teachers and clerical workers in the depression.

Ralph Bond for information about Lily Webb and the organisation of the unemployed.

Keith Hindel for information about Stella Browne.

Finally for their encouragement, criticism and labour:

Anne Scott and Val Clarke who between them transformed my messy drafts into typewriting.

Richard Kuper, comrade and publisher, who disentangled my anarchical use of tenses and scrupulously made clear his political disagreements while still helping me to say what I wanted to say without imposing his own views.

David Widgery whose patience and sustained interest in my outpourings amazes me and who read the text as it was being written, between snatched Guinnesses when he emerged exhausted from being a house-surgeon and from his own writing and organising.

And to all the women in women's liberation and without, whose action, ideas and organisation while this was being written directed many of the questions I was asking about the past. In particular the Fakenham women who occupied their factory, the London cleaners who went on strike, and the women in the claimants union who in campaigning against the cohabitation clause are confronting patriarchy and the state.

Introduction to the American Edition

Two problems presented themselves with the American edition of *Hidden from History*. American readers are not likely to be familiar with the people and events described, which relate very specifically to England. It is also possible that the manner in which I approach the past may be removed from American experience. While an English reader would not necessarily be aware of how I came to think historically, the contours could fairly easily be filled in. A new introduction for this edition seemed to be needed to overcome this distance. I was unable to draw parallels or delineate differences between your past and ours because I am still woefully ignorant of American history. Perhaps you will do this for yourselves as you read. I have instead tried to give you an indication of how I began to begin by describing the kind of history I had encountered before I wrote *Women, Resistance and Revolution* and *Hidden from History*. Writing them has helped me to think about the problems of writing history in which women are included. The question of a feminist approach to the past has been discussed recently in the women's movement in England, though most of the empirical work being done has not yet appeared. In the second part of this introduction, I have brought together tentatively some of the points raised in those discussions and some problems which I have pondered over in isolation. I hope this will be helpful to anyone concerned with developing a marxist feminist view of history and contribute to your own discussions. Since the ideas here were thought out after *Hidden from History* was written, you may find it more useful to read this after, rather than before, the book itself.

1

My earliest memories are a ragbag of stories and pictures: King Alfred burning the cakes and Robert Bruce of Scotland learning to 'try, try and try again' from a spider making its web after he had been defeated and driven into hiding. Boadicea, with flaming red hair, driving her chariot in battle against the Romans or Queen Elizabeth dancing and rather vainly pretending not to see a foreign courtier watching her from the gallery. Young Queen Victoria comes down the stairs, demure, pure and gracious in her nightdress and shawl to learn that she has succeeded to the throne. It was mainly kings and queens this childhood history; the common people hardly figured at all. There was Nell Gwyn though, the mistress of King Charles II. Her picture was on the jar of a particular brand of marmalade. I found out as much as I could by asking grownups about this beautiful marmalade person with her orange haircap and ringlets and her tray of oranges under her bosom. Behind her picture there was darkness. I imagined dim, winding streets and adventure. The stories the grownups told about her could never illuminate those streets. I think I hankered even then for a history that would enable me to follow her down them, to find out where she came from. But my first conscious memory of having an idea about what history was came as an abrupt blink of excitement. We read a story in school about the Phoenicians discovering how to make purple dye. I realized quite suddenly a world without the obvious, a world in which everyday things were absent, in which nothing was purple.

I was lucky at school between eleven and fourteen for, though history became less exciting, it was never completely killed for me. It was still more than just space on the timetable. Wars and explorations left me cold. I was interested only in how extraordinary events penetrated the lives of ordinary people. I was quite happy to imagine being a peasant in the Peasants' Revolt or the Wars of the Roses, a young lady at Bath in the eighteenth century in a family with Jacobite connections or a revolutionary 'agitator' skirting English villages during the Napoleonic Wars.

As I grew older, history began to run more strictly along examination routes. I took 'O' level exams when I was fifteen and 'A' levels before I left school at seventeen. The first exams consisted of a large number of subjects, but by the second you studied only two or three. I was exceptionally lucky in my history teacher, Olga Wilkinson, who saw exams as hurdles to be surmounted with history growing undeterred over and around them. Her own background and views were closely bound up with the kind of history she felt at home with. She came from a farming family in East Yorkshire, and was a Methodist and a liberal, who disliked enthusiasm and fanaticism and liked baroque architecture and classically tailored clothes.

The history she taught belonged to the present, not to history textbooks. For example, in 1956 she poked fun at Eden for going into Suez as she described Palmerston bringing out gunboats to protect British prestige. The Nation and Empire, hitherto unquestioned and sacred, began to stagger before my eyes. The Union Jack, the Dambusters, Winston Churchill, the Royal Family, Gracie Fields began to crumble and disintegrate. Jimmy Porter in John Osborne's play *Look Back in Anger* was to give them their final prod. I doubt if Olga realized at the time how subversive one historical irony could be. Now it seems almost inconceivable how outrageous it still was to someone from a conservative, small business background like mine simply to laugh at patriotic trappings and symbols.

The school I was at was Methodist and we were exposed to the popular history of Methodism, Wesley's life and the splits with the Primitives. Through Olga, a sociological dimension to the history of religion opened up. It was not simply a matter of God, faith, grace and redemption. The church and the various doctrinal strands and their historical fortunes emerged as part of the more general development of society.

She also had a radical view of the kinds of sources we could learn to use. She put us to work in the country archives at Beverly with enclosure maps and accounts of local misdemeanours; she taught us to see buildings as historical records, steering us around Norman churches and stately homes and landscape gardening as well as into deserted villages and Dominican sewers. I always wanted to be more adept at this digging up kind of history. I envy people now who can make sense of the countryside, who can spot ridge and furrow and the structure and shift of settlement. I was rather dim and slow at it, however much I tried. But at least I glimpsed that this tramping and plodding in Army Surplus anorak or late 1950s plastic mac over field and moor in the English rain was part of the historical craft. It was an unusual glimpse at the time and by no means the normal stuff of historical schoolteaching.

My rebellion came at first sporadically and only gradually acquired coherence. Olga Wilkinson's beginnings were very different from mine. She had been reared in the reaction against the first generation of radical English social and economic historians like Tawney and the Hammonds. It was not the task of the historian to moralize or to judge. Red lines scarred my essays in a continuing war against sentimentalism and purple passages. I discovered *Religion and the Rise of Capitalism* when I was about seventeen and devoured it enthusiastically to Olga's resigned dismay. But her inoculation against the Hammonds was more successful. Several years later when I finally came to read *The Village Labourer* I felt that she had cheated me of good history by mocking their indignation against enclosure. She would have been the first to tease me for accepting her views so unquestioningly, and it is true that they could not have had such an effect if they were not confirmed elsewhere. In her insistence against judgement and sentiment she reflected assumptions which were very much part of the idiom of much economic and social history in the 1950s. It was considered naïve to be critical of the actions of people in the past, though significantly this was always seen as applying to the upholders of the status quo, not those who were trying to change things. One consequence was that poverty and suffering appeared inevitable if vaguely regrettable.

I went to Oxford, which little social and economic history seemed to have reached even by 1961. It was very bewildering. We had to read Gibbon, Macaulay, de Tocqueville and Bede the first term, after which we launched into the Romans and Anglo-Saxons and European diplomatic intrigue in the nineteenth century. The syllabus changes slowly at Oxford, and I suppose we were still being prepared to serve in the early twentieth-century Indian Civil Service or the foreign office, or perhaps for nothing in particular. So far as I know, people who go to Oxford still suffer under this bizarre syllabus.

I was fortunate, however, to bump into bits of history along the way which did interest me. The education which has been manufactured to prepare such an imaginative ruling class as the British is sufficiently oiled to allow for odd accidents. I thrived on these accidents. There was, for instance, quite a shuffling of tutors as we were farmed out to other colleges for tutorials as well as within our own. What you were taught for your weekly essays thus depended on the luck of the draw and the draw varied. Glimmers of light came through in my second year with the Peasants' Revolt, religious heresy and the Puritans.

I sought my own history too as I met people who were socialists who argued with me. I tried to find my bearings by reading about socialist ideas and movements in the past, mainly in nineteenth-century Europe. I learned how different ideas had arisen, the crosscurrents of argument, schisms and heresy. I entered an echo chamber of contested orthodoxies and tragic conflicts. Familiar and fascinating stuff for someone reared on biblical criticism and Wesley's theological doctrines, or the proud and bitter feuding between orthodox Methodism and the dwindling remnants of the Primitive persuasion.

When I read Marx, I found something more than descriptions of arguments. The arguments sprang from the real world. The early political economists presented their vision of the world as it was then and claimed that this was as it must always be. But even within their growing world its impatient opposite was also developing in the creation of the working class and the assertion of labour as a source of value. There was such a density of detail combined with great sweeps of contempt, a playful irony and the continuing slow accumulation of the structure of Marx's theory. I was interested in the significance he gave to class conflict and the way in which he exposed the arrogant and preposterous swindle which had been perpetrated against the sellers of labour power—to sell your whole capacity to make and then be bound by religion, law and morality to be grateful and respectful to Mr. Moneybags and his henchmen.

His view of history was inseparable from his view of the present. It was possible because of Marx to begin to see a pattern behind the way I myself had come to see the past and the present. He seemed to share my lack of interest in purely political events like Lord North's period in office or the diplomatic manoeuvring of Austria and Prussia.

The difficulty with Marx was one of scale. On one side you had his kind of history, like a gigantic organ with all the stops out; on the other you had your weekly essays, tiny little things dealing with short periods in detail. It was like trying to stop the organ for a minute to find out the right moment in its accumulative crescendos to ping the triangle in the school band.

I often found myself puzzling over some controversy which appeared to have originated many issues back in the *Economic History Review*. The arguments presented themselves in their own chronology. Each article had to be remembered intact. It took me years to know what so-and-so was saying or why. The sources of these controversies were mysterious. Quite often they seemed to have originated in something Marx had said or that someone had decided he had said somewhere. But since in those days it was not the thing to put Marx in your footnotes even if he had started the whole thing off in the first place, the terms of argument were not always explicit. The trouble was that many more historians seemed to have been produced who were eager to show you how wrong Marx was. The ones who agreed with him were sparse indeed. You were left in your half week or so with a mountain of empirical evidence showing how this or that could or could not be said. Capitalism had always existed or it had never existed at all; things always went from bad to worse or progress was built-in so why waste time fretting about a few handloom weavers drinking nettle soup in hard times? E. H. Carr's *What Is History?* was the only criticism I came across in the early 1960s contesting these views. They were never presented as methods of looking at history explicitly, but as objective, unbiased common sense.

It was very difficult to study history which was not about Parliament and the growth of the treasury or about cabinets, treaties and coalitions, partly because we barely questioned how we should be taught and partly because a different kind of history was still in the making. It was before the days of student militancy —all sheepish and meek we were, no alternative syllabuses or shares in decision-making for us. We had to make our own individual solutions, so that any questioning could evaporate into guilt and an overwhelming sense of personal inadequacy. This was particularly true of us women, who were a tiny minority in a male stronghold and subtly taught our place by being told how privileged we were to be there at all.

Much labour history has accepted a strictly political definition of what history is about too, merely substituting working-class leaders and institutions for those of the dominant class. This bias towards the people at the centre or the history of organisations has affected both social-democratic historians, who look towards the creation of working-class institutions as part of the gradual accretion of reforms, and marxist historians, who have studied the party as representing the most conscious among the working class. It is reinforced by the accessibility of sources. Formal organisations leave records. This kind of source produces a particular kind of history, which excludes people who have not been prominent in formal labour organisation. From this point of view women's role has invariably been supportive and secondary. While consciousness is seen in a pyramid of levels, women are always seen as on the bottom and in need of being hitched up.

Another kind of history was shaping, though, and I learned it awkwardly, half from books and half from people I met. In the early sixties, ideas from France about the kinds of sources which could be used and a different type of historical question were having a belated influence in England. Historians of the 1789 Revolution and of the later revolutions in France were enquiring about the composition of the revolutionary crowd, the organisation of the sans-culottes, the movement of population, the incidence of cholera and revolt. This kind of history appeared for me in the person of the historian of the revolutionary army, Richard Cobb. One of my tutors sent me off to him for tutorials. Strange and exciting events they were as he leapt over the sofa saying, 'The Spanish people will rise again', with me wondering momentarily quite how he was going to land. Richard Cobb hunted down food hoarders and police informers gleefully, sided with risings of the left and right, arbitrarily sauntered down a prostitute's beat or probed a sans-culotte's anti-Semitism or dislike of homosexuals. About the same time a few historians working on the British labour movement were moving away from the strictly political history of labour and the history of official institutions. They were beginning to explore the relation between religious heresy and dissent and early political protest. They wrote about class consciousness as it was expressed in action and in the records of local meetings, or as it was reported by informers. They described not inevitable and impersonal forces, but real men and women acting in specific situations.

Their appearance was not accidental, though at the time it appeared so to me. Edward Thompson's *The Making of the English Working Class* was the most massive single work and exerted a tremendous influence, not only in its particular theme, but in making the undergrowth of consciousness and organisation a subject for enquiry. Both Edward and Dorothy Thompson's history, like that of other marxist historians of their generation, was nurtured by the Communist Party historians group. This combined in their case with contact with their students in the Workers Education Association and with the radical political tradition of the area round Halifax in the West Riding of Yorkshire, where they lived in the 1950s and early 1960s.

The existence of historical work which was using marxist ideas in a non-dogmatic fashion meant that there was a context in which to learn an alternative kind of history. These historians formed a very loose grouping who by the early sixties were more likely to be without than within the Communist Party and to have political roots in the New Left. The meetings of the Labour History Society were a means of communicating the work which was being done. As the decade rolled on the Society became increasingly august and the study of labour history itself began to be respectable. In the late sixties more informal gatherings at Ruskin College, a trade union college in Oxford, where worker students read papers which related to their own lives and work experience, became important to younger people who had been radicalised by the student movement and the Vietnam Solidarity movement and were searching for some way of locating their own politics. The Ruskin History

Workshops grew larger and larger, becoming half political gathering, half celebration—hundreds packed on the cold floor with a diet of bread and cheese and a sleeping bag at night.

But although implicit within this history, which in various ways focused on work and community struggles, popular action and the submerged consciousness of people without power, was the possibility of studying the position and action of women, the female historical experience was still only glanced at.

Interest in women's position in the past has grown as women's liberation has grown, partly because women within the movement have started to study women in the past and partly because the existence of a new feminist movement has stimulated enquiry among other historians. When the women's movement began in Britain in 1969 it was so small and there was so much to be done that interest in the detailed study of the past was necessarily limited to just a few of us, though the idea of calling the first conference, which was held a Oxford in February 1970, came out of a meeting of women at one of the Ruskin History Workshops and included two papers on women and history.[1]

When I turned to women's past I learned the extent to which I had been unconscious of how the history I had studied before had been so neglectful of women. We were always led to believe that women were not around because they had done so little. But the more I read, the more I discovered how much women had in fact done. Because I was a socialist I started by trying to find out what role women had played in socialist movements in the past, and *Women, Resistance and Revolution* came out of this. I wanted particularly to learn whether women had questioned their role as women as well as trying to make a new society. It was difficult to know where to start. Alice Clark's *The Working Life of Women in the Seventeenth Century*, Edith Thomas' *The Women Incendiaries* and Wilhelm Reich's *The Sexual Revolution* and the references to Alexandra Kollontai which I followed up from Reich's book were invaluable. They provided starting points which gave me some inkling of the vastness of the silence about women in the past. As I discovered more, I became more and more excited. It was apparent that women had used forms of opposition which did not come within a strictly political definition —hence the word 'Resistance' in the title. Yet even by 1972–1973, when I wrote *Hidden from History*, I was unable to follow up these less political forms of resistance because I was still writing a general study based mainly on secondary sources.

1 One of these has been published: Jo O'Brien, *Women's Liberation in Labour History*, Spokesman Pamphlet no 24, Nottingham nd.

Since *Hidden from History* was published, there have been several meetings of people studying women in the past in Britain and it is evident that the rediscovery of our history is an essential aspect of the creation of a feminist critique of male culture. I think that in America you are ahead of us in terms of the amount of work done, circulated and published. But I do not think that the question of a feminist approach to the past is an easy one or that any of us has produced an adequate definition of what such an approach would be.

I know that my own urgency towards the past is not an isolated eccentricity, but is shared by other women in Britain and in the women's movement internationally. We are privileged to be able to think, write and communicate in such a context, which, though limited, is still *there*.

Some of our difficulties come from the newness and closeness of the subject of women in the past. We are, after all, young as a political movement, scarcely born as a critique of the whole of existing male culture. Our existence is flimsy. There is the danger that by overdefining a tenuous reality you produce dogma. An existing culture, asserting.the world as it is, is rich in ambiguity, fertile in contradictions, moist, malleable, elastic. A critical culture, which springs from people without control in the world, is, on the contrary, fragile, brittle, taut with the effort which has gone into its creation. There is the closeness, too, between search and subject. The search for what happened is out there, but we are the subject in here. We ourselves are there even as we look at them, the others, in the past.

There is a tension between any conscious radical commitment to the creation of new social relations and the writing of the history of an oppressed group. It is possible for such a political commitment merely to force history into its own mould, to manufacture a past to fit its own present. The idea that the writing of history is a utilitarian process, that its only purpose is to produce neatly capsulated lessons for political dilemmas in the present, is destructive of anything more than exhortation. The opposing reaction to this tension is to say that we should bury our heads in documents and just do more work. It is important to do more work and particularly important to do more work about women in the past because our knowledge is so meagre. But it is an illusion that the collection of facts alone will change the orientation of our views of the past, for there is no such thing as an empirical study which does not come from a particular vision of the world. 'Unbiased' history simply makes no declaration of its bias, which is deeply rooted in existing society, reflecting the views of the people of influence. A radical critical history has to be clear about the distinctness of the assumptions with which it begins. It does not imply a dismissal of the craft skills of historical work. It does not know all the answers. It requires a continuing movement between conscious criticism and evidence, a living relationship between questions coming from a radical political movement and the discovery of aspects of the past which would have been ignored within the dominant framework.

Feminism—the assertion of the need to improve the position of women—has had various political strands appearing historically in different forms. Just as there are several feminisms there are several feminist approaches to history, which it would be interesting to try to unravel, for this would show the impact of political ideas on the writing of women's history. In the feminist movement of the late nineteenth century, for instance, there was a popular myth of the universal, total subjugation of women in the past. This undifferentiated view of women as completely weak and helpless was a projection backwards of the contemporary lot of middle-class women. It was not recognised that women could be aggressive and take part in production even though they were subordinate to men. As the study of economic history developed, the participation of women in the guilds and their part in agricultural production in precapitalist society were described by the first generation of economic and social historians, who were themselves challenging the scope of history.

A great deal of what was accepted then and now as history excludes most people. It has really been only since the working class became a force to be reckoned with in capitalism that the confines of this narrow definition of history could be challenged. In the nineteenth century, Carlyle criticised history which was only about kings and queens. He wanted a history of people who had made a name for themselves—Let us now praise famous men. In 1924, Eileen Power remarked in *Medieval People* that he should have gone further:

> 'He did not care to probe the obscure lives and activities of the great mass of humanity upon whose slow toil was built up the prosperity of the world, and who were the hidden foundations of the political and constitutional edifice reared by the famous men he praised. To speak of ordinary people would have been beneath the dignity of history.'[2]

For Eileen Power, the history of ordinary people included women along with men. The work she and other historians did was important in showing that women were not always excluded from labour as the women of the Victorian middle class were.

2   London 1924, p 1. For the influence of Marx on the development of social and economic history, see E. J. Hobsbawm, 'Karl Marx's Contribution to Historiography' in Robin Blackburn, ed., *Ideology in Social Science*, New York 1973.

The feminist movement in the early part of this century thus coincided with a period of substantial historical questioning. In the case of Alice Clark's *The Working Life of Women in the Seventeenth Century*, published in 1919, this resulted in an examination of the nature of women's productive activity during he period when the capitalist division of labour was just beginning. Alice Clark was a Fabian socialist who begins her work with an admission of feminist partiality.

> 'It is perhaps impossible to divest historical enquiry from all personal bias, but in this case the bias has simply consisted in a conviction that the conditions under which the obscure mass of women live and fulfil their duties as human beings have a vital influence upon the destinies of the human race.'[3]

Among the people she thanked was the feminist Olive Schreiner and her book *Woman and Labour,* which Alice Clark says 'first drew the attention of many workers in the emancipation of women to the difference between reality and the commonly received generalisations as to woman's productive capacity'.[4]

By enquiring into the effect of capitalism upon the economic position of women, Alice Clark questioned women's relationship to the state in capitalist society, 'which regards the purpose of life solely from the male standpoint'.[5] Though she does not seem to have been able to pursue this idea in her writing of history, her book does show very clearly how the developing division of labour in capitalism removed the productive role of women and fragmented productive activity. She contrasts the lot of the woman in family industry with that of the wage-earning poor. Perhaps her assumption that family industry was so widespread in the late Middle Ages exaggerates, for it is possible that in certain regions the number of wage-earning poor people was larger than has been thought. It was not a straightforward transition from family industry to landless labourer, but greatly modified by the region and type of agriculture. But the central point remains—a challenge to the view that women had been universally subordinated without seeing that subordination can assume different forms depending upon how particular societies organise production.

Mary Beard, an American, is another example of a historian whose interest in women's position in the past made her question the emphasis implied by some histories that women had been silent and suppressed before the struggle for the vote in the nineteenth century. Her *Woman as a Force in History* is, she says, a 'study of the tradition that women were members of a subject sex throughout

---

3   London 1968 (first edition 1919), Preface.
4   *ibid.*
5   *ibid,* p 308.

history'.[6] She locates the source of this tradition in diverse places, including the feminist movement influenced by Mill and the socialists who followed Bebel, though she adds that the marxist socialists did qualify this by accepting the idea of mother right. Because she is studying a 'tradition', she darts around the centuries, from ancient times to German fascism and American women in the Second World War. Her case that women have always been a force in history is confused by the fact that she does not distinguish between women of different classes. She approaches medieval history through the history of law, literary evidence, education and organisation of the guilds. But these sources mainly throw light on the lives of upper-class women or those of a middling status. Nor does she disentangle the differing nature of women's influence. Economic activity and education are not synonymous with political power. Thus, while it is true that women have been a force in history and that the notion of universal passivity and subordination is ahistorical, there are also differences between classes, and in the particular cultural shape of subordination.

Both Alice Clark and Mary Beard, though, provide interesting examples of how contemporary assumptions which came out of political movements, in this case feminism, can contribute towards a history which asks large questions.

The modern women's movement has produced an immense popular enthusiasm about women's history as part of the challenge to masculine cultural hegemony. History is part of the way in which we have been defined by men. There are two channels in the course of this feminist history at the moment. One is to identify romantically with women in the past. The strength of this impulse is that it is defiantly popular. It refuses to address itself to a limited audience. Its enthusiasm is important because it insists that history belongs to an oppressed group and is an essential aspect in the cultural pride of that group, just as the working-class and black movements celebrated their past and as gay people are beginning to discover themselves. The dangers in this identification are that we become impatient with the time it takes to do careful research and substitute present assumptions for the unravelling of what happened. The other channel consists in the quiet burrowing, yet to see the light of day, of innumerable lonely women making meaning of remote academic credentials by studying women in the past. Here the perils are reversed. The pursuit of the past can become a substitute for trying to change the present. It can become divorced from its original radical impulse and we might find ourselves creating just another academic subject. We need somehow to avoid

6   New York 1971 (first edition 1946), Preface.

letting this divergence become too extreme. We need to combine popular enthusiasm and directness of style with painstaking research, even though present-day society, with its pressures of work, money and political activity, makes it difficult for one person to supply both.

Within both channels of this new feminist history there are the implicit assumptions that women's history will be done by women and be about women. I think that these assumptions are disorienting and can actually restrict the radical implications of a feminist approach to the past when they are presented as unchanging principles. I think that we should distinguish between a principled definition of feminist history in these terms and a tactical choice we make at this point. There are tactical reasons for demanding that at particular times women should be employed rather than men as teachers of history because we have been so discriminated against. This is different, though, from a general principled commitment to women writing our own history. This commitment can misfire because it is possible to find women who are anti-feminists and because it restricts human consciousness to biology in a deterministic manner, forgetting that a man writing history can be transformed by the existence of a feminist movement. The criticism of a male historian who does not inform his history by an understanding of the questions raised by the women's movement would be the same as the insistence that historians who are middle-class must learn from the action of workers if they are to interpret the history of the working class. Equally, simply studying women in the past does not necessarily question the whole scope of history. It could mean that we study exceptional women or that we study only the political aspects of the women's movement in the past or that we simply stick women onto the study of the labour movement. There is also a chance, if we interpret feminist history in this way, that we pursue an abstract category called 'Woman' through history and isolate women from social relations in the family and at work.

But just as we need tactically to insist in certain cases that a woman rather than a man be set to work, we need to focus particularly now upon the role of women in the past because of the overwhelming neglect and ignorance which exists. The manner in which we go about these immediate and tactical moves, though, is crucial to their outcome. In saying that a woman should be employed to teach women's history we also have to question the mode of teaching, not try to create a female equivalent to a professional elite whose academic knowledge has no relation to the social needs of most people. Similarly, in saying that we choose to study woman's past we should not perpetuate a notion of

'Woman' as an isolated, frozen category, an unchanging historical entity. Instead, we should begin to transform our approach to the past by starting from the different material conditions of women, recognising that these have not been the same under all systems of production and have varied also according to class. The social relations of women have altered over time, just like those of men, but most history looks at women through the situation of men. A primary focussing on women is tactically necessary in order to disentangle ourselves from this all-pervading identification of the norm with the specific predicament of men. A conscious feminist commitment, thus, is crucial if this identification is to be challenged.

But feminism alone is not enough to encompass theoretically the forms of oppression women have shared with men. Class exploitation and the cultural indignities which have accompanied it have affected both men and women in the working class. The fate of all women has not been the same. If we start from the material circumstances of women's lives and try to work out how they maintained and reproduced the means of continuing life, how they saw themselves and the world, how they resisted or acquiesced in their fate, how the movements of women differed from those of men, it does not mean that we can ignore class or race. Nor does it mean that we do not look at the social relations between men and women. But it does mean that our understanding of men as well as women in the past gains a new perspective. If we are to begin to integrate the study of the social relations of men and women we need this conscious commitment to what is specific and what is shared. At present we not only lack such a perspective, we barely know what has happened in the lives of the great mass of women.

What follow are suggestions of some ways of looking and means we could use as starting points for enquiry. None of these is trouble-free, they all have their snags. By using them the snags will become more evident and we can change or discard them.

Marx's thinking about history and his understanding of the significance of class conflict as a crucial factor in historical transformation have exerted a continuing influence on all people who have pitted their humiliation in the world as it is against the hope of the world as it could be. His particular comments about what happened in the past have provoked voluminous controversy among historians. These are worth studying and unravelling, but more immediately relevant are where he thought historical enquiry should begin and how he saw it proceeding. In *The German Ideology* in the 1840s, he says that it starts with 'the real individuals, their activity and the material conditions under which they live, both those which they find already existing and those produced by their activity'.[7]

His view of history was inseparable from his view of human social existence:

'. . . men must be in a position to live in order to make "history". But life involves before everything else eating and drinking, a habitation, clothing and many other things. The first historical act is thus the production of the means to satisfy these needs, the production of material life itself.'[8]

The production of needs is a social action, their satisfaction making new needs possible. This production of life, both of one's own labour and of new life through procreation, decides how production is organised and how men and women are bound to one another within a system of production. History is, thus, the study of this everyday human activity:

'In each stage . . . there is . . . a sum of productive forces, a historically created relation of individuals to nature and to one another, which is handed down to each generation from its predecessor; a mass of productive forces, capital funds and conditions which on the one hand is indeed modified by the new generation, but also on the other prescribes for it its condition of life and gives it a definite development, a special character. It shows that circumstances make men just as much as men make circumstances.'[9]

Here the emphasis is on objective social change, but he also believed that the action of human beings changed the course of history. In *Capital*, for instance, he said that force was the midwife of every new society pregnant with a new one. Men and women make history, but not always in conditions which are under their control. There is a continual tension within his thinking about history between material circumstances and the action of human

7   Karl Marx and Frederick Engels, *The German Ideology*, London 1965, vol 1, p 31.
8   *ibid*, p 39.
9   *ibid*, pp 50–51.

beings. The emphasis varied depending on the problem he was considering and the purpose for which he was writing. Thus, in 'The Communist Manifesto' in 1848 he stresses the action of the working class and in his 'Preface to a Contribution to the Critique of Political Economy' in 1859 he says that the dissolution of a social order can only occur when all the productive forces which can be contained within it have been developed.

He did not see human consciousness as removed from this material movement of society. Historical consciousness arises from the totality of the social relations of production. The dominant class creates the world in its image. It owns and controls language and culture as well as the means of material production. The struggle of the oppressed is thus material and ideological. Material existence, the particular mode of production and the relations between human beings are inseparable from specific visions of the world.

Marx's view of history opens up the possibility of including the mass of women within its scope and provides a means of understanding how women have only sporadically been able to challenge the dominance of men in all culture. Women's subordination is not only material but is expressed in a subordinated consciousness. But the specific oppression of women remains implicit. Marx was primarily concerned with the social consequences of class antagonism, not conflict between men and women. By the time he wrote *Capital* he concentrated on the exploitation and alienation of the worker who sells his or her capacity to labour to the owner of capital, who gives only part back in the form of wages. Though this covers the situation of the working-class woman as a wage earner, it does not explore the position of the woman working in the family, the sexual relations between men and women, women and women and men and men or our relationship to our bodies. In *Capital* Marx takes for granted the necessity of women's labour in maintaining and reproducing wage earners, but he does not examine this in any detail or discuss its implications for women's consciousness.[10]

Although there have been repeated attempts to relate class exploitation and alienation as Marx described them to other aspects of human life and experience and although it is apparent that we can have only a partial view even of class consciousness if we neglect childhood, these questions remain in considerable confusion and obscurity. Marxism has only sporadically illuminated those areas of women's activity which are outside the point of production

10   These arguments are developed in Jean Gardiner, *Political Economy of Female Labour in Capitalist Society*, paper delivered at the British Sociological Association Conference, Aberdeen 1974, unpublished.

and only indirectly linked to class-conscious organising. Consequently, marxists have shared the neglect of other historians of sexuality, maternity, production and reproduction in the household and the family.

While some social historians have very recently begun to examine these aspects of life, they have been for a considerable time integral to the subject matter of studies of precapitalist societies, perhaps because the separation of these human activities from politics and production is less pronounced than in capitalism and because the anthropologist does not look towards written records. Some of the questions an anthropologist would ask are obviously relevant to the study of the position of women in the past. For instance, what do beliefs and practises of witchcraft or the ritual pollution of menstruating, pregnant or nursing mothers or ideas about the mystical strength of women, the voracious ferocity of the vagina, reveal about men's view of women and the social relations between men and women in precapitalist societies?

Anthropology, however, is not neutral or ahistorical. It bears the marks of its Western colonial origins. It developed as a subject which assumed the superiority of Western capitalism. Even when this was challenged, it remained a means of understanding and thus controlling the colonised. Also, because the oppression of women is not just a product of capitalism, the societies studied are themselves male-dominated. It requires a specifically feminist commitment to uncover this, for much of the work has been done by men and seen through their eyes.[11]

It has been difficult to make a marxist critique of this Western capitalist orientation because marxism itself was so much a product of nineteenth-century capitalism and because in its subsequent development it tended to remain isolated from non-marxist empirical work in anthropology. Marxism has been stunted in the areas in which anthropology has grown and developed. Marx's preoccupation in *Capital* is with capitalist society, a society in which labour power is sold to the owner of capital as a commodity. He is only peripherally interested in other forms of production within capitalism, such as housework, and in precapitalism. Subsequently, marxists tended to concentrate on the wages system. This orientation was reinforced by a schematic interpretation of marxism which took Marx's analysis of capitalism as providing generalisations which could be applied willy-nilly to every form of society, projecting laws of development specific to capitalism backwards. It also contributed to a dogmatic isolation in anthropology. Marxist

11   See Michelle Zimbalist, Rosaldo and Louise Lamphere, eds., *Woman, Culture and Society*, Stanford 1974.

anthropology for so long meant a fundamentalist faith in Engels' categories about the evolution of primitive society in *Origin of the Family*[12] that marxists have only recently begun to engage critically with the main currents in anthropology and to question the assumptions that anthropologists should bring to a society. Instead of asking how does it function, how does it continue, or only looking at the ideas of the dominant people in a community, they have also begun to look at the conflicting views of people who are not responsible for maintaining the status quo. The impulse behind this challenge has been the disintegration effected by imperialism and the rebirth of non-dogmatic marxism. The penetration of capital has made a static, functional approach unable to explain social changes, whereas marxism provides a means of understanding transformation and its effects on people's consciousness. It has been Marx's writing in the *Grundrisse* on precapitalist economic formations, not Engels', which have influenced this anthropology.[13]

Anthropologists have devised ways of understanding consciousness which is not explicitly stated through political organising. This has a particular relevance to women, for our consciousness has dwelt hidden in a twilight world. The notion that people who do not have a coherent intellectual philosophy can still have a picture of the world has begun also to influence historians working on the sixteenth and seventeenth centuries. Their work opens up new ways of looking at women in the past. Lawrence Stone, for instance, in a review of recent studies of witchcraft including Keith Thomas' *Religion and the Decline of Magic* and Alan McFarlanes' *Witchcraft in Tudor and Stuart England*, suggests that magic and witchcraft can be seen as part of an underground view of the world held by the common people. He sees this search for *'mentalités collectives'* as an essential part of social history.[14]

Similarly, in *The World Turned Upside Down*, Christopher Hill describes the extreme democratic views of the sects during the English Civil War. He also discovered from writing this book that these ideas could be traced back into the Middle Ages, a continuing subversive vision of how things should be.[15]

By seeking the kind of clues and signs of consciousness which anthropologists have struggled to decode, it is possible to find out

12 For the historical background of Engels' views, see Joan Bamberger, 'The Myth of Matriarchy' in *ibid*. See also chapter 13, 'Socialism, the Family and Sexuality', below.

13 For a more detailed statement of these currents in anthropology, see Raymond Firth, 'The Sceptical Anthropologist, Social Anthropology and Marxist views of Society', *Proceedings of the British Academy*, vol LVIII.

14 'The Disenchantment of the World', *New York Review of Books* 2 (1971)

15 Christopher Hill and Lawrence Stone, *The Listener*, October 4, 1973.

about women's resistance and about relations between the sexes. For instance, witchcraft and magic provide a means of understanding how people conceived their relationship to nature. They indicate how far they felt they could placate or control the external world. Similarly, various forms of community ritual and folk beliefs were a way of regulating social and sexual relations and of defusing conflicts.

The problem of uncovering this hidden experience can be approached in more recent periods simply by talking to older people. It is true that there is always the problem that time passing will affect how people remember, but this is also a disadvantage with written sources like evidence to Royal or other commissions of enquiry or biographies. Oral history could be an important means of discovering what women thought and felt in the immediate past. It could also restore aspects of experience which are seen as too trivial and everyday to be recorded elsewhere. Menstruation, pregnancy, and menopause, for instance, are rarely the subject of history as it is taught in schools and universities. This concealed dimension of living has an obvious bearing on women's history. The women's liberation movement has insisted that all aspects of female experience be recognised, considered and redefined. Once stated, many of these neglected areas appear as quite obviously important. They have always been important to the women who experienced them, but because the ideas in society of what is significant and what is trivial exist within a male-dominated context, it has been easy to ignore these kinds of female experiences. Oral history can cut right through this, especially when one woman is talking to another woman, because this could make it easier to talk about things that a man would not always notice.

It is not just the commitment to personal testimony but the theories about the economic and social position of women within the new feminism which affect what we recognise as important in the past. For instance, the women's movement has shown that housework is economically essential to capitalist society, though it is rarely seen as part of production. Because of the relation between man and woman, mother and child, the work women do in the home is seen as a purely personal rather than an economic activity. The extent to which the nature of the work has changed even in this century is often forgotten too. A woman who comes to a morning class I teach on social history for the Workers Education Association in London interviewed her mother-in-law about her childhood in a respectable working-class family during the period around and immediately after World War I. Her mother-in-law's memories of washing are so vivid that they communicate much more than any general statement about the change in household technology.

'Washing and cleaning in the home really were heavy chores. To do the washing you first had to save everything that would burn to stoke up the stone copper or stone and cast-iron copper. My mother-in-law remembered that her mother was friendly with the owners of the corner shop who would give her wood in the shape of boxes. Once you had your fuel, you had to fill your copper by hand and when the water was hot you ladled it out into a tin bath where you would use a rubbing board and blocks of soap.

'Once all the washing had been rubbed it went back into the refilled copper together with bleaching soda and ordinary soda and would be left to boil for twenty minutes. It was a steaming job pushing it down every so often with a copper stick. As the children went out to work and there was a little more money, her mother would use Hudson's Soap Powder instead of the two sorts of soda.

'When the wash had finished boiling it would be lifted out into a bath of clean water to be rinsed and "whites" would be "blued" with Reckitt's blue bag or starched and finally it would all be wrung out through a hand-operated mangle.

'After the wash had been dried it would be ironed on the kitchen table on an old piece of blanket with a sheet or piece of cotton over that. The irons would be hot irons heated by the fire and the only sure way to see if they were hot enough would be to spit on them.

'In 1923, her mother had to have an operation for breast cancer and a neighbour, whose husband was a dock worker and more often than not was not chosen to work, came in and did all the washing, not the ironing, for 2s.6d. The neighbour came at 8 A.M. and left at 1 P.M. and would only stop for a glass of beer and bread and cheese half-way through the morning.'[16]

When you focus on the woman's role in production in the family, all this hidden labour comes to light. Alice Clark's study of seventeenth-century household production revealed women doing a wide variety of tasks because more things were produced in the home. In her introduction to *The Household Account Book of Sarah Fell*[17] she showed how an account book could be used to retrace the actual extent of this labour. Statements of its effect on consciousness are relatively rare. Lucy Larcom, who went to work in the Lowell mills at the age of eleven, described a period of domesticity in her life: 'I felt myself slipping into an inward apathy from which it was hard to rouse myself.'[18]

If the first step is to discover and reveal aspects of woman's life in the past which have been ignored, we need also a means of understanding how this has related to the lives and activity of men and to children. Woman's production in the home has a double

16   Marilyn Clark, 'Interview With My Mother-in-Law', unpublished interview.
17   Norman Penney, ed., Cambridge 1920.
18   'Lucy Larcom's Factory Experiences', from *Lucy Larcom: A New England Girlhood*, Boston 1889, quoted in Nancy F. Cott, ed., *The Root of Bitterness*, New York 1972, p 139.

character. It maintains the other members of the family and makes it possible for them to reproduce the means of life through labour. It also involves reproduction in the sense of procreation. The relationship between this form of labour and other forms of production and reproduction is not usually made without a feminist orientation and commitment. Although this double character of women's productive capacity is implicit within the marxist view of the social relations of production, the sexual sphere is often subsumed within economics.

This affects consideration both of the question of women's social contribution through the reproduction of the species and of the relationship between procreation and the reproduction of the means of life through labour. It has left marxist historians particularly vulnerable to the criticism of those non-marxist historians who tend to abstract population from other factors in production. When population is detached it can be presented as the sole determinant of historical change and the complex interaction between human action and the social and natural world is reduced to a model of stimulus and response. Demography becomes a separate school of study. While an understanding of demography as a technique is vital in the development of any history which includes the family and woman's reproductive activity, this does not mean that history can be streamlined into a technical or statistical process.

In asserting the need to see reproduction in the family as part of material production and reproduction as a whole it is important not to reduce relationships within the family to a purely economic activity. For the woman's position within the family is not simply an affair of either economic or sexual production. To see it only in those terms would be to impose a materialist determinism which falsely excludes the personal and social relations within families.

But here again there is a theoretical absence within marxism which raises several problems if this aspect of women's lives in the past is not to be ignored. Relationships within the family have been neglected by marxist historians and seen by non-marxists in isolation from the society outside. There are very few precedents which could help us to study family relationships interacting with other forms of social relationships in various historical periods. This is an obvious difficulty not only for women's history but for the history of childhood.

The existence of women's liberation can help to make this kind of connection, though this is still one-sided and we would need to know about men's relations to women as well as women's relations to men and the relationships between fathers and sons as well as between mothers and daughters. Women's groups have begun to integrate the personal experience of childhood and motherhood with the collective social experience of what it means to be a woman in a particular society. This could have important implications for how we look at history. After all, if our memories of our own mothers' lives and even their mothers' are part of how we became women, it is not such a step from this to regard our own and other women's memories as a source for women's history in the recent past.

There are many examples which could be given in illustration, but one account by an American black woman writer, Alice Walker, describes it very clearly.

> 'In the late 1920's my mother ran away from home to marry my father. Marriage, if not running away, was expected of 17 year old girls. By the time she was 20, she had two children and was pregnant with a third. Five children later I was born. And this is how I came to know my mother, she seemed a large soft, loving-eyed woman who was rarely impatient in our home. Her quick violent temper was on view only a few times a year, when she battled with the white landlord who had the misfortune to suggest to her that her children did not need to go to school.
>
> 'She made all the clothes we wore, even my brothers' overalls. She made all the towels and sheets we used. She spent the summers canning vegetables and fruits. She spent the winter evenings making quilts enough to cover our beds.
>
> 'During the "working" day, she labored beside—not behind—my father in the fields before sun up, and did not end until late at night. There was never a moment for her to sit down, undisturbed, to unravel her own private thought, never a time free from interruption by work or the noisy inquiries of her many children. . . .
>
> 'Yet so many of the stories that I write are my mother's stories. Only recently did I fully realize this; that through years of listening to my mother's stories of her life, I have absorbed not only the stories themselves but something of the manner in which she spoke, something of the knowledge that her stories—like her life—must be recorded.'

Alice Walker says that her mother's own artistry was expressed even within the tight confines of her life, through gardening:

> 'Before she left home for the fields she watered her flowers, chopped up the grass and laid out new beds. When she returned from the fields she might divide clumps of bulbs, dig a cold pit, uproot and replant roses, or prune branches from her taller bushes or trees—until night came and it was too dark to see.'[19]

The women's movement also has begun to question the tendency in our society to divorce sexual emotion from culture, to see sex as somehow outside history. Sexual love continues to be seen as an unchanging, natural factor in human existence, not a social creation. This is deceptive, for in reality sexuality and the feelings generated by the particular sexual relationship come out of the totality of human social relations. The women's movement

19   Alice Walker, 'In Search of Our Mothers' Gardens', *Radcliffe Quarterly* vol 60, no 2 (June 1974), pp 4–5.

has concentrated on the distortion which the social dominance of men over women has had upon sexual relationships and upon our affections. This emphasis can lead us to consider how we would begin to think about the kinds of feelings of people in societies where the working relationship was often synonymous with the sexual relationship. It was only with the development of capitalist society, in which the capacity to labour is exchanged on the market like any other commodity, that personal emotion for the mass of the people can appear as separate from work and production and as inhabiting an ideal sphere outside society. What appears to us as normal and obvious would be quite strange to a medieval peasant. Marx and Engels noted the historical appearance of the idea of romantic love. But we have to dig deeper than conscious systems of ideas. Our very sexual responses and ways of relating are not removed from society or history; they are learned as part of our sexual culture and are thus open to change.

> 'It is not just the ideology of the age which is produced within the mode of production; the type of feeling is specific and bounded too. It is not just bourgeois ideology about love and sex, or bourgeois morality and conventions that sustain bourgeois sexual practice; it is the very structure of our most intimate and powerful perceptions, emotions and ways of acting.
>
> 'Imagine how differently sex must be felt to connect with emotional and other attachments to people in a kinship society where sex is a matter for public initiation, deflowering an occasion for solemn communal rejoicing, a *social* act on behalf of the collective hope for fertility, not a private act of emotional commitment or sensual pleasure between two individuals.'[20]

The women's movement has made the need to uncover every aspect of women's experience an immediate political issue and in doing so has started to redefine what is personal and what is political, questioning the present scope of what is defined as politics. This new feminism has made enquiries which have not been made so persistently before, enquiries which can initiate new historical questions. Women are hidden from most history in the same way as the lives of men of the poor are obscured, because of class. But we are also hidden as a sex, and it takes a specifically feminist consciousness to come to terms with the full extent of this.

History which includes women will mean that we study the role of women in movements which are usually described from the point of view of men, for example, the part women have played in revolutions, in political organisations, in trade unions, as well as women's own movements for suffrage or for peace. Similarly, we need to know how periods of change and upheaval have affected

20 *The Politics of Sexuality in Capitalism*, Red Collective Pamphlet, Russell Press, Nottingham (obtainable from 104 Greencroft Gardens, Flat 6, London N.W. 6).

women, war, revolution, the growth of capitalism, imperialism. But more than this, we have to go outside the scope of what history usually is. We need to look at folk beliefs, at magic, at the means by which people sought control over sexuality, fertility and birth. The personal testimony of any woman who can remember—not just women who have witnessed major political events—is a source for this history. It is also a source which can enlarge our concept of what we are looking for. Our definition of women's work will include not only production paid in wages, but the unpaid labour of women in the home which makes work outside possible. We have to understand the relationship in different historical periods between procreation, the production of new life which will make existence possible in the future, housework, the labour in the home which enables workers to go out and continue to labour in the wages system in capitalism, child rearing, making the survival of the future makers of new life possible, and women's work outside the home for wages, which in modern capitalism is becoming more and more general. We can only understand women's part in production when we can trace changes and grasp the interactions between these various aspects of women's labour.

Women's history, though, is not just about production in a material sense, for human beings create and re-create themselves in the effort to control, to bring the material world within the grasp of consciousness. Here too we inherit what we seek to go beyond and what defines our limits. We are the daughters of the tales our mother told us and drop easily back into the same way of seeing and telling even if the tales are changed by our transformed circumstances. We learn how to relate through our families and with children who themselves come from families. These relationships affect us not as external ideas but from the innermost self—feelings in our bones. They are nonetheless part of the movement of society. Our views about love between men and women, women and women, men and men, parents and children are historically shaped as much as our views about government, poverty, the organisation of production. Moreover, not just our conscious ideas of love but our unconscious experience of loving relationships, the manner in which we express sensual feelings, are also socially learned and as such are the proper if buried subject matter of history.

Much of this is such an uncharted province that to ignore any maps and compasses which exist, however imperfect, would be feckless. My own suggestions of how to begin are necessarily bounded by my own ignorance, the contours of my own history: the writing of earlier feminists, Marx's theories about history and class consciousness, anthropological studies of production and reproduction in precapitalist societies, new work in social history which seeks to uncover the everyday perceptions of the poor, demographic history, oral history. It is one thing to announce that all these could be useful and beyond any present knowledge. However, it is quite another thing to *use* them. The writing of our history is not just an individual venture but a continuing social communication. Our history strengthens us in the present by connecting us to the lives of countless women. Threads and strands of long lost experience weave into the present. In rediscovering the dimensions of female social existence lost in the tangled half memories of myth and dream, we are uncovering and articulating a cultural sense of what it is to be a woman in a world defined by men. We are tracing the boundaries of oppression and the perpetual assertion of self against their confines, the erosion and encirclement, the shifts and tremors of new forms of resistance. We are heaving ourselves into history, clumsy with the newness of creation, stubborn and persistent in pursuit of our lost selves, fortunate to be living in such transforming times.

S.R.

May, 1974

Preface

This book comes very directly from a political movement. The decision to work over some of the territory I had gone through and find out more came out of discussions in women's liberation and on the left about the situation of women in contemporary capitalism. I felt it would be helpful to try and unravel historically some of the questions we kept raising. This was both because of my own uncertainties and because I felt it could help to make our discussions less abstract. Thus throughout I keep asking in different ways—in what conditions have women produced and reproduced their lives, both through their labour and through procreation; how has the free expression of this activity been distorted and blocked by the circumstances of society? I have tried to explore both what has been specific to women as a sex and the manner in which class has cut across this oppression.

Capitalism brought new relationships of property and domination. It brought into being a class which did not own the means of production, 'free' labourers who had to sell their labour power on the market. It started to dissolve all previous forms of ownership. But men still owned their women body and soul long after they themselves ceased to be the property of other men. Men continued to own and control female creative capacity in the family and to assume that the subordination of women in society was just and natural—though the consequences of this for women from different classes were not the same. Patriarchy, the power of men as a sex to dispose of women's capacity to labour, especially in the family, has not had a direct and simple relationship to class exploitation.

In the attempt to explore this contradiction, I kept coming across many related questions which are also surfacing in the women's movement today; for example, the conflict between population control and the right of women to control their own reproductive capacity; the political implications of separating sexual pleasure and procreation; the difference between developments in the working-class and the middle-class family; the connection between sexual self-determination and control over production; the manner in which our work in the family has affected our position outside, both in terms of our place in the labour market and our relationship to male-dominated trade-union organisation; the changing role of the state in the oppression of women; and finally problems of organisation and strategy: how to retain our autonomy without isolating ourselves from other movements; how to connect immediate demands to the long term creation of a society in which nobody is oppressed.

I don't think there is an absolute answer to any of these questions in the present. This book certainly does not provide them for the past. They involve, rather, a continuing enquiry. *Hidden from History* began as a pamphlet and it is still a kind of pamphlet, or perhaps a bundle of pamphlets, bursting out of their binding with unfinished problems. It begins when it does, not because I think the oppression of women began with capitalism, but because I think its forms in the recent past relate more nearly to our predicament now. It stops in the late 1920s and early 1930s, partly because I was getting short of wind and energy, but more legitimately because the last great feminist wave of the late nineteenth century finally faded then. I restricted myself to Britain, and in fact really to England, for reasons of space, ignorance and time, not from chauvinism.

In writing about such a wide sweep of our past I am necessarily skimming the surface of things, piecing together what I can find from diverse sources, most of them secondary. I am turning up the top soil in the hope that others will dig deeper. I know that already the women's movement has made many of us ask different questions of our past. The results of this questioning are only just beginning to appear.

1

Work, the Family and the Development of Early Capitalism

Britain in the sixteenth and seventeenth centuries was still an agricultural society. Most people lived on the land, and a large proportion of the population only produced enough for bare survival. Work could be spasmodic, malnutrition was common—oddly enough among the rich as well as the poor because of their theories about diets. 'Green sickness' or anaemia affected women particularly. But diseases of all kinds, including the plague, ensured a high death rate. Division between rich and poor was extreme.

However by the seventeenth century trade was breaking down the contained local communities. The division and specialisation which made for more efficient production had begun, and was to accelerate. Tendencies towards new kinds of social differentiation, apparent before in the organisation of production, became marked. The group of people who were neither rich nor poor grew larger and more self-confident, both in the countryside and in the towns.

As the division of labour became more complex and specialised the richer yeomen's wives tended to withdraw from agricultural labour, though responsibility for the dairy and catering for the farm servants who lived in and ate off their board meant that they were still very busy. In the towns, as the units of production became larger, the amount of capital a small master needed to start off on his own became greater, and so fewer journeymen could hope to become employers of labour. This affected the organisation of the guilds and the regulation of trade. Separate organisations developed to protect the masters, and the terms of entry became formalised. It was consequently more difficult for journeymen's wives to be informally involved in the workshop, or for the master's wife to supervise the apprentices, and less customary for widows to take over from their husbands.

Although apprenticeships were generally reserved for males there were certain women's trades in which the women were protected against male competition. These were often trades which related directly to the work of women in the household because at this stage domestic and industrial life were not clearly separate. Women thus carried on food, drink and clothing production. Descriptions of these jobs have since become archaic or changed their meaning. 'Brewster' meant a female brewer, and a spinster was not an old maid but a woman who supported herself by spinning. But as the division of labour became more complex, and the workshops became bigger, informal customary arrangements were broken down and competition among the men intensified. Gradually women were forced out of the more profitable trades. Women's work became associated with low pay.

This was not a single, once and for all process, but went on throughout the eighteenth and early nineteenth centuries. However, from the seventeenth century women were on the defensive and for a variety of reasons found themselves at a disadvantage in the new organisation of industry which developed with early capitalism. They resisted changes as they encountered them piecemeal, and fought to protect themselves against the consequences of the new class and sexual division of labour which capital brought into existence. Sometimes it was the separation of the workplace from home which reduced women's productivity because it was harder to work and have the children around and work could not so easily be combined with housework. Sometimes it was the introduction of a new and heavier machine which secured the barring of women workers. In other cases the superior craft organisation of the men drove the women out.

Young printers for example were protesting against the women in the unskilled printing processes in the 1630s and had virtually excluded them by the mid-seventeenth century. It became no longer common for wives and daughters to help out the master printer. But there were wide variations from place to place, and trade to trade. There were still a few girl carpenters in the second half of the seventeenth century, for instance. In the woollen trade women retained quite a strong position though by the seventeenth century they were no longer employed in all sections, and were being restricted to carding and spinning at home, while men did the sorting and dyeing. As the newly formalised rules were used against women the appeal to custom lost its force. In 1639 Mary Arnold went to jail because she had continued to brew contrary to an order of the brewers of Westminster. Women were excluded from the brewing trade by the end of the century.

These changes in the trades were accompanied by the transformation of craft skills and folk lore into professional work and science. There were still women surgeons at the end of the seventeenth century, but women healers were increasingly associated with witchcraft and the practice of the black arts. As medicine became a science the terms of entry into training excluded women, protecting the profession for the sons of families who could afford education. Women were forced to the bottom. Midwifery, an exclusively female branch of medicine, was taken over by the male doctor when rich women gave birth. The female mid-wife attended only the poor. When the women midwives protested, they asserted their craft experience against the men's abstract theory. But in the new world science meant control of ideas which gave power. Craft experience was not valued so highly.

The peasant judged his woman by her capacity to labour and to breed more hands for toil. Only the wife of the lord was decorative, and even she was sought after for the land she brought with her. But from the seventeenth century the idea gained currency that men should be able to support their wives from their wage. Although many women still continued to work alongside their husbands their role in family production came increasingly to be regarded as supplementary. By the eighteenth century women in the growing strata of 'middling people' were already being reared for the leisure and sensibility we associate with the Victorian middle class. Leisure for women became an indi-cation of status just when the bourgeois man elevated the dignity of labour against the indolence of the aristocracy and of the poor. The beginnings of capitalism required singleness of purpose and ceaseless uninterrupted endeavour. Young men should not be interrupted by domestic concerns. They must not divert themselves with useless arts. Locke, the wily exponent of the interests of the new middle class, warned young men against music and poetry. Music should be left to women and acquired as an accomplishment for the recreation of their men folk, or be performed by specialised musicians and exchanged as a com-modity. The confinement of women in the interior world of the family left bourgeois man 'free' to accumulate capital.

These changes in the organisation of work affected the household, the legal and social position of women and the dominant ideas in society about what was 'feminine'.

In the sixteenth and seventeenth centuries the homes of people who were neither very rich nor very poor grew bigger, became more important, and began to be subdivided. The houses started to have two floors, there was some differentiation of function, new amongst the peasantry. It became common for yeomen farmers, for example, to have bedrooms, an important move towards the notion of individuality and sexual privacy. A stable monogamous home unit appropriate to capital-ism was thus being created before the industrial revolution and played a part in the growth of capitalist industry. But many regions remained untouched by the new kind of family and household. In Wales, Ireland and Scotland quite different family arrangements persisted well into the eighteenth century until English capital brought a new way of life to the lands it had colonised.

Legally, patriarchy retained its power. The notion that men had property in women was not dissolved when the idea that men were not part of the property of others lost any basis in society. Instead, as the social, economic and political control of the manor grew weaker, the power of the lord passed over to the centralised state or to the father.

In feudal society the woman's chastity was jealously guarded. There were obvious economic reasons for this. Not only did men see themselves as having property in women, but among the upper classes marriage was used to consolidate property in land, and so the seduction of an heiress carried a severe penalty, and women from noble families were disinherited if they lost their virginity. Among the poor, because illegitimate birth meant a dependent mother and child, even the peasant girl had to pay a fine if she became pregnant. But the lord's authority and responsibility was not just an economic relationship. The concept that a woman had the right to dispose freely of her person was completely alien to feudalism, because the relations between lord and peasants were bond relations, with obligations and duties, not the 'free sale of labour power by the wage contract'.

Property in women did not disappear but was maintained in a different form as capitalism developed. The law reflected the subordination of women. It was biased against women as it was biased against the poor. Within the family the father assumed the authority of the lord. Among the rich and middling people he guarded the chastity of wife and daughter. Bastardy could still cause property disputes. Primogeniture made it important that the paternity of a child should not be in dispute. Seduction and adultery were a form of theft. Women were part of a man's property and had to be kept inviolate. Though the value of a man was the price of his labour power on the open market, or his skill in business the value of a woman was still bound up with her chastity. 'Wives lose their value, if once known before.'[1]

Among the peasantry women were essential in the family economy. The peasant's wife bore children which meant more hands to toil and she laboured herself. She was like cattle, a means of production. Because of her labour she was valuable, and the peasant woman thus had a degree of bargaining power. She was never excluded from production. A woman without a man was in a weaker position, especially if she had a young child or was old. The young woman could be more easily integrated into the community if a man could be found for her. But old women were the responsibility of the local community. As the manorial system disintegrated the Tudor poor rate replaced customs which had

---

1 Keith Thomas, 'The Double Standard', *Journal of the History of Ideas,* Vol XX no 2, April 1959, p 210.

allowed widows support in kind. In the sixteenth and seventeenth centuries there was considerable ambiguity about the position of the poor. Alms and charity were still considered an essential part of religious life but vagrancy and poverty were also seen as crimes. There was considerable conflict between communal ideas of ownership and individual property. Old rights to pick peas or collect wood became the subject of controversy.

During the seventeenth century many women were persecuted as witches. In Scotland the punishment was death, but in England public humiliation was more common. In England too, unlike on the continent, violence against witches was spontaneous rather than organised by the church or state. It was believed that if you drew blood by 'witch pricking' you weakened the witch's magic and power for evil.

'Witch mania' provided a way of resolving conflicts within the community by finding victims, and by assuaging religious guilt about poverty by defining some of the poor and dependent as evil. It developed in a period when traditional certainties were being eroded. Even within the Catholic church ritual magic was being questioned. Protestantism constituted an onslaught on this aspect of popery. But it attacked the basis of sacred magic and the mysteries of ritual at a time when people were still impotent in the face of natural disaster and when changes in the organisation of production were breaking up the traditional communities. Many of the women who were accused of being witches were old and poor. Disputes arose between neighbours and when misfortune came people looked for someone to blame. Old women who argued back were obvious targets. Reginald Scot in his *Discoverie* said the witches' 'chief fault' is that 'they are scolds'.[2] They could also be felt to be trying to gain powers or control which did not suit their station. Thus 'wise' and 'cunning' women became suspect. Curing by ointments was indistinguishable from charms and magic. Midwives had to take an oath not to use magic while they attended pregnant women in the sixteenth century.

In some of the confessions of the witches they admitted to making pacts with the devil. The devil seemed to get the best of the bargain. He tempted them in affliction when they were starving, or when their husband had died, and urged them to steal, kill children they could not feed, or promised them riches and sexual satisfaction in return for their souls. In a tightly-knit community the consequences of accusation could be severe. Sir George Mackenzie, in his *Criminal Law* published in 1678, says a woman told him she had confessed not 'because she was guilty, but being a poor creature who wrought for her meat, and being defamed

2   Quoted in Keith Thomas, *Religion and the Decline of Magic*, London 1971, p 530. The following account of the English witches is based on *Religion and the Decline of Magic*.

for a witch, she knew she would starve, for no person thereafter would either give her meat or lodging, and that all men would beat her and set dogs at her, and that, therefore, she desired to be out of the world.'[3]

Thus although the bonds in the local communities had become less close, the immediate dependence of people on their neighbours for better or worse still remained.

The economic helplessness of old women meant they were common targets. How far witch mania was an attack on sexual deviance is not altogether clear. Although the demonologists were fascinated by the sexual aspects of the bargain with the devil, these seem to have been less important among grass-roots witch prickers in the local communities. It seems that only in the case of the notorious professional witch-finder Matthew Hopkins who set himself about denouncing and trying witches in East Anglia between 1645 and 1647 with the aid of informers did the English witch-mania dwell on the sexually titillating stories which were a feature of witch-hunts in other countries. However the mythology of diabolic copulation, naked orgies, and visitations by obliging incubi and succubi enjoyed a flourishing life of its own. It served a function rather like the ham moralising of the popular press now. People could be shocked and stimulated at the same time. Possibly some of the stories came out of farmers' descriptions of the beggars drinking and dancing when they congregated in barns at night. There was considerable fear in the sixteenth and seventeenth centuries about the 'Infynett numbers of the wicked wandrynge Idell people of the land',[4] who stole sheep and stopped carts of cheese.

Chastity and monogamy belonged to the alien customs of property owners, and found no place among the wandering poor.

There was also in the seventeenth century a repeated male complaint about the sexual insatiability of women. 'Of woman's unnatural, insatiable lust what country, what village does not complain', declared Robert Burton in his *Anatomy* in 1621.[5] Stories of an enormous devil's penis, or clitoral stimulation by the devil's agents grew up in the context not of a belief of female passivity but of masculine fears of women's voraciousness. The old proverb said that women were 'saints in the church, angels in the streets, devils in the kitchen and apes in bed'. In early folk songs like 'Room for a jovial Tinker' and 'The Scolding Wives' Vindication', the women are as interested in sex as the men; in fact the vindication of the scolding wife for cuckolding her husband is that 'he nothink at all would do', but has

3   Quoted in Charles Mackay, *Memoirs of Extraordinary Popular Delusions*, Vol II, London 1852, p 137.
4   Edward Hext, 1596, quoted in R H Tawney and Eileen Power, *Tudor Economic Documents*, Vol II, London 1963, p 339.
5   Quoted in Thomas, *Religion and the Decline of Magic*, pp 568-69.

> lain like a log of wood
> in bed, for a year or two

when she was in her 'blooming Prime' and 'loth be to lose my Teeming Time'.[6]

Apparently old beliefs of feminine sexual evil combined with a common view that the active vagina and insistent clitoris were too much for any man to cope with. In the eighteenth century the middle class produced an alternative myth of female sexual passivity, but this still did not penetrate popular sexual folk-lore even in the nineteenth century.

6   'The Scolding Wives' Vindication', in (eds) V de Sola Pinto and A E Rodway, *The Common Muse*, London (Penguin Books) 1965, p 54.

2

Puritans and Prophetesses

The puritan movement developed within the Anglican church as a means of restoring simplicity in worship and purifying abuses and corruption in the church by an appeal to the inner spirit or conscience. The puritan assertion that man could communicate directly with God without any intermediary challenged not only the Catholic church but the English Anglican compromise. During Queen Elizabeth's reign puritanism was contained. However under the Stuarts religious grievances combined with political and economic factors. England was divided by Civil War. The puritans led by Oliver Cromwell emerged victorious and executed the king. The divinity which surrounded the monarch was never really restored.

The puritan revolution in the mid-seventeenth century brought to the surface very fundamental questions about the whole structure of society, even though the main body of puritans never saw their revolution as being truly popular. The very poor remained outside the revolution. They did not share the economic and social interests of the possessing classes who supported puritanism, or the values of thrift, diligence and discipline which appealed to the men who had a 'calling' to their name and the 'liberty' to dispose of their property as they wished.

The puritans challenged the authority of priest and king by asserting the primacy of conscience, but they did not generally extend their notion of democracy to include people without property. The propertyless must be dependent and therefore could not have liberties. Women and children were thus automatically excluded. The head of the household was responsible for their moral and economic welfare. Legally their interests were inseparable from his. In some ways puritanism strengthened patriarchal authority; there was need of a substitute for the shaken rule of priest and king. The father assumed a new importance in the hierarchy of authority. The puritans saw children as naturally sinful, and believed they had to be beaten into holiness. As formal educa-tion replaced informal teaching, home and school became increasingly important as the two agencies for instilling godliness and thrift. The puritans attempted to impose the monogamous family against the values of the aristocracy and the poor. They stressed the importance of the wife's role in sustaining the breadwinner. The stable, monogamous family unit was vital if the 'middling people' were to accumulate wealth. The puritan family ideal reflected the reality of the small farmer or the tradesman with a small independent business. The man was the head of the household and had control over wife, children and servants.

Though patriarchal authority was explicitly asserted in the puritan family, in the context of the seventeenth century monogamy and stability did not mean that the position of women became worse. The alternative, with no welfare provision or contraception, was more oppressive. The puritan wife was at least a partner, albeit an unequal one. In the small farm or business a diligent wife was a valuable asset who could increase the family's substance. She was a help mate, a yoke-fellow.

The puritan attitude to women was also more humane than earlier conceptions, in which women of the poor were close to cattle. Their attack on old customs like the churching of women to cleanse them after pregnancy and upon the popular religious belief that women were natur-ally shameful and unclean represented a new humanity. A woman's soul in the sight of God was equal to that of a man even if her place on earth was inferior. But while the main stream of puritanism indicated a new notion of human individuality, this conception remained paternal-istic. The male head of the household defined the woman's place and the nature of her 'freedom'.

But the radical wing of the puritan movement began to push against the boundaries of this limited democracy. They started to take ideas like the rights of conscience of all believers and spiritual equality to their logical conclusion. This began in their own religious practice. Some of the small puritan sects included women in decision-making, some allowed children and servants also to influence the government of the religious group. The emphasis on conscience, on the inner spirit against the institutional authority of the church or the letter of the law meant that St Paul's prohibition on women preaching was overruled. The inspired could claim instead the revelation of the spirit. Among the Quakers for instance the women not only prophesied they preached as well. This revelation and enthusiasm provided an outlet for the sup-pressed female spirit. Because the men subscribed to the same faith, they were not able to silence this explosion of prophecy and spirit-possession.[7]

7   For examples of spirit-possession in other societies where women are politic-ally subordinate, see I M Lewis, *Ecstatic Religion*, London (Pelican Books) 1971.

Jane Holmes, a Quaker, had a fever which transformed her into a 'wild eyrie spirit, which . . . kicked against reproof'.[8] The prophetess could always claim that the spirit entered her. She was not responsible for herself. To try and suppress her religious outpouring was to act against God.

However female prophecy had social implications which contemporaries were quick to note. These democratic visitations of the spirit had worldly consequences. Anne Wentworth, for instance, who wrote delirious mystical verse, was regarded as 'an impudent hussy, a disobedient wife . . . one that run away from her husband and the like'.[9]

The spirit might move a woman to celibacy, or to challenge the husband's right to govern her conscience, or to tell her where to worship. The spirits had little regard for the respect due to worldly patriarchy, they recognised only the power of God.

Worse, the prophetesses' insubordination was encouraged by some of the arguments of radical puritanism. One pamphleteer held that '. . . every infant at the hour it is born in, hath a like interest with the greatest and the wiseth men in the world . . . not to speak of women, especially virgins, who by birth have as much natural freedom as any other, and therefore ought not to lose their liberty without their own consent'.[10]

If this were true parents and teachers had no right to control or punish children, fathers had no property in their daughters, or husbands in wives. If people were born 'free' they had the right to participate in governing, regardless of qualifications of age, sex, or property ownership. In fact during the Civil War women did take collective political action petitioning parliament and demonstrating. They justified this by referring to their equality in the sight of God and the fact that the war was affecting them as much as men. A vigorous pamphleteering controversy both pro- and anti-feminist ensued.

The 'left' puritans attacked more than patriarchy in the family and the state. They questioned the virtues of industry, of every man having a 'calling', of accumulating property, and being his own master. Against discipline, deferred gratification, and individualism, they stressed inspiration, ecstasy and community. The Diggers, for example, believed the land belonged to the people and should be cultivated co-operatively providing enough for all. Another group, called the ranters, questioned monogamy and chastity. Innocence was within, purity was an affair of the inner spirit.

8   Quoted in Keith Thomas, 'Women and the Civil War Sects', *Past and Present*, no 13, 1958, p 326.
9   *ibid*, p 327.
10 *ibid*, p 336.

'Till you can lie with all women as one woman, and not judge it sin, you can do nothing but sin.'[11]

Sin was thus not the act but the attitude behind it. Diggers and ranters were the only puritan groups to stir the people who had no calling. They appealed to the wandering poor, who squatted and were hunted as vagrants, for whom the mainstream puritan stress on industry and monogamy had no social meaning. But in challenging the ideas of thrift, abstinence and deferred gratification the ranters were attacking not only the basis of the new world the middling people were making, but pressing far beyond the material resources of the seventeenth century. Winstanley, the digger, criticised the ranters because their insistence on absolute freedom dissolved the necessary self-discipline of the Diggers' co-operative community struggling to make a living in a situation of material scarcity. He also noted the consequences of men's freedom for women.

'The mother and child begotten in this manner is like to have the worst of it, for the man will be gone and leave them, and regard them no more than other women . . . after he hath had his pleasure. Therefore you women beware, for this ranting practice is not the restoring but the destroying practice of the creation . . . By seeking their own freedom they embondage others.'[12]

As Christopher Hill observes: 'Sexual freedom, in fact, tended to be freedom for men only, so long as there was no effective birth control. This was the practical moral basis to the puritan emphasis on monogamy.'[13]

Imagination leapt out of material reality for a time, only to be forced back into a more proper circumspection. The ranters' critics were quick to point out the connections between their doctrines and 'immorality'. Drink and tobacco smoking, which apparently induced ecstatic trances, combined with sexual promiscuity to call forth moral censure. According to the pamphlet *The Ranting of the Ranters*, the woman ranter '. . . speaks highly in commendation of their husbands that give liberty to their wives, and will freely give consent that she should associate herself with any other of her fellow creatures which she shall make choice of . . . she topeth of her glasses freely, and concludeth there is no heaven but the pleasures she injoyeth on earth, she is very familiar at first sight'.[14]

The danger of childbirth and inadequacy of contraception meant that ideas of sexual liberation were necessarily constrained. The possibility of separating pleasure from procreation was still remote when capitalism was beginning to develop. The material predicament of women made

11   Quoted in Christopher Hill, *The World Turned Upside Down*, London 1972.
12   *ibid*, p 257.
13   *ibid*.
14   N Cohn, *The Pursuit of the Millenium*, London 1957, p 328.

sexual freedom male-defined. It is not clear whether the ranter women really enjoyed their pleasures or whether the men who opposed them liked to imagine that they did. Opposition to the most limited forms of female religious or political unorthodoxy has often taken the form of accusations of sexual abandon, or alternatively of sexual frigidity. This connection is not surprising because the subordination of women has been sexual as well as political.

3

The Restoration

After the Restoration the old order was brought back but as the basis of a new capitalist society. The democratic vision of women like Mary Cappe in 1645 was obscured.

'The time is coming,' she said, when 'not only men but women will prophesy; not only aged men but young men, not only superiors, but inferiors, not only those who have university learning but those who have it not, even servants and handmaids'.[15]

From 1660 patriarchy was once more secure and the agitation of 'inferiors' was suppressed. The division of labour developed further and continued to exclude women from the new professions and from business. Science retained its mystery and subdued the ignorant. The servants and handmaids were silenced again. The dangerous ideas of the Civil War about the equal rights of all believers to inspiration, and the democratic effects of this in society, were rejected by the church. For a time dissenters were excluded from education. Contemporary conservative writers like Lord Clarendon denounced the insubordination which existed during the puritans' period of power: 'Children asked not blessing of their parents . . . the young women conversed without any circumspection or modesty . . . Parents had no manner of authority over their children.'[16]

It is hard to say whether this represented reality or his own fears—though there were signs of tension within Quaker families, at least between sons and fathers in the seventeenth century. At a more popular level, the author of *The Womens Fegaries* in 1675 took up the same theme of the consequences of female insolence:

> When Men unto their Wives make long beseeches
> The Women dominere who wear the Breeches

15 Hill, *The World Turned Upside Down*, p 259.
16 Thomas, 'Women in the Civil War Sects', p 340.

Their tongues, their hands, their wits to work they set,
And never leave till they the conquest get.
. . . Nothing will serve them when their fingers itches
Until such time as they have attain'd the Breeches.'

In Restoration comedy the relations between the sexes were viewed with wit and cynicism. Property marriage made the married woman sexually desirable. If she was unfaithful her husband was a cuckold who had been foolish enough to allow himself to be robbed. The relations between husband and wife and between parents and children were very clearly connected to the ownership and inheritance of property.

The mainstream of dissent, driven underground, assumed quieter forms or accommodated itself to the culture and values of the dominant class. However some of the puritan ideas survived. The right of everyone to knowledge and the idea of marriage as a companionship became quite widely discussed and gained some popularity among the increasing body of people in the towns who belonged neither to the aristocracy nor the labouring poor. Daniel Defoe, for instance, educated at a dissenting academy in Stoke Newington, defended the right of women to education in his *Essay upon Projects* in 1698:

'I have often thought of it as one of the most barbarous customs in the world, considering us a civilised and a Christian Country, that we deny advantages of learning to women. We reproach the sex every day with folly and impertinence; while I am confident, had they the advantages of education equal to us, they would be guilty of less than ourselves.'[17]

He took up the argument of equality of souls. God had surely not made women only to be 'stewards of our houses, cooks and slaves'. But he hastened to add, 'Not that I am for exalting the female government in the least, but in short, I would have men take women for companions, and educate them to be fit for it'.

These ideas of course only applied to the women of his own class. The women of the poor were outside the terms of his argument.

In the late seventeenth and eighteenth centuries the right of women to education and opposition to marriage as an affair of property were frequent themes in a growing pamphlet and journalistic literature. The growth of the novel with its new audience of middle-class women with leisure anxious to become part of polite society, also served to question aristocratic arranged marriages.

In 1697 Mary Astell, author of *A Serious Proposal to the Ladies*, put forward a scheme for a kind of academic convent where women could retreat from the world and become learned. She rejected the idea that women should be merely decorative. Swift satirised her proposal and she did not collect enough money because although her convent was a secular institution, it was feared that any woman's academy would

17   Brian Fitzgerald, *Daniel Defoe: A Study in Conflict*, London 1954, pp 101-2.

encourage catholicism which was feared. Also learned women were the subject of caricature and mockery, although during the eighteenth century several women of letters, or 'blue-stockings', became part of the London intellectual and literary world. One of these, using the penname 'Sophia', wrote *Woman not inferior to man* in 1739 and took the attack on male privilege into the economic and financial sphere. Exclusion from education was connected to exclusion from employment and politics.

However the economic and social helplessness of women became increasingly presented in the eighteenth century as inevitable and 'natural'. Lord Chesterfield could say for example in 1748, that 'women then are only children of a larger growth'.[18] The other side of this paternalism was the popularity of the brothel. Bernard Mandeville, an early writer on political economy, wrote *A Modest Defence of Publick Stews* in the early eighteenth century, arguing for state-regulated brothels, to protect 'our wives and daughters'.[19] The rake and seducer valued virginity and chaste women as much as potential husbands did—the harder the conquest the higher the stakes. According to established morality if a woman lost her 'purse'—her chastity that is—it was still the affair of her kin, represented by father or husband. As families who made money in finance and trade invested in land, the marriage portion played an important part of the consolidation of estates. The dowry and virginity were part of the stock paid over when a girl married. As the marriage portion went up, many girls remained unmarried.

The conflict between natural spontaneous affection, 'love' and family obligations and parental authority appears in many eighteenth century novels. Novels expressed the alternative morality of the middle class, which was critical of the sexual double standard and rejected the traditional kinship pattern of the aristocracy in favour of the idea of individuals in charge of their own destinies, in love as in business. The middle-class notion of virtue extended the concepts of chastity and monogamy to men, rejecting the cynical hypocrisy of upper-class sexual intrigue. Words like 'indelicacy' and 'sensibility' were part of a new language of feeling created by the middle class. Pamela's 'bashfulness', for example, revealed that she was not 'of quality'. Women were brought up to cultivate modesty and passivity. Those who were unable to achieve them were compelled to pretend. The aristocracy despised these bourgeois sallies into gentility. 'Prude' was a courtly word originally for a female hypocrite.[20]

In Richardson's novel *Clarissa*, the man who seduces her, Lovelace, is cynical about sex and marriage in the tradition of restoration comedy.

18   Quoted in W Lyon Blease, *The Emancipation of English Women*, London 1910, p 2.
19   Quoted in Thomas, 'The Double Standard', p 197.
20   See R P Utter and G B Needham, *Pamela's Daughters*, London 1937.

He has a shrewd assessment of where power is to be found in society.[21]
'Poverty is generally susceptible', he says, though he recognises the real
value of the people who produced wealth that others enjoyed. 'Were it
not for the poor and middling the world would probably long ago have
been destroyed by fire from Heaven.'[22] Thus Clarissa's persistent virtue
also represents real morality and thus 'humanity', but she places herself
at a disadvantage in worldly terms. Both she and Lovelace place themselves outside the protection of their class and thus outside 'freedom'—
the security of wealth and class. Clarissa disobeys her kind, and Lovelace
refuses to play the game of property marriage. Compromise and acceptance would have been possible if Clarissa had been willing to marry the
repentent Lovelace. But instead she sought solace only in her own
conscience, not in the outward forms of polite behaviour. 'Let me wrap
myself about in the mantle of my own integrity, and take comfort in my
unfaulty intention.'[23] The puritan inner voice thus reappears in a secular
and moral context.

Nor were the prophetesses completely silenced in the age of
'reason'. But their visions became more personal and less social, and
declined in political significance. French protestants fleeing from persecution arrived in England in 1706 and began prophesying the fall of
Babylon (the Roman Catholic Church). In 1711 they aroused the fury
of the London mob, who threw stones and dirt at them, beat drums
and blew horns, and even entered their meeting place in the Barbican
on horseback. But they gained some following including the beautiful
Betty Gray, a candle snuffer, and Pudding Pie Moll who sold penny pies
in the street. In July 1707 the Great Whore of Babylon entered Betty
and got her to take off all her clothes before the prophets and beat
everyone with her fist. The spirits directed John Lacy, prophet, to leave
his wife and children for Betty. When one of the faithful fell ill and
died they took it as an omen that the millenium was coming and He
was to rise again. Accordingly 20,000 people assembled on Bunhill Fields
to wait for the second coming, along with two regiments of train bands
and sellers of gingerbread and oranges. When the world did not end
most of their following melted away. Betty Gray and her prophet moved
to Manchester where they formed a cell.

Thirty years later a group of enthusiasts who broke off from the
Quakers, called Shakers because their worship took the form of jumping
and shaking, started to gain followers in Manchester. Amongst the
recruits was the daughter of a blacksmith, Ann Lee. She had had no
proper schooling, working first in a cotton factory, then as a cutter of

21   Christopher Hill, 'Clarissa Harlowe and her Times', in *Puritanism and
     Revolution*, London 1962, p 373.
22   *ibid*, p 379.
23   *ibid*, p 385.

hatter's fur, and finally as a cook in the infirmary. She married a black-smith called Abraham Standley and had four children by him. But they all died. The last child was delivered by forceps and Ann lay for several hours as if she were dead. When she came to she said she would never have sexual intercourse again. Her relationship with her husband was already unhappy, he drank a lot and treated her badly. Out of this physical and spiritual suffering she emerged reborn, 'as helpless as an infant', seeing 'colours and objects' like a child. The Shakers hailed her as the vehicle for the divine female spirit which they believed would be Christ's form in the second coming. After being imprisoned for Sabbath breaking, for the Shakers' tumultuous worship upset both neighbours and the authorities, Ann saw a vision of Adam and Eve having sexual intercourse which convinced her sex was the root of human evil and that the Shakers as the chosen must be celibate. She and her husband with a small band of followers emigrated to America, because she saw it as the new world in a vision, but Standley deserted her in New York—celibacy was not to his taste. The sect began an adventurous and hard life in the United States.

Ann Lee was by no means the last. Joanna Southcott for example appeared in the early 1800s. She was a Devon farmer's daughter and a domestic servant, and gained most supporters from among the poor. The old imagery of the Whore of Babylon revived, and there was a hint of placing the 'true heirs' in possession of the land. Millenarian feeling reached a peak in 1814 when she had an hysterical pregnancy and promised to give birth to Shiloh, but she died soon after, doubting her voice and the spirit within her.

There are similarities between these prophetesses and the female shamans studied by anthropologists in quite different societies. Very often the spirit comes after a period of suffering, the body is purified by tribulation. Celibacy sets the shaman apart from the world, and indicates the closeness of the bond to God.[24] Joanna for example uses the metaphor of marriage. 'The bride is come. The Bridegroom now receives the marriage seal. The law and gospel now unite. The moon and sun appear.'[25]

In Betty's case the spirit obligingly found her a mate. Ann Lee's spirit made her sexual rejection of her husband socially acceptable to the faithful. For women participation in the sect or group compensated for their wider social subordination. The prophetess could gain respect because the spirit chose her. The humblest of God's handmaidens could speak his word.

Women continued to be possessed by spirits, and spiritualism, mes-

24 See Lewis, *Ecstatic Religion*, London (Pelican Books) 1971.
25 E P Thompson, *The Making of the English Working Class*, London 1963, p 386.

merism, and other heretical off-shoots of established religion remained curiously intertwined with radicalism and socialism. However, the development of working-class political organisation and the recognition that a secular Jerusalem needed to be planned and made, meant that religious ecstasy declined in significance as a form of protest. Increasingly as radicals assumed that the actions of human beings and not an external deliverer, decided the course of things political organisation and strategy changed. Although women never achieved real equality within these new movements the cultural assumptions which made spirit possession an acceptable activity grew weaker with industrialisation. They continued instead on the periphery of working-class culture.

4

The New Radicalism of the Eighteenth Century

In the course of the eighteenth century campaigns in support of the American rebels in the War of Independence and agitation for the vote, provided a practical focus for the emergence of a new kind of political radicalism. Out of the puritan attack on church hierarchy had come the basic constituents of political democracy. The puritans had asserted the right of people to have a say in their own governing within church and state. In the eighteenth century this notion crystallised as the demand for the vote—no taxation without representation. The 'middling' people could still make common political cause with the 'little' people—the people with small means. For it was not only the poor who were excluded from the franchise, but the business and trades people and some of the more prosperous farmers as well.

The demand for the vote was not only a practical political notion. Behind this demand there were important shifts in the whole structure of intellectual thought. The philosophers had begun to interpret society in fundamentally different ways. Already in the seventeenth century the assumption that societies could be made by human beings and the confidence that man could control the external natural world in his own interests had appeared. The social and economic development in agriculture and industry in the eighteenth century led many thinkers to believe that progress was natural and inherent in human society once the obscurantist remnants of aristocratic rule and culture were swept away. Politically this took the form of demanding participation in government. The new reformers, however, like the puritans, tended to set limits to the scope of participation. Many of them still felt that there must be certain criteria for democratic rule, and retained qualifications of property, class and sex.

During the French Revolution the 'little' people in Europe moved for the first time into sustained political activity for what they defined as their 'rights'. Similarly women began to include themselves within the scope of radical argument. Male radicals, influenced by the idea of men controlling nature and society by science and reason, did not necessarily see that this had implications for women. They tended to assume that a man would reason for his woman and children, just as the puritans had assumed that democracy would only involve heads of households who owned property.

Against this optimistic faith in reason and progress—albeit with its various shades and qualifications—came a more ambiguous and less optimistic response to the emerging industrial capitalist society. The pessimists are not clearly of the right or of the left. Instead of the need to control and subdue nature, they wanted to restore man to his lost connection with nature. The politically conservative interpreted this as opposition to the concept of human rights, because such a notion shattered the 'natural' social order. But political radicalism could combine, as it did in Wordsworth's early poetry, with a passionate hatred of industry for destroying man's direct communion with nature and a sense of horror at the growth of large towns which it was felt broke down all bonds and neighbourliness between people.

The optimistic and reasonable believers in progress stressed the capacity of human beings to change, but continued to identify humanity with men. The pessimistic critics of capitalism saw human nature as an innate quality corrupted by society. But this natural man was their own creation, abstracted from time and historical reality. It was very easy to idealise the 'natural' ignorance of the rustic poor and therefore to deny them the possibility of choosing change. Equally it was easy to follow Rousseau and devise a distinct role for women and call it natural. It was after all convenient to argue that a woman's function was to please and serve man, not to reason and act in her own right. Such a notion was peculiarly acceptable to the men in the middle strata of society who had to make themselves in a competitive market and who looked to women for the sensibility and feeling impossible in the world of work. The ideal of the helpless languishing woman of leisure replaced the puritan yoke-fellow. It provided a rationale for a division of labour which was excluding middle-class women from production and a secular justification for patriarchal authority.

In the context of the French Revolution a woman called Mary Wollstonecraft produced her *Vindication of the Rights of Women*, extending radical ideas about the need for all human beings to decide their fate, and the influence of environment upon 'human nature'. Women had to be able to decide what was their own interest, rather than depending on men. If men were to 'contend for their freedom and to be allowed to judge for themselves respecting their own happiness, be it not inconsistent and unjust to subjugate women, even though you firmly believe

that you are acting in the manner best calculated to promote their happiness'.[26]

She was forced to counter the arguments which said women's
subordination was inevitable and natural. Mary Wollstonecraft used all
the men's assumptions and demanded that women be included within the
radicals' 'reason'. Sharing the faith in education as a means of changing
human consciousness, which was an important aspect of radicalism, she
was, not surprisingly, contemptuous of Rousseau's proposals for natural
female education and commented acidly:

> 'I have probably had the opportunity of observing more girls in their
> infancy than J-J Rousseau—and can recollect my own feeling and I have
> looked steadily around me; yet so far from coinciding with him in opinion
> respecting the first dawn of character, I will venture to affirm that a girl,
> whose spirits have not been damped by inactivity, or innocence tainted by
> false shame, will always be a romp, and the doll will never excite attention
> unless confinement allows her no alternative.'[27]

She was 'fully persuaded' that women would not be so fearful and
fragile if they were brought up like boys. It was not only the inadequacy
of formal education but the way in which girls were treated from childhood. She attacked the whole cultural conditioning of girls.

Mary Wollstonecraft was not certain how this situation had come
about. But she was dimly aware that the sexual roles girls learned were
connected to much deeper and less apparent social factors. She describes
the powerlessness which came from the exclusion of women from production. Women have been 'insulated, as it were . . . stripped of the virtue
that should clothe humanity they are decked with artificial graces that
enable them to exercise a short lived tyranny'.[28] She saw some relationship between the oppression of women and existing property relations.
The uneven distribution of property meant that some lived in wealth
and idleness and the rest remained 'chained' under them. Despite her
antagonism to Rousseau she shared his ideal of equality between small
independent property owners. She thought dependence of one section of
society upon another corrupted both dependents and those on whom they
depended.

She believed that, as society was, men had more scope for freedom
than women. '. . . There are some loopholes out of which a man may
creep, and dare to think and act for himself, but for a woman it is a
herculean task, because she has difficulties peculiar to her sex to overcome which require almost superhuman powers.'[29]

In her own life Mary Wollstonecraft faced many of these difficulties. Her father was an alcoholic who mistreated her mother. She

26   Mary Wollstonecraft, *Vindication*, London 1792, p ix.
27   *ibid*, p 87.
28   *ibid*, p 70.
29   *ibid*, p 329.

worked as a governess for a pittance when she was young and hated the lack of freedom. After writing the *Vindication* she fell desperately in love with a man called Imlay who deserted her, leaving her alone to look after the child she had by him. She did not live long enough to confront the degeneration of the French Revolution and the despair of its radical supporters. But she did watch it in the early stages being consumed in factionalism. She lived with the radical philosopher Godwin, marrying him when she became pregnant, only to die in childbirth.

Her views brought her obscene parodies from establishment writers. There was only a small circle of friends who shared her ideas. Amongst them was a woman called Mary Hays who also attacked Rousseau's ideas of feminine nature in her novel *Emma Courtney*. Although the *Vindication* was to influence radicals later the English Jacobins were not primarily concerned with the rights of women. However one Jacobin, Spence, addressed propaganda to working women. He defended 'the rights of infants' or the 'right of mothers to such share of the Elements as is sufficient to enable them to suckle and bring up their young'. Spence saw that political reform would not necessarily affect the personal life of men and women in the family. 'What signifies Reforms of government or Redress of Public Grievances, if people cannot have their domestic grievances redressed.'[30]

However such connections, or propaganda aimed specifically at working women, were the exception. Mary Wollstonecraft herself drew back at significant points. Her ideas of sexual equality in education are limited to girls from her own estate and condition. It was inconceivable to her that the daughters of the poor could be taught to become rational beings. Also she cannot imagine in the *Vindication* that women will organise themselves. Although she recognised theoretically that women must decide their own interests, in practice she appealed to men to release women from dependence.

30   Thompson, *The Making of the English Working Class*, pp 182-183.

5

The Agricultural and Industrial Revolution

At about the time Mary Wollstonecraft was writing, the 'middling people' were becoming conscious of themselves as a distinct estate, or condition. By the early nineteenth century they saw themselves as a class. They did not distinguish between their interests as a class and the progress of society in general. They were proud of their industry and achievements and began to challenge the aristocratic idea that leisure was the mark of status. Against the idleness of the aristocracy and the holders of public offices they asserted their usefulness.

The growth of a distinct middle-class consciousness was mediated by the close connection in England between business and landed property. Business men became capitalist farmers and landowners invested in canals and mines. Moreover, during the eighteenth century gentleman farmers took an active interest in the management of estates which amazed foreign observers. They were concerned to increase the value of their investments and applied industry and science to schemes for increasing the yield. As agriculture became more heavily capitalised, many of the smaller farmers were either swallowed up or prospered themselves and grew big. The break up of the old family which included farm servants living in and eating off the table, was thus hastened. Farm buildings reflect the change with the small dining room for the immediate family replacing the great kitchen of the old farmhouse.

The mark of status for the wives of these industrious farmers was leisure, not only for the gentry but for the smaller farmers as well. Already by the end of the eighteenth century the agricultural enthusiast Arthur Young noted some of the new prosperity being lavished on the wives and daughters of farmers, copying the upper classes. He grumbled that he saw pianofortes in the parlour and that the farmers' daughters went to boarding school to learn accomplishments rather than the business of the dairy or the farm. The whole process of social mobility and the withdrawal of women first from labour outside and finally from domestic production, was of course uneven, affecting different regions and different families at various times. By the mid-nineteenth century Young's grumbling was taken up in a rhyme satirising the aspirations of the farmers and their families:

> 1743
> Man, to the Plough
> Wife, to the Cow
> Girl, to the Yarn
> Boy, to the Barn
> And your Rent will be netted.

> 1843
> Man, Tally Ho
> Miss, Piano
> Wife, Silk and Satin
> Boy, Greek and Latin
> And you'll be Gazetted.[31]

As agricultural productivity increased there was no need for the whole family to be involved in production. The increase in population in the second half of the eighteenth century together with the smallholders, forced off the land, provided a supply of cheap labour which did not have to be boarded. As prices went up it was cheaper to pay a low wage than keep labourers in the farm house. The sexual division of labour, already clearly defined, was transposed into educational and leisure roles. The girls learned accomplishments, the boys received an academic education.

Thus from the nineteenth century the dominant feminist theme was to be an attack on the exclusion of women from education, the professions and generally from the work of men of the middle and upper classes. Connected to this was resistance to the continuing fact of male property in women. The legal system expressed and maintained patriarchal authority. Without the vote women could not change the laws.

However these concerns did not directly relate to the women of the poor. Capitalism had different consequences for them. Far from being excluded from production their life was one of ceaseless labour. Their complaints were rarely recorded. Their silence is the silence of class and sex oppression. It was only the occasional discerning eye like that of the rural poet John Clare who saw the unending cycle of poor women's work. Because of this historical obscurity the poetic testament of Mary Collier, a washerwoman living in Petersfield, Hampshire, is particularly valuable.

In 1739 she wrote, *The Women's Labour; an Epistle to Mr Stephen Duck; in answer to his late poem called The Thresher's Labour*. Mr Duck had dismissed the extent and significance of women's labour, much to Mary Collier's indignation. In his poem he had

31 Quoted in Ivy Pinchbeck, *Women Workers and the Industrial Revolution 1750-1850*, London 1969, p 37.

> . . . let our hapless sex in Silence lie
> Forgotten, and in dark Oblivion die;
> But on our abject State you throw your Scorn,
> And Women wrong, your verses to adorn.

He had implied that women agricultural workers had '. . . their wages paid for sitting on the ground'. Drawing on her own experience she put him right with some precision, pointing out that they sat down to eat after the hay was exposed to the sun.

> I hope that since we freely toil and sweat
> To earn our Bread, you'll give us Time to eat,
> That over, soon we must be up again
> And nimbly turn our Hay upon the plain.

Mary Collier describes how the work in the fields was by no means the end of work for women.

> When Ev'ning does approach we homeward hie
> And our domestic Toils incessant ply;
> Against your coming Home prepare to get
> Our Work all done, our House in order set,
> Bacon and Dumpling in the Pot we boil,
> Our Beds we make, our Swine to feed the while;
> Then wait at door to see you coming Home,
> And set the Table out against you come.
> Early next morning we on you attend;
> Our Children dress and feed, their Cloths we mend:
> And in the Field our daily Task renew,
> Soon as the rising Sun has dry'd the Dew . . .
> . . . Our tender Babes into the Field we bear,
> And wrap them in our Cloaths to keep them warm,
> While round about we gather up the Corn.

At night the men could 'sup' and go to bed in peace but the women stayed awake with the children's crying.

Mary Collier was conscious of no 'uselessness'. She felt women's labour was equal to, if not greater than a man's. She resented the notion that women of her class were leisured.

> What you would have of us we do not know:
> We oft' take up the Corn that you do mow;
> We cut the Peas, and always ready are
> In ev'ry Work to take our proper Share;
> And from the Time that Harvest doth begin,
> Until the Corn be cut and carry'd in,
> Our Toil and Labour's daily so extreme,
> That we have hardly ever Time to dream.

Women were not only employed during the harvest. After it was done they would go off 'to the House', and toil away washing the fine linen, muslins, laces and edgings, with the lady of the house telling them to save on soap and fuel, and not tear her cambrics and ruffles. Or they would get busy cleaning her pots and brass, preparing vessels for brewing, or pump water. At the end of all this their meagre wages left them no prospect but 'Old Age and Poverty'.

Mary Collier glimpsed economic exploitation behind this wretched injustice. The rich grew rich at the expense of the poor, who used up their lives in return for a pittance:

> Their sordid Owners always reap the gains
> And poorly recompense their Toil and Pains.

Mary Collier, with no time to dream, could see no solution either to the exploitation of her class, or the double load of women's work at home and outside. But the women of the poor were by no means passive. They played an active part in the continuing struggle of the eighteenth century crowd to maintain the right of the poor to a cheap loaf. A fair price for bread was the concern of the women as provisioners. Bread was the main item in the diet of the poor. There was little margin between high prices and severe hunger. Conflicts around consumption continued well into the nineteenth century and were part of the local bargaining of the community against the 'laws' of supply and demand which were always weighted in favour of the rich property owners.

Women pelted unpopular dealers, playing not only on the fact that some of the local gentry shared their distrust of new forms of commerce, but also on what the poet Southey described in 1807 as 'the privilege of sex'.[32] It was often difficult to bring soldiers quickly to the scene of turbulence and the troops were inclined to falter when faced with a crowd of angry women. These protests over consumption erupted spontaneously sometimes because the women encountered the dealers short-weighing or selling bad goods. There is evidence of preparation on certain occasions as well. The women were roused by a woman with a stick and a horn, handbills and notices were pinned on church or inn doors. In Wakefield for instance, in 1795 this notice appeared:

> '. . . To all Women and inhabitance of of Wakefield they are desired to meet at the New Church on Friday next at Nine O'Clock. . . . to state the price of corn. . . . By desire of the inhabitants of Halifax Who will meet them there'.[33]

Crowd action required not so much sustained organisation as a tacit assumption that revolt was legitimate. The poor retained a notion of a fair price and the right to reasonable provision against the 'free' market economy of the middle class. Because the women of the poor had an immediate connection to consumption they were prominent in these class struggles of the market place.

32   E P Thompson, 'The Moral Economy of the English Crowd in the Eighteenth Century', *Past and Present* no 50, Feb 1971, p 116.
33   *ibid.*

As the factories appeared, and with them machines that could produce more goods than was possible by handicraft work, the separation between the women's work in the family and work for wages appeared clearly. But the industrial revolution did not have an immediately uniform effect on working women's production. There were variations according to region and according to trade. For instance when the spinning Jenny was introduced in the 1760s it was still small enough to fit into cottages and women used it. However, after the mule was introduced the machine became heavier and men took over the women's jobs. The consequences for cotton spinners who were not independent producers were not so severe because there was alternative employment in the cotton industry. 'Spinsters' who lived in the districts where machines were introduced were thus able to find work. However the location of the new factories was not always the same as the old scattered home industry. Workers in some parts of the countryside had to tramp miles to get work. The women who were independent producers resented the loss of status entailed by factory work and persisted in using their hand wheels in the outlying areas.

Married women shared the economic situation of their menfolk. If a spinster was married to a weaver she was compensated for her loss in earnings because, at first, the new machines brought a lot of work to weavers. Some spinsters also became weavers during the French wars. The trade expanded and many of the men went off to fight. This could temporarily make up for their loss of earnings in spinning, but it lowered the pay of weavers.

After 1815 a combination of factors reduced the strong bargaining power of the handloom weavers. Men came back from the wars, to find weavers no longer in short supply. Women and children, along with agricultural labourers, forced off the land by capitalist farming methods, and Irish immigrants starved out by English colonisation, had all flocked into the trade. They were grateful for whatever wages they could get and consequently threatened the privileges of the skilled craftsmen. It was in this context that the employers started to introduce the power loom, and the handloom weavers faced the alternatives of unemployment or factory work. Weaving was thus devalued as a trade.

The weavers resisted but it was a matter of organising the unemployed. Some tried petitioning parliament. For instance in 1820 cotton weavers petitioned for a tax to be put on 'a machine called a power loom', and asked for a fund to be set up which could provide land for unemployed weavers. David Ricardo the economist said the government's job was to encourage industry,[34] and that the weavers' proposal would

---

34 Quoted in (ed) Lionel M Munby, *The Luddites and Other Essays*, London 1971, p 43.

'violate the sacredness of property, which constituted the great security of society.

The new political economy of the middle classes always presented the interest of the employers and propertied people as the interest of the whole of society. Workers referred back to a lost golden age, an altern-ative moral economy which kept prices down and in which everyone did the work of their fathers and mothers before them. Neither model fitted reality completely. Pre-capitalist forms of production continued mutation-like within the capitalist factory system, and non-capitalist attitudes survived, albeit in strange forms. Nor was the past as glorious as the workers confronted with the new machines and factories imag-ined. But both these models had an important influence upon how people of different classes came to conceive their separate class interests.

When petitions had no effect workers turned to the alternative of direct action. 'Collective bargaining by riot' could be effective when transport and communications remained undeveloped and inefficient. The women supported men who broke machines because their liveli-hood was bound up with the men's. For instance in riots in Lancashire in 1826 thousands of men and youths were out marching to destroy the power looms and some women accompanied them. At Chadderton the soldiers shot a woman who 'bled to death'. The men told a magistrate: 'We are starving now, and our children are famishing at home. We have nothing to eat and nothing to do. Speaking will fill no bellies.'[35]

The economic organisation of the family still made all hands neces-sary in order for them to survive. Men and women looked back with nostalgia to the time when they all worked at home. It was not that the conditions of production at home were good but they were still often preferable to factory work. For instance, the father of a girl called Jane Ormerod, aged 14, told the Factory Commission in 1843 that she worked from 5am to 9pm with an hour for breakfast and dinner and was apt to fall asleep at her work. Her wages by this time were half what they would have been as a power loom weaver but he would rather 'see his daughter hanged up than in a mill'.[36]

The new machines had to be minded and operated by workers who would submit to a different rhythm of work from the long but irregular hours of domestic industry. The factory owners tried to make their work-force appendages to the machines; they wanted their workers broken into an unvarying regularity. They introduced rules against late-ness, against talking. Punishment was severe. Workers were fined heavily or beaten. Physical violence existed within the family but there it fitted into a customary pattern of relationships. In the factory it became symbolic of a new industrial relationship, the impersonal discipline of

35   *ibid*, p 45.
36   Quoted in Pinchbeck, *Women Workers and the Industrial Revolution*, p 182.

the cash nexus. In the factory too, women and children were under the control of overseers and employers, not fathers or husbands. This meant the man's social control in the working-class family was threatened.

Employers were quick to find that women and children were easier to subdue than craftsmen, proud of their trade and tradition. The existence of this reserve of cheap labour led factory owners to employ them—sometimes in preference to men—while congratulating themselves on not tempting women out of their traditional sphere because they paid them less than the men. The conditions of factory work were only tempting to desperate people with no other alternatives. Capitalism was generous with its freedom to starve. Nonetheless factory production did mean an independent wage for women and children. Although this was pitifully small it meant they were no longer dependent on the male breadwinner at certain points in the family cycle. Young women without children and adolescents, for instance, could achieve a precarious independence. Though as soon as young children came along there were more mouths to feed and parents were forced to send them out to work very early.

Working-class hostility to the factory system in the early years of the nineteenth century was not merely economic in origin. It was bound up with the desperate defence of a way of life, in which fear of the independence of wives and daughters working under another roof with other men, coming back with their own wages, mingled with a notion of the family as a producing unit and protest against the sheer brutality of conditions in the early factories.

Social and personal resentment against capitalism's attack on popular culture appears in folk song. The poor cotton weaver tells of his poverty and the rebellion of his wife Margaret.

> We lived on nettles while nettles were good
> An' Waterloo porridge were best of us food.

The bailiffs were sent in and 'looked sly as a mouse'. They had no furniture, nothing to lie on, and no means of livelihood because they had been forced to sell their looms.

> Our Margit declares if hoo'd cloas to put on,
> Hoo'd go up to Lundun an' see the great mon.
> An if things didn't alter when hoo had been
> Hoo swears hoo would fight, blood up to th'een,
> Hoo's nought agen th'king but hoo likes a fair thing,
> An' hoo says hoo can tell when hoo's hurt.[37]

But even the proud handloom weavers had to face the final humiliation of sending their daughters into the factories, or find their sons were courting factory girls. In one song which still has the air of a rural folk song the father asks his son how he could fancy a factory worker.

> How can you say it's a pleasant bed,
> When nowt lies there but a factory maid?

37   Quoted in A L Lloyd, *Folk Song in England*, London 1967, p 326.

The young man answers in defence of his choice,

> A factory lass although she be,
> Blest is the man that enjoys she.[38]

As the factory workers settled in the towns the countryside remained a memory. In hard times they would still tramp out to get nettles for nettle soup, and the Lancashire cotton workers who studied natural history tramped out before work to find specimens. But soon the pre-industrial world was nothing but a haunting melody, the meaning of which was only half remembered.

The industrial revolution brought a generation of country people into the cities. Their children learned to identify themselves as urban wage-workers. Work in the family was clearly separated from work for wages in industry. The new capitalist organisation of labour was transforming not only relations between classes but between the sexes.

38   *ibid*, p 323.

6

New Means of Resisting

Trade unions were illegal between 1799 and 1824. Furthermore it was difficult to form permanent combinations because the rapid fluctuations in the trade cycle made long-term organising a problem. The growth of workers' organisation had produced the Combination Act in 1800 banning trade unions. Workers continued to combine secretly taking oaths never to reveal the membership. After 1824 organisation among factory workers really started to develop. Workers campaigned too for political reform, for a free press, for a reduction in hours, and the repeal of the hated Poor Law. These movements culminated in the Chartist movement in the late 1830s and 1840s. Thus while community direct action continued it was accompanied with forms of organising which required long-term commitment, and a consciousness not only of what was to be defended but what was to be made.

Although women participated in these new kinds of organisation the old unity between work and home, where action over consumption was not distinct from action over production, was lost. The women's loyalty was divided. A long strike meant hardship for the family. The results of trade unions were hard to see. In the bread riot you got food immediately. But if you joined a trade union you could be victimised and unable to defend your wage. Political reform seemed remote too. Like 'our Margit' the women perhaps thought that if they could only get up to 'Lundun' to see the 'great mon', all hardship and grievances would disappear.

Nonetheless women did begin to organise in trade unions and participate in radical politics. Women were among the victims of the great demonstration for political reform in St Peters Fields, Manchester, which the soldiers charged—the 1819 Peterloo Massacre. The first Female Reform Societies were formed in Lancashire between 1818 and 1819. In a spinners' strike in 1818 the women drew strike pay equally with the men, because they were part of the same union. However there was trouble between the men and the women in 1829. The men said they had failed to keep union rules and condemned them as 'black legs'. The women were excluded from the men's union and urged to form their own. However they did not organise at all when left to their own devices. Conflict and competition between male and female workers was to continue to be an obstacle to joint unionisation.

Unions were regarded by the middle class with horror, but when women organised it was seen as a threat not only to class power but to the whole basis of authority in society. The tentative and spasmodic militancy of women workers threatened the hold of men over women, as well as the hold of employers over workers. In May 1832 for example the *Leeds Mercury* was worried by a strike of 1500 female card setters. 'Alarmists may view these indications of female independence as more menacing to established institutions than the education of the lower orders.'[39]

Sadly the women were far from realising their power. The ruling class saw the social and political implications of female militancy at work more clearly than most workers. The attempt by the Glasgow Spinners Association to negotiate equal rates of pay for men and women was quite exceptional—an important early recognition of the need for solidarity in the working class to overcome the divisions capital had created between the family and work, home and the factory, male and female.

The early trade unions were not seen just as a means of improving pay and conditions but as organisations which could secure for workers control over the produce of their labour. In 1834 there was an attempt to federate all the unions into a combination of the whole working class. Trade unionists saw this class combination as a way of creating a society in which there was nobody at the top and thus nobody at the bottom. They also thought of taking a general 'holiday' or strike. They understood that their labour was their power. Women were included within this conception of the union. Rule xx of the 'Grand National Consolidated Trades Union' provided for Lodges of Industrious Females. However this ambitious scheme collapsed very quickly because strikes and lockouts throughout the country exhausted its limited resources. For instance, in Derby 1,500 men, women and children were locked out. The union did not collapse without resistance. In Oldham for example there was an uprising and demonstrations for an eight-hour day in which women played an important part. There was some organisation of women in the 1830s on a Friendly Society basis, combining sick and burial benefits with a kind of social club. The women went on outings, drinking beer in pubs—much to the disgust of upper-class observers. These Friendly Societies had strange names, 'Female Druids' and 'Ancient

39   Wanda F Neff, *Victorian Working Women*, London 1966, p 32.

Shepherdesses'. It was very difficult for both men and women to sustain trade-union organisation over a long period in the first half of the nineteenth century because the economy was still subject to rapid slumps and booms in trade which made regular employment unusual. But even allowing for this women's unionisation lagged behind that of the men.

Women had a double responsibility for work and home. Not only did this mean they had twice as much work as the men but that they never quite came to see themselves as wage-earners. Many men shared this view and resisted the entry of women into the factories. Women workers meant even more competition on the labour market. Although men depended on their wives' earnings many of them felt that capitalism owed them a living wage which came to be seen as a wage that was enough to keep themselves and their families. The desire to be master in their own home merged with the feeling that women should be protected from the factories. All these factors held back the growth of women's trade unionism and prevented male workers from supporting them. But the lack of trade-union organisation among women was also a result of the kind of work women did in the nineteenth century. Apart from the cotton workers who benefited from the Ten Hour Act in 1847, women were mainly outside the unions which became strong between 1850 and 1880 when groups of engineers, carpenters, and iron-foundry workers amalgamated. Women in small pottery workshops, or scattered in rural areas lace-making or straw-plaiting for instance, or working in the agricultural gangs or doing dressmaking in the towns in sweat shops or even at home, were not in a strong position to organise.

For though the accumulation of capital concentrated industry, bringing workers together in factories, disciplining them to work the machines, it also threw up whole areas of work where it was still cheaper to use low-paid labour, and which had a dependent relationship to factory production. Women were employed in many of these jobs, finishing off operations, or serving the consumer demands of the growing prosperity of the middle class. Domestic service also still absorbed many women workers for the homes of the middle and upper classes grew bigger and employed a larger retinue of servants. In London much of the work women did was seasonal so girls changed jobs rapidly. Union organisation on anything other than a temporary basis was thus virtually impossible.

*   *   *

Soon after Peterloo, according to the radical Samuel Bamford, women were among those voting in radical meetings held outside on the moors. The Female Reform Societies demonstrated with the men and swelled numbers at radical meetings. They passed resolutions and gave addresses. But their role was essentially supplementary, giving moral and occasionally financial support to the men, making banners and caps of liberty which they presented with great ceremony. This pattern appears to have continued in the Chartist movement. Although the Chartist William Lovett included women in the first draft of the Chartist petition to parliament in 1837 he was later persuaded to drop this. However the Chartist newspaper, the *Northern Star*, carried regular reports of female Radical Associations. The women carried their own banner on a demonstration in Nottingham in 1838. There was also a Chartist Chapel Sunday School which women helped to organise.

Although the Chartist movement was the first concerted mass organisation of workers on a continuing national basis, like earlier movements it was as much a protest against what the factory and city had taken away as a radical assertion of a new world. Radical workers came to a political consciousness in which past and future mingled with a moral myth of the good old days. Thus male workers who would defend the political rights of women could also lament the passing of the old pre-industrial family, and regard women going out to work as a sign of the callousness of the new capitalist order. Not only were conditions bad enough for men, but women increased competition. Their place was at home. Out of this came the idea that a fair wage was a wage that would support a man and his family. A good husband protected his wife and children and provided for them, and a system which made this impossible was unjust and had to be destroyed.

The Nottingham Female Political Union printed a letter in the *Northern Star* on 8 December 1838 which shows that some of the women shared these views:

> '. . . Urge on your husbands, fathers, brothers, friends and neighbours and be prepared and ready for the conflict, urge upon them the necessity of calm reflection and duty to be sober, frugal, patriotic and to consider themselves bound by the sacred ties of Nature to protect and shield their wives and children from that system of cruelty and starvation now stalking through the land alike degrading the legislature and the region of the country.'[40]

Although the mobilisation of women was in support of their class and did not raise questions which related specifically to women, like all mass popular movements which involved women it nonetheless raised the whole question of women's active participation in politics. The Female Political Union from Newcastle-on-Tyne said in 1839: 'We have been told that the province of woman is her home, and that the field of politics should be left to men; this we deny; the nature of things renders it impossible, and the conduct of those who give the advice is at variance with the principles they assert. Is it not true that the interests of our fathers, husbands, and brothers, ought to be ours? If they are oppressed

---

40 Quoted in Jo O'Brien, *Womens Liberation in Labour History*, Spokesman Pamphlet no 24, pp 14-15.

and impoverished, do we not share those evils with them? If so, ought we not to resent the infliction of those wrongs upon them?'[41]

The Newcastle women also quote Shelley—an indirect link with Mary Wollstonecraft.

> Well ye know
> What woman is, for none of woman born
> Can choose but drain the bitter dregs of woe
> Which ever to the oppressed from the oppressors flow.

They had already had experience of political protest against slavery.

> '. . . When told of the oppression exercised upon the enslaved negroes in our colonies, we raised our voices in denunciation of their tyrants and never rested until the dealers in human blood were compelled to abandon their hell-born traffic; but we have learned by bitter experience that slavery is not confined to colour or clime.'[42]

Mass political campaigns provided an exceptional context in which old attitudes appeared in a new light. These new forms of working-class organisation provided a popular climate in which it was possible for women to insist on their right to political activity, partly because the men needed their support, but also because their claim to have a joint interest in what happened obviously made sense. The radical movement again meant that women could use their common predicament with men to insist on new rights as they had done during the Civil War. Male radicals defended the women not because they claimed new rights for women but because they asserted a notion of the customary relations between the sexes. For example when the early female reformers were attacked as 'petticoat reformers', 'degraded females', for prostituting themselves by 'deserting their station' and discarding 'the sacred characters' of wife and mother 'for turbulent vices of sedition and impiety', William Cobbett, who was no feminist, exploded in his radical paper *The Political Register*, 'just as if women were made for nothing but to cook oat-meal and to sweep a room'.[43] The female Chartist reformers were attacked on a similar basis by Punch—which has a long tradition of opposing women's rights.

41 Address, in Dorothy Thompson, *The Early Chartists*, London 1971, p 128.
42 *ibid*, p 128.
43 Quoted in Thompson, *The Making of the English Working Class*, p 417.

7

Birth Control and Early Nineteenth Century Radicalism

In the context of the struggle for a free press the specifically female questions of conception and childbirth were raised in the early radical movement. Birth control information to working-class women appeared in the 1820s and was distributed along with other 'seditious' and 'blasphemous' stuff by the radical network of wandering sellers, and agitators. It was from the start a controversial question amongst male radicals because the idea of limiting population was associated with the hated middle-class political economy. Malthus had written his *Essay on the Principle of Population* in 1798 'proving' by economic 'laws' that the poor must inevitably remain poor, and would continually overtake the resources available to feed them. Distribution of wealth was presented not as an arrangement in the interests of the ruling class but as natural. All the poor could do to avoid starvation was, in his view, to marry late and keep down their numbers by abstinence. Malthus's ideas gained support among the middle class and also influenced some workers. James Mill, the economist, followed Malthus but hinted that a more effective method of limiting population should be found. In 1822 Francis Place, the radical tailor who had campaigned against the Combination Laws, advocated the use of 'precautionary means' to 'prevent conception' and prevent the population growing beyond Malthus's 'means of subsistence'.[44] Place also advocated contraception because he felt sexual abstinence had a bad effect on women physically. He claimed girls who were still spinsters at 26 tended to get 'disorders of the Uterus'.[45]

In 1822 Richard Carlile, the editor of a paper called *The Republican*, wrote to Place asking him for information about contraception because he was writing an article about it. He was afraid that it might encourage young girls to be unfaithful after marriage, because they

44 Quoted in Peter Fryer, *The Birth Controllers*, London 1965, p 81.
45 *ibid*, p 82.

were only kept 'chaste' out of fear of conception. Place replied that chastity was non-existent among the lower classes and that their conditions of existence made it impossible. Overpopulation kept wages so low that girls grew up in squalid poverty and men dared not marry.

Place convinced Carlile, who shifted the argument for contraception away from Malthusian fears of the surplus poor to the right of men and women to control their families and have sexual relations without the fear of an unwanted child. Carlile published an article, 'What is Love' in his paper. It described as contraceptive methods a vaginal sponge, the 'skin' or glove, and withdrawal.

Not only did he upset people who wanted to keep working-class men and women in fear and dependence, but he also annoyed radicals. William Cobbett for instance attacked both Place and Carlile for encouraging 'young women to be prostitutes before they married'.[46] For him birth control was a device of the upper classes to put off other kinds of social reform and an unnatural interference in the rights of the poor. In 1831 he wrote a comedy called *Surplus Population* in which a great Anti-Population Philosopher says,

> Pray, young folks of procreation,
> Of breeding children, shun the woes
> Check the surplus population
> Restraint that's moral interpose.[47]

To which the young men and girls reply,

> Hang that THIMBLE what can he know?
> The Bible bids us to increase:
> Back to London, then may he go;
> And let us live in love and peace.

Thimble and his new-fangled metropolitan ideas had to slope off.

The anti-Malthusians asserted the good old ways and said if only the resources of the country were equally divided everyone could have as many children as they wanted. Supporters of contraception were seen as stooges for the political economy of the employers. The case for and against birth control in radical circles never freed itself from this original connection to Malthus's ideas about population control. The necessity for women to choose how many children they wanted, the idea that sexual pleasure should not always involve procreation, had to wait for a century or more.

The immediate influence of birth control propaganda is hard to judge. It had no effect on the birth rate but possibly a few women heard of contraceptive methods. In 1832 a Yorkshire textile worker told a parliamentary committee that '. . . there are certain books which have gone forth to inform depraved persons of a way which they may

46   *ibid*, p 89.
47   *ibid*, p 90.

indulge their corrupt passions and still avoid having illegitimate children'.[48] Factory women, he maintained, had fewer children than women in other circumstances. This kind of evidence is made dubious by the common prejudice against factory women and the conviction that factories encouraged sexual insubordination and economic independence among women. Certainly someone was reading the books on birth control though. In Manchester a survey of 'Immoral and Irreligious Works' sold during 1834-35 showed that 600 copies of *The Bridal Gem*, Charles Knowlton's *Fruits of Philosophy*, and Robert Dale Owen's *Moral Physiology* had been bought. Paine's *Age of Reason* and *The Rights of Man*, radical political classics, had sold 400 and 800 copies respectively. But presumably if information did pass among working women much of it was by word of mouth—'women's talk'. Possibly a few women told others. The tradition of 'wise women' did not disappear with the growth of big towns. Abortion and infanticide were the only alternatives and there were cases of these throughout the nineteenth century, although the penalties for abortionists were severe, and the conditions of abortion horrifying. Quacks with herbal abortifacients proliferated.

48   *ibid*, p 95.

8

Feminism in the Radical and Early Socialist Movement

There existed a strong minority tradition in radicalism which questioned the whole social and sexual position of women. This was linked to the ideas of Mary Wollstonecraft, the movements of utopian socialists in France and co-operators and community builders in Britain and the United States, and was the secular descendant of religious millenarianism. It emerged in distinct opposition to the middle-class radicals, who were called utilitarians, and wanted reforms which would make capitalism more effective.

James Mill, the middle-class economist and philosopher, could see no utility in women and children having legally separate interests from husbands and fathers. In reply William Thompson published his *Appeal of one half of the human race, women, against the pretensions of the other half, men, to retain them in political and thence in civil and domestic slavery* in 1825. Thompson was a remarkable defender of people whose interests were not his own. He was an Irish Protestant who supported Catholic political liberties, and a landowner who believed in peasant co-operatives. Against middle-class political economy he defended the workers' right to their produce and he was one of the earliest radical thinkers to perceive the psychological consequences of capitalist production long before they were fully evident in society.

In the *Appeal* he defends women with a rare passion. He dedicates the book to a woman called Anna Wheeler. Like him she was an Irish protestant. She had left her dipsomaniac husband after twelve years of unhappy marriage in which she bore six children, four of whom died. Despite her isolation in the countryside she had read widely, including Mary Wollstonecraft, Shelley, and the French rationalist philosophy, much to the disgust of the neighbours. She finally ran away and went to live with a relative in Guernsey in 1812, and was to be an important mediator between several different tendencies in radical thought. Like

Mary Wollstonecraft she was both a feminist and a radical. Thompson remembers Wollstonecraft and Mary Hays in his dedication. He regrets Anna did not write herself and is very conscious that he does not share her oppression directly. 'Though I do not *feel* like you—thanks to the chance of having been born a man . . . though I am free from personal interest in this question; yet can I not be inaccessible to the plain facts and reason of the case.'[49]

Thompson believed women's physical weakness and the task of rearing children had placed them at a disadvantage and made it hard for them to compete with men. This disadvantage had been increased by the exclusion of women from knowledge, from work and from property ownership and political rights. The existing system of marriage and the way women's minds were 'moulded' by a culture in which men were supreme had also further contributed to subjection. He attacked the hypocrisy of men who described the home as bliss but found their pleasures outside, and the unequal sexual code which condoned this. Women were economically and legally helpless in the home. How could women be 'happy' when their happiness depended on the whims of another. Thompson went on to demand political rights for women. He was also critical of the idea that masculinity meant domination and feminity submission.

In fact behind the *Appeal* there is an attack on the whole basis of competitive society, which he believed would continue to keep women at a disadvantage. Under the existing system men would be afraid of the competition of women's work. Women needed also some recompense for the labour in bearing and rearing children which the wages system could not provide. Women would remain dependent on men for support unless care was made social. It was the 'dread of being deserted by a husband with a helpless and pining family'[50] which often forced women to submit to the barbarities of an exclusive master.

> 'Though nothing short of "voluntary association" or the "mutual co-opera-
> tion of industry and talents in large numbers" could entirely heal the
> flagrant evils of our present artificial social system, and particularly the
> desolating injustice practised on women; yet would the mere removal of
> restraints of exclusions and unequal laws, so improve their situation and
> the general aspect of human intercourse, that they would be no longer
> recognised for the same.'[51]

The distinction between reforms to be won while the structure of society remained based on private profit and competition, and a fully co-operative society is important. If particular 'negative advances' were

49 William Thompson, *Appeal of one half of the human race, women, against
    the pretensions of the other half, men, to retain them in political, and thence
    in civil and domestic slavery*, London 1825, pp v-vi.
50 *ibid*, p 200.
51 *ibid*, p 151.

made, education, legal changes, domestic rights, access to jobs, it would be more possible for women to struggle for the 'positive replacement of existing social institutions'. Until these initial reforms were achieved, women were not fully human. 'To be a woman is to be an animal.'[52]

Thompson makes the comparison with slavery. Female oppression was determined by birth, 'like the skin of the Black'.[53] The unequal social relationship between men and women meant that men could 'brand' women with 'mental incapacity' and call it 'nature'. Women often accepted men's definition of their 'natures'. Thompson called on them not to submit to masculine versions of female inferiority. Once women became conscious of this cultural imposition which defined them as inferior, the 'fetters' would be 'loosened'. He added, 'their magic depends on your ignorance, on your submission'.

He did not neglect the inadequate understanding of specifically female oppression even within the radical movement.

'What wonder that your sex is indifferent to what man calls the progress of society, of freedom of action, of social institutions? Where amongst them all, amongst all their past schemes of liberty or despotism is the freedom of action for you?'

Women must make men relate to them differently:

'. . . You must be respected by them; not merely desired like rare meats to pamper their selfish appetites. To be respected by them you must be respectable in your own eyes; you must exert more power, you must be more useful.'[54]

Thompson mentions the influence of the French utopian socialist Fourier. He had also come into contact with the ideas of another utopian thinker and his followers, Saint-Simon, when he travelled abroad in the early 1800s. Anna Wheeler had been a member of a Saint-Simonian circle in Caen in 1818.

Fourier advocated great phalanxes or communes, where he wanted work to be organised to allow people to pursue their interests and express their feelings. In this society of free association people would be housed in large buildings which would be equipped with various services including crèches. Young children would be cared for communally. There would be communal restaurants and public rooms, but each family was to have its own apartment. Fourier's first book *Théorie des Quatre Mouvements* was published in 1808 but he was still writing in the 1820s and gained a following in France which included working women. He often used the words 'mutualisme' and 'association', to describe his ideal society—terms which Thompson also uses. Hugh Doherty, who popular-

52   *ibid*, p 165.
53   *ibid*, p 165.
54   *ibid*, p 196.

ised Fourier's theories in England, called the new society 'socialism' and the new forms of relationship 'solidarity'.

Fourier was among the amateur originators of anthropology. In his *Theorie* he tried to explain how the existing social order had come about by searching for its origins, and working out various social stages. He believed the position of women was an important indicator of the level of civilisation achieved by the different societies, an idea the young Marx borrowed, changing as he did all his intellectual loans from a moral to a social notion. Fourier became more cautious as time went on about the emancipation of women but the testimony of his early writings remained.

Saint-Simon believed in a union of the classes involved in industry against the 'parasite'. He did not make any clear distinction between employers and workers. It was still possible to see their interests as being socially united because the system of small workshops predominated. When he died in 1825 he left his followers with a book called *The New Christianity* which predicted an era of peace, industry and internationalism. His followers soon began to split over the economic question of the workers' right to their produce as opposed to the employers' right to profits. One group split off under a man called Enfantin who saw himself as the 'master' or father of the group, which was extremely hierarchical in structure. Enfantin developed the idea that God was both male and female and that female equality followed from this. In order for the new era to begin, a female messiah, or mother, had to be found to complement the father. The Saint-Simonians went on to attack inherited property and Christian marriage as an oppressive institution. Marriages should be ended at will. They lived as a 'family', sharing their possessions, and men and women wore similar clothes, tunics over floppy trousers. They were persecuted by the French government for their beliefs and life-style.

The situation in the 1820s and 1830s was remarkably fluid. Ideas passed to and fro across the Channel and even across the Atlantic and although there was much argument and inter-sect sniping between Saint-Simonians, Fourierists and followers of the English co-operator Robert Owen, there was much common ground and much interchanging of ideas. There were connections between the idea of a female messiah which appeared among the socialists, and the millenarian visions of Joanna Southcott too. In Ashton-under-Lyme 'Shepherd' Smith, a preacher, met one of Joanna's disciples, John Wroe, and was attracted by the idea of a female deliverer. He later came in contact with Anna Wheeler and set off on a quest for the 'free woman'. He believed male spiritual power was exhausted and was to be superseded by the feminine-materialist world. Smith noted the great number of female messiahs in recent times and said the new era would be the 'age of the Bride'.

However he shared with other searchers for the 'Mother' a feeling that no man was really worthy of the role of deliverer.

> 'Is there a woman in England who can represent her sex? If there be let her come forth, for be assured that until she appears there is no salvation even for men. It is needless to reproach man for not doing woman's work. Woman has a work of her own to do. She has her own feelings—she only can express them; she has her own wrongs, she only can describe them.'[55]

Saint-Simonian 'missionaries' arrived in Britain in 1833-34. They directed their propaganda to women and to workers. They hired the Burton Lecture Rooms for socialist and feminist addresses and on one occasion the speaker was a mechanic's wife. Lectures included 'Organisation of Industry versus Community of Goods', 'The Fallacy that Owenism is Practical Christianity', 'The Saint-Simonite Attitude to Trade Unions', and 'Female Emancipation, Matrimony and Divorce'.[56] They alienated middle-class radicals like J S Mill by appealing to the workers, and were suspected by many trade unionists and working-class radicals for their ideas about industry, religion and feminism. However 'Shepherd' Smith supported them in his paper *The Shepherd* and the Owenite paper *The Crisis* printed Anna Wheeler's translation of an article from the Parisian women's paper, *La Femme Libre*. It was headed with the statement:

> 'With the emancipation of women will come the emancipation of the useful class.'

The women argued,

> 'Up to the present hour, have not women through all past ages been degraded, oppressed, and made the property of men. This property in women, and the consequent tyranny it engenders, ought now to cease . . .'

> 'Let us reject as a husband any man who is not sufficiently generous to consent to share with us all the rights he himself enjoys.'[57]

The article called on women of every class to spread the 'principles of order and harmony everywhere'.

The Destructive and Poor Man's Conservative—despite its title a radical paper—replied to this. It did not accept the connections made between the liberation of women and the useful classes, but claimed that 'change in the institution of property must precede every other great change'.[58] These 'new-fangled dogmas' could not be turned to practical account and merely confused people.

> 'Why talk of making women rational until we have first made ourselves rational? Or why talk of restoring them to their social rights, till we have

55   W Anderson Smith, *The Universalist*, London 1892, p 66.
56   Richard Pankhurst, *The Saint-Simonians, Mill and Carlyle*, London (no date), p 109 and pp 125-6.
57   *ibid*, p 109.
58   *ibid*, p 110.

first obtained our own? We may sigh for the conditions of women as we did for the poor Poles, but until we secure our rights of citizenship we can do nothing for them.'

The women might well have replied it was not what the men could do for them, but what they would do for themselves. The missionaries must have achieved some success however in popularising Saint-Simon's ideas, for a cheap edition of *The New Christianity, or the religion of Saint-Simon*, translated by none other than 'Shepherd' Smith with a portrait in colour of 'A Saint-Simonian Female' in her short dress and pantaloons was being advertised by a Manchester book seller, Abel Heywood, in 1839, along with Shelley's poetical works and pamphlets by Cobbett and Owen.[59]

Owenite millenarianism took a more clearly secular and rational form. The new moral world had to be made by the efforts of men and women in the here and now. By the 1830s and 1840s Robert Owen had moved far away from the enlightened manufacturer who in the early 1800s had tried to create a model factory community at New Lanark, and his own ideas had been taken over by working-class Owenites.

In the course of agitation for co-operatives, for the Grand National Consolidated Trades Union, and for a National Equitable Labour Exchange, which Owen thought would secure for workers the value of their labour, Owenism changed from an external paternalistic creed into a propagandist force which came out of the radical working-class movement. Owenism was more than Owen. By the late 1830s, it was a large and growing sect, organising branches and meetings for lectures and discussions, sending out travelling missionaries into remote places, issuing cheap printed propaganda. It was a living witness to Owen's original impulse—the idea that human character was infinitely perfectible. Like subsequent working-class movements they adopted the Methodist system of class meetings, informal gatherings where a class leader would set off discussion and everyone participate in the debate. Women were not excluded. In Huddersfield for instance in 1838 the Owenite classes included wives and female friends and relatives. Owenite Halls of Science provided a radical alternative to the Mechanics Institutes patronised by employers and Owenites pioneered co-operative infant and nursery schools where the children were taught not by a system of terror, rewards and punishments, but by making learning pleasurable. There were Co-operative Sunday Schools too, for both adults and children.

Owenite education was inseparable from the creation of the 'New Moral World', it was part of the making of a co-operative community and was necessarily in opposition to the existing state of society. Owen disassociated himself from the people who formed infant schools to

59 Dorothy Thompson, 'La Presse de la Classe Ouvrière Anglaise, 1836-48', in Jacques Godechot, *La Presse Ouvrière*, Paris 1966, p 20.

inculcate respect for God and employers into children at an early age. Although he was one of the earliest advocates of national education he did not see education only as a formal learning process in institutions. He believed people learned through the way they lived, through their whole culture. Thus, if one was serious about making a new world, one had to attack the means by which its values were maintained and reproduced.

Like Mary Wollstonecraft he saw education in its widest sense, but unlike her he was not confident that the small family unit of parents and offspring which was being created by industrialisation could be the basis of a society in which men and women were equal. Instead of supporting this new middle-class ideal of the family, where people were free from kin ties and supposedly had free choice, even though men and women performed different tasks and women were not equal to men in society, Owen saw the family which was appearing in the early nineteenth century as an obstacle to co-operation. Small isolated family units promoted individualism and competition and thus held back the possibility of a co-operative society. Owenites envisaged a much larger family —they wanted to extend the home and break down the division between the contained family circle and the community as a whole.

It was not merely that the existing structure of the family maintained capitalist ideas; the family was also the means of handing on private property.

> '. . . Separate interests and individual family arrangements with private property are essential parts of the existing irrational system. They must be abandoned with the system. And instead there must be scientific associations of men, women and children in their usual proportions, from about four to five hundred to about two thousand arranged to be as one family.[60]

Like William Thompson the Owenites opposed the existing system of sexual morality with its different standard for men and women. With the Saint-Simonians they were against Christian marriage which they believed would have to be ended before the 'New Moral World' could come about. It was this emphasis on consciousness and cultural change before the coming of the new society which meant they stressed the significance of relations in the family and the rituals of old forms of personal life. Christian morality prevented frank relations between the sexes and encouraged 'prudery' and false shame. Marriage without feeling was prostitution. Owenites had to struggle against existing culture as part of the creation of the co-operative community. Thus these cultural changes were not to be deferred until after male workers had achieved political or economic rights within the existing society.

60   Robert Owen, *Book of the New Moral World* (1844). J F C Harrison, *Robert Owen and the Owenites in Britain and America*, London 1969, p 59.

Owen put forward these ideas in his 'Lectures on the Marriages of the Priesthood of the Old Immoral World' in 1835. But the Owenites believed in practising what they preached. In *The Crisis* on 4 January 1834 an advert appeared for an Owenite wife. She had to be 40 years of age and possess an income of £50 a year and her 'womanhood'. The editor added in a note, 'Virginity we suppose is not necessary—no socialist could insist upon it.'[61]

Owenites sometimes performed their own marriages, using the civil ceremony and thus took over some of the functions of religion over personal life. A marriage took place for example at the John Street Institute in London in 1845. They did not believe marriages should be binding on partners who no longer cared for one another and consequently favoured easy divorce. Like Place they thought celibacy was unnatural, leading to diseases of body and mind. It is not clear what part Robert Owen played in the birth control movement, though William Thompson supported contraception and Robert Dale Owen, Owen's son, was the author of a popular book on birth control which was among the immoral and seditious works sold in Manchester in the 1830s.

Owenite strategy was rather different from William Thompson's, with his 'negative' and 'positive' notions of change. Owenites were not interested in any intermediary reforms, they thought people should set about the whole task immediately. As faith in the possibility of building a completely new world faded, and after the defeat of the Chartist movement, these ideas about transforming relations between the sexes and struggling in the area of personal life faded in the working-class movement until the socialist movement was reborn at the end of the century.

61   Harrison, *Robert Owen and the Owenites in Britain and America*, p 61.

9

Middle-Class Women Begin to Organise

Feminism came, like socialism, out of the tangled, confused response of men and women to capitalism. Feminism protested against the continuation of man's property in woman. It contained an essential ambiguity however, for the feminist attack on man's continued possession of woman did not necessarily imply a rejection of the private ownership of capital or of the wage-system. On the contrary women could well ask for admission into that system on terms of equality, but this would mean that men of all classes faced competition from women. It would also shatter the middle-class image of woman and the family as a retreat from the hostile competition of the world outside. The model of the free market and freely competing economic atoms required sentiment to give it cohesion, as long as this emotion was kept in its proper place. Otherwise bourgeois man was left with a Hobbesian world which dissolved under its own rationality.

The Victorian middle classes found their sentiment in their womenfolk encased in their crinolines. The Victorian wife was quite literally insulated from the sources of her man's prosperity. As the century progressed not only women's clothes but also the household became larger and more upholstered. It was the visible sign of the wealth and security of the middle-class man. The number of servants multiplied and by the 1870s there were complaints that women were no longer involved in even supervising them. Although the circumstances of middle-class women improved with the growing power in society of their men, their relationship was one of increasing economic dependence. In this sense patriarchy was strengthened. The women were part of the man's belongings, their leisure the sign of his conspicuous consumption.

This situation had no sooner started to develop however, when some women came to regard it as intolerable. Even in the 1830s and 1840s women had come to question their relationship to men and their position in society not because they wanted to transform all forms of domination but because they wanted particular improvements which were apparently consistent with capitalism. An ex-governess, Anna Jameson, observed that it was absurd to educate girls to be 'roses' and then send them to pass their life in an arctic zone.[62] It was evident that women's situation was an incongruity. A few years later Anne Lamb criticised the idea of spheres of influence for women and the way women were treated as children, angels, or playthings to be discarded when they ceased to amuse.

A new ideal of the relationship between men and women, reminiscent of the puritans, and of Defoe's notion of wives as companions appeared very clearly by the middle of the century. In Tennyson's 'The Princess' the old man asserts the traditional notion of patriarchy. Women, once promised, were property to be taken by force if they resisted. But the young man wants to possess the proud, independent woman in a different way. He wants to possess her through her feelings and subdues her with a kiss. The Victorian bourgeois hero thus played 'the slave to gain the tyranny'.[63]

As the idea of marriage as a companionship developed, direct patriarchal power became unacceptable to many middle-class women at a time when their actual economic dependence on men was increasing.

The similarities between the slave as property and the woman as property were brought out by the anti-slavery agitation. In 1840 an anti-slavery conference was held in London, and although Lucretia Mott and Elizabeth Stanton were delegates from the US a vote taken at the conference excluded women from the discussion. This decision provoked antagonism. The general connection between the English anti-slavery movement and subsequent feminist organisation remains unexplored. In America it was very close. Though less important than in the US it has probably been greatly underestimated.

As the reports on women's conditions in industry, especially the 1842 report on the mines appeared, the idea of feminine incapacity and delicacy was made to look increasingly absurd. In *Shirley* by Charlotte Brontë, the heroine longed for a trade—even if it made her coarse and masculine—instead of the vacant, weary, lonely life of a woman of her class. Out of this despair over uselessness came the energy of middle-class women, bustling about doing charity work. At worst they were interfering intruders, at best they found a kind of peace through activity and learned to respect the workers they sought to reform. But they remained aliens. The gulf between them is hard to imagine now. The cultural values and life style of the middle class in the nineteenth century

---

62 John Kilham, *Tennyson and The Princess; Reflections of an Age*, London 1958, pp 113-114, 134-135.
63 Tennyson, 'The Princess', quoted in *ibid*, p 135.

was as remote from the working class as it was from the African tribes which this same middle class was conquering and 'converting'. Indeed they saw themselves as colonisers winning the workers for civilisation— *their* civilisation of thrift, abstinence and hard work. In the mid-nineteenth century most middle class people involved in charity still believed the unequal distribution of wealth was justified by the personal failings of the poor and by economic law. Poverty was intimately connected to sin. However, within the limitations of this framework they were beginning to search for a 'scientific' approach to charity. Cautiously women began to argue in the meetings of the National Association for the Promotion of Social Science that women should be educated for charity work.

'It has now become the fashion to advocate the industrial training of girls of the lower classes. The need of it is nearly as great amongst the upper', declared Mrs Austin at a Conference of the Association in Birmingham in October 1857. She argued that educated women should be appointed to administer the female workhouses and that committees of visiting ladies—there was already one in West London—should be set up. She believed that this would not only improve the conditions of women and young girls in the workhouses but would also provide an outlet for the 'longing for practical work' that 'comes to us all'. She noted that it was not only ladies who were idle and useless but the wives and daughters of trades people as well:

> 'Young women of this class do not now, as formerly, occupy themselves exclusively with household drudgery, as it is called, and no longer follow the good old paths of their grandmother in the care of the house and family.'[64]

The notion that social service was a secular and scientific task that required its own investigations and its own training, rather than a religious duty based on spiritual purity began to undermine some of the assumptions of earlier charitable endeavour. The Congresses of the National Association for the Promotion of Social Science provided an intellectual outlet for the women who participated and were early testing grounds for the talents of several who were later to become active feminists.

Women started to campaign for particular reforms in the nineteenth century not because they saw themselves as feminists but because circumstances in their own life forced them to protest. An aristocratic woman for example, Caroline Norton, struggled tirelessly to limit the legal control of husbands over wives. Her alcoholic husband whom she had left prevented her from seeing her dying child. In 1839 children were declared in Parliament not to be the property of their fathers in

64 Workhouses and Women's Work reprinted from the Church of England Monthly Review . . ., London 1858.

certain cases. Another Act in 1858 allowed a woman who left her husband to retain anything she inherited or owned after separation. The married woman was still not affected by this legislation. However, they were eventually allowed to keep their own earnings, and in 1882 finally came into independent ownership of their own property.

But while some of the legal power of patriarchy was whittled away, the control of men over women in society was evident in education, work and politics. The long struggle of women for entrance into schools and colleges was heartbreakingly slow.

The vote seemed to be the key. If women could vote they could change man-made laws. The working-class agitation for the franchise raised the hope that women might be included. When J S Mill, the author of *The Subjection of Women*, became an MP he introduced an amendment to the 1867 Reform Act by substituting the word 'person' for the word 'man'. When this was defeated, supporters of women's suffrage started a legal case to establish that words of the masculine gender legally included women. In Manchester the Suffrage Society began a great campaign to get women to register, but the judges decided that only in cases of punishment and obligations were women included under the term 'man'. Patriarchy remained supreme. Another bill was introduced but blocked by Gladstone. The women had to wait until 1884 for the issue to be raised in Parliament again when a new bill to widen the franchise was introduced. Gladstone threatened to drop the whole bill if the women's amendment was not taken out. At the end of the 1880s there was another bill, but again the women were disappointed. Women were not to be included in the franchise in the wake of the working-class man. The militant feminist movement was to come out of these constitutional setbacks.

For in 1889, exasperated by the apologetic caution of the leaders of the suffrage movement, a new group, The Women's Franchise League, was formed. Among its council members was Mrs Emmeline Pankhurst, encouraged by her husband Richard Pankhurst, but still afraid of public speaking. The Franchise League took up the rights of married women. The feminists had tended to seek reforms for the unmarried—the failures —even excluding married women from their demand for the vote. The League campaigned for complete equality of women in divorce, inheritance and custody of children. The politics of the League were radical-liberal, although the Pankhursts had already had some contact with the socialist movement and were soon to join the Independent Labour Party.

10

Feminism and Rescue Work

Conservative opponents of women's suffrage were quick to see a connection between political rights and the social and sexual position of women. *The Saturday Review*, for example, was of the opinion in 1871 that women's votes would 'endanger the institution of marriage and the family'.[65]

In fact liberal feminism in the late nineteenth century was reticent on the question of women's sexual liberation, although these ideas were being again discussed in the socialist movement. Liberal feminists faced such overwhelming opposition to their most cautious demands that they were unwilling to face the public notoriety of a Victoria Woodhull, who attacked sexual hypocrisy and defied Mrs Grundy in America in the 1870s.

Moreover many middle-class women were more inclined to insist that men observed their own moral code than to demand the right to love freely. Upper and middle-class women who became involved in 'rescue' work could not help but confront personally the responsibility of men of their own class in making girls take to prostitution. In the 1860s the roads of Oxford Street, Haymarket and the Strand were full of street-walkers, while in Rotten Row the fashionable Miss Walters paraded. She was called 'Skittles' because she had told some drunken guardsmen who insulted her that 'if they didn't hold their bloody row, she'd knock them down like a row of bloody skittles'.[66] Kept by Lord Hartington with her own income of £2,000 a year, Miss Walters was at the top of her profession. The future poet laureate, Alfred Austin, even wrote a verse about Skittles' sexual bravado,

65   Women's Votes, the *Saturday Review*, 6 May 1871, quoted in J A and Olive Banks, *Feminism and Family Planning in Victorian England*, Liverpool 1964, p 109.
66   Letter from Sir William Hardman to Edward Holroyd, quoted in James Laver, *The Age of Optimism*, London 1966, p 69.

spurning frown and foe
With slackened rein swift Skittles rules the Row
Though scowling Matrons stamping steeds restrain,
she flaunts Propriety with flapping mane.

There was a middle stratum in prostitution, the women of the business classes, kept in suburban villas on the new railway lines in London. Less openly provocative than the upper-class mistress, the half-respectable kept women still presented a threat to the middle-class wife's position.

Venereal disease, unmentionable and yet impossible to ignore, lurked behind the Victorians' moral code. In 1864 a bill to prevent Contagious Diseases in the armed forces was introduced. This bill meant that any woman who was said to be a prostitute could be forcibly examined and imprisoned if she resisted. If she had VD she could be kept in the 'Lock Hospital' for three months. There was no compulsion on men to be treated for VD. Instead of being innocent until proved guilty, the women were defined as guilty and had to prove their innocence. However, the supporters of the Bill believed these measures would help in the rescuing of fallen women as well as reducing venereal disease in the armed forces. They included Elizabeth Garrett Anderson, one of the tiny minority of women doctors.

Opposition began to develop when the bill became law in 1869. Among the opponents of the Contagious Diseases Acts were people who had been involved in rescue work among prostitutes. Josephine Butler was the daughter of a prosperous Northumberland radical who had been connected to the Anti-Slavery agitation in the 1840s. In 1866 her husband moved to Liverpool, her daughter had died tragically while still a child, and Josephine Butler had thrown herself into rescue work as a release from her personal grief. She accepted the position of national organiser of a new society formed to campaign against the Acts with considerable apprehension, knowing that she was going to become publicly notorious.

Not only did the campaign against the Acts make the middle-class women aware of the hypocrisy of male dominated morality towards women of their own class and the evils which, in Josephine Butler's words, 'bore with murderous cruelty on other women',[67] it also gained working-class support. The complacency of middle-class men about the prostitution of working-class women was in marked contrast to their concern about the virginity of their own daughters. 'The Working Men's National League' enrolled 50,000 members, and the TUC supported repeal.

67   Quoted in Banks, *Feminism and Family Planning in Victorian England*, p 109: see Marion Ramelson, *Petticoat Rebellion*, (Chapters 10 and 11), for a longer account of this, London 1972.

The campaign thus attacked sex and class dominance within one of the most taboo areas of Victorian sexual culture. What is more it was led by a woman who was determined to insist that upper class men were to be subject to their own moral code. Not surprisingly it provoked much antagonism. Sir John Elphinstone MP said, for instance, 'I look upon these women as worse than prostitutes'.[68] Knowledge and activity among women of their own class threatened the control ruling-class men could exercise over all women.

The insistence by the campaigners that moral codes should apply without discrimination was to be a persistent theme in feminist propaganda. Many women went into the feminist movement because they felt it was wrong that existing morality was defined by men. This was part of a wider movement for the sexual protection of young girls. In the 1870s the age of consent was still 12 years of age and child prostitution was common. In 1881 a committee reported on prostitution among working class girls and the sale of girls to foreign brothels. In 1885 W T Stead, a radical journalist, wrote a series of exposures of the white slave traffic. These radical moral campaigns represented an attack on the sex and class power of the upper-class men, but they were also acceptable within the general framework of the Victorian attitude to women as helpless and in need of protection.

The prevalence of child prostitution inevitably meant that there were extremely young unmarried mothers who had to choose between the grim discipline of the workhouse or the streets. Before 1873 no mother of an illegitimate child could take any action to make a man in the army or navy financially responsible and civilian fathers could only be made to pay 2s 6d a week in the unlikely event the girl got them to court. In the 1880s the first charitable homes for young unmarried mothers were set up. The girl was still assumed to have 'fallen' but at least she was thought to have a right to some alternative to the workhouse or prostitution.

Middle-class reformers by the 1880s and 1890s were being forced to look towards the structure of capitalist society rather than at individual failing as the cause of social problems. Some turned to the collection of empirical data, believing that conditions could be changed if only they had the 'facts'. Though some were merely confirmed in their support for the status quo others moved towards the new socialist groups. The women were no exception. Middle-class investigators began to look at the economic situation of working-class girls. They exposed the conditions of home work and sweated industries, the exploitation of women in the dangerous trades like lead-making. They demanded more legislation and women factory inspectors and magistrates to enforce the new

68 Quoted in Ray Strachey (ed), *Our Freedom and its Results*, London 1936, p 181.

laws. Some of them attacked the condescending patronage of upper class philanthropy. Isabella Ford was a Leeds feminist and socialist active in the Women's Trade Union League. In a pamphlet written in the 1890s called *Industrial Women and How to Help Them*, she pointed out that the whole education of girls taught them to be submissive and patient.

> 'The general tone of this influence is against the idea that women should assert their rights as human beings, or that they should be loyal to a cause, and to their comrades, known and unknown in that cause, sooner than to their own immediate interests.'

This was reinforced by many teachers and charitable people:

> 'The earnest-minded band of women who spend their lives in rescue work ... end to perpetuate the evil they detest, since everyone who works on curative rather than preventive lines must do so in some degree . . .'
> 'The industrial woman . . . must be roused to desire and work out for herself her own salvation.'

The role of 'persons not of the proletariat class' was to help working class women to 'find a voice' to 'express their needs'.[69] This kind of attitude represented an important shift in progressive middle-class attitudes to social work which was to lead some middle-class men and women into Fabianism, the Independent Labour Party (ILP) and even into the Marxist Social Democratic Federation (SDF).

69   Isabella Ford, *Industrial Women and How to Help Them*, nd pp 7-19.

11

The Position of Working-Class Women in the Nineteenth Century

Capitalism broke down the old forms of social relations both at work and between men and women in the family. The consequences were, however, different for the working class than for the middle class. Middle-class women found themselves cut off from production and economically dependent on a man: working-class women were forced into the factory and became wage-labourers.

So although patriarchal authority was actually strengthened among the dominant class, the economic basis of the working-class man's ownership of his woman was undermined by the wages the woman could earn outside the home. The concern of the middle-class rescuers to protect working-class women frequently ignored the economic and sexual realities of working-class life. The rescuers persisted in seeing the values of their own class as universal and in seeing the state—their state which enforced their class interests—as a neutral body. The working class very often saw the factory inspectors, the housing investigators as alien interfering intruders who would reform their livelihoods away. Also the rebellion against patriarchal authority evoked little immediate response among working-class women for here capitalist development was undermining such authority in brutal and inhuman ways and many working-class men and women resisted what they felt to be a violation of natural bonds between men and women, parents and children.

One of the frequent complaints in the early stages of the industrial revolution was that although women and children could find work, the men could not. This had very direct effects on authority in the family. But as Engels points out in his *Conditions of the Working Class in England* of 1844, wage-labour in early nineteenth century capitalism brought not freedom, but a reversal of the economic position of men and women. They were still tied not by affection but by economic necessity. Because other social changes had not accompanied the alteration of economic power in the family, the man felt degraded and humiliated and the woman went out to work for less pay, and consequently greater profit for the employer. For although the factory system began to undermine the economic and social hold of the working-class man over the women in his family, patriarchal authority continued in society as a whole. The ruling class could benefit from the assumption which was still strong that women belonged to men. Thus the unctuous Ure wrote *The Philosophy of Manufactures*, delighting in the prospect of workers becoming appendages to machines and justifying women's low wages.

> 'Factory females have in general much lower wages than males, and they have been pitied on this account with perhaps an injudicious sympathy, since the low price of their labour here tends to make household duties their most profitable as well as agreeable occupation and prevents them from being tempted by the mill to abandon the care of their offspring at home. Thus Providence effects its purpose with a wisdom and efficacy which should repress the short-sighted presumption of human devices.'[70]

Capitalism in dividing work from home had produced a contradictory need. There was a new demand for female labour in the factory, but somehow children had to be cared for, and families fed. Women were not able to turn this contradiction to their advantage. Instead they were forced to labour both at home and at work.

From the 1830s the agitation for protection for women at work gained some success. Slowly hours were reduced, and women and children barred from the mines. Later efforts were made to extend protection beyond factories and mines. Humanitarian feeling combined with fear that the family was disintegrating. Shaftesbury believed that, if the factory system were allowed to go unchecked, 'Domestic life and domestic discipline must soon be at an end; society will consist of individuals no longer grouped in families; so early is the separation of husband and wife'.[71]

Single women began to fear that women would be banned from working altogether and that all women without men to support them would have to emigrate in search of husbands. Protective legislation concentrated on reducing hours, and men's hours tended to follow the women's. But there was often initial distress because the protectionists failed to provide any alternative sources of income. Women told the Commission of 1842 that they did not like work in the mines but they needed some other employment before they could stop going down the pit. In isolated mining districts, especially in East Scotland where there was no other employment, women dressed up as men and sneaked down the pit.

Not only did capitalism affect the economic relations between the

70   A Ure, *The Philosophy of Manufactures*, quoted in Wanda Neff, *Victorian Working Women*, London 1966, p 29.
71   Quoted in Pinchbeck, *Women Workers and the Industrial Revolution*, p 297.

sexes. As the cities grew rapidly the old kinship networks of the country-side and the small towns disintegrated. Popular sexual customs which belonged to a non-industrial society lost their function and their force. Upper-class opposition to the factories often connected the pathetic wage of the factory girl with sexual insubordination but there was both confusion and hypocrisy here. They assumed *their* morality was normal and the sexual culture of the poor was a deviation. In fact the sexual mores of the middle class were alien to the pre-industrial poor and to the new working class in the cities. In *The Manufacturing Population of England* Gaskell says,

> '. . . Sexual intercourse was almost universal prior to marriage in the agricultural districts. This intercourse must not be confounded with that promiscuous and indecent concourse of the sexes which is prevalent in towns and which is ruinous alike to health and morals. It existed only between parties where a tacit understanding had all the weight of obligation—and this was that marriage should be the result.'[72]

The large towns made old understandings harder to enforce. The factory wage, small as it was, meant girls could leave home and set up with boys very young. The upper and middle-class shock and horror about the pathetic and momentary 'freedom' of the factory girl was profoundly hypocritical. It was the flicker of independent sexual choice they feared in the mill girls for the sons and fathers of the rich took their pleasure with the female servants who were dependent on them and then deplored the tawdry gaiety of factory workers.

The life of women in the countryside before the industrial revolution was very hard. The poor had only the bare necessities and complaints about the decline of housekeeping and the neglect of children, both idealised the pre-industrial family and forgot that the rural poor had had no say in the new forms of capitalist exploitation. Many of the campaigners for protection were more concerned about social stability than the real situation of working-class women.

Without idealising the past it was still true that the cumulative effects of the new manufacturing towns, and the specific kind of poverty of the town-dweller meant a different species of wretchedness. For women the separation of work and home and the new discipline of the factory made their diverse activities less easy to combine. The factories created special problems for nursing mothers, or women with very small children. Engels describes the women rushing home in the factory break to feed their babies. Not surprisingly they stopped breast-feeding as soon as they could. Instead the babies were fed with watered-down, often infected cow's milk. Later, after the 1870s they were given condensed milk, and a pap of bread and water sweetened with sugar or treacle.

72 Margaret Hewitt, *Wives and Mothers in Victorian Industry*, London 1958, p 54.

When women had to go out to work the children were left with old women, grandmothers or baby minders. The minders crammed as many children as possible into a small space and kept them quiet with laudanum. Infant mortality was very high, and pregnancy was dangerous throughout the nineteenth century. A few nurseries were started in the factory districts, but they were usually far beyond the women's means and did not begin to cope with the problem. Instead of providing nurseries most middle and upper-class people blamed women for neglecting their children, not seeing that they were forced to send their children out to baby minders and when they were older into the factory because wages were so low. They blamed the women for being bad housekeepers, not asking how women could keep a house when they worked sixteen hours, and earned so little money they had nothing to keep it with.

Marx pointed out that it was absurd to blame working-class parents for sending their children out to work. Against abstract morality about a woman's 'natural' place, he supported protection for all workers because this was a way of preventing employers extracting more surplus value.[73] In *Capital* Marx wrote that it was 'modern industry, in overturning the economical foundation on which was based the traditional family, and the family labour correspondingly to it (which) had also unloosened all traditional family ties'.[74] These consequences sprang from the capitalist mode of production and not from the 'immorality' of working-class men and women.

Capitalism left women stranded in an ambiguous situation that was neither fully exposed to the cash-nexus nor completely freed from the older form of property ownership. The man's ownership of the *persons* of his woman and his children and his complete control over their capacity to produce was broken in the immediate relations of the working-class family. They ceased to be directly means of production for the man. However their low wage was still supplementary in the commodity system. Women could not enter commodity production on the same terms as men. Like the man they sold their labour power now as a commodity. But they still worked to maintain the labour force at home. In the early years of the industrial revolution the work of women in reproducing the men's and children's capacity to labour was drastically reduced. With protective legislation and fewer hours in the factory, women workers spent more time doing housework in the family. The need for women's labour in the family, in reproducing and maintaining labour power thus exercised a certain restraint on the direct exploitation of women's labour power in industry. But women's social usefulness was

73   See Henry Collins, C Abramsky, *Karl Marx and the British Labour Movement*, London 1965, pp 115-120.
74   Karl Marx, *Capital*, Vol I, translated by Moore and Aveling, London 1957, p 495.

never recognised or recompensed. Instead their dependence on the male bread-winner and their work in the family reduced their capacity to organise. They were thus placed at a double disadvantage.

Also men still dominated in society. Although the economic basis of patriarchy was weakened, cultural and sexual attitudes about female inferiority continued and contributed to women's economic compliance. In a competitive labour market the men had an obvious interest in keeping women out of the labour force. When the demand for labour power made this impossible men managed to exclude women from the skilled, highly paid jobs where they were organised. Consequently, women and foreign workers, the Irish and later the Jews, were forced into low paid work.

The man's direct ownership of women and children in the family was also modified by the state. By the end of the nineteenth century the 'free' market economy was being increasingly influenced by state intervention. While the short-term interest of the individual capitalist was to extract as much surplus value from workers regardless of age, sex or physical strength, the long-term interest of capital demanded some protection and guarding of future capacity. Thus not only protective legislation against the exhaustion of human body and mind at work, but public health measures, national education, and various efforts to protect small children from neglect were introduced.

Contemporaries often confused these changes with socialism, and indeed it was often trade unionists, radicals and socialists who forced them through. They were obviously important defences against the expansion of capital at the expense of human physical and mental capacity. Changes in education, public health and later in the beginnings of welfare also made possible the emergence of a working class which bargained with a new scale of expectations. But they brought also an extension of state power and a direct relationship between the central ised bourgeois state and everyday life, and represented a newly assumed responsibility by capitalism for preserving capacity and skills for a more 'rational' exploitation.

Already in the last quarter of the century the state began to take over some of the family's former responsibility for upbringing and education. This was only the beginning of a process which was to become more marked in the twentieth century. As the state became more involved in the physical welfare and cultural attitudes of the working class, public health, municipal reform and national schooling assumed a new importance and began to challenge the old policy of laissez-faire which had been the ideology of the earlier years of the nineteenth century.

12

Women and Trade Unions

After sections of the working class got the vote in 1867 there was pressure to remove the legal restraints on the trade unions: in the first half of the 1870s there was an expansion in trade-union membership along with the trade boom. This took the form not only of the increasing strength of existing unions, but also of the growth of unions in new areas like agriculture, and among unskilled workers.[75]. In 1872-74 as in the period 1833-34 there were attempts to recruit women. In 1872 the Edinburgh Upholsterers Sewers Society was established, an all-women union which survived for some considerable time. In 1874 Emma Paterson, daughter of a school teacher and married to a cabinet maker, formed both the Women's Protective and Provident League to encourage trade unionism among women, and the National Union of Working Women in Bristol. She had got the idea of women's unions from the Female Umbrella Makers Unions in the United States. She was opposed to mixed unions like those in the cotton industry because 'the women paid only half contributions and were excluded from management'.[76]

When in 1874 a strike of unorganised woollen weavers broke out in Dewsbury against a cut in wages, the League moved in and the women won. In the following year several small unions among London women bookbinders, upholsterers, shirt and collar makers and dressmakers were formed. In 1876 Mrs Paterson and Mrs Simcox, from the London Society of Bookbinders, Upholsterers and Shirt and Collar Makers, took their place in the TUC. At first they were welcomed but conflict soon broke out. The League got its funds from 'middle-class friends', the male trade unionists were suspicious of the influence of middle-class women. Men like Broadhurst, who was a prominent trade-union leader, were

75　See Sidney and Beatrice Webb, *The History of Trade Unionism*, London 1919, pp 336-337.
76　Barbara Drake, *Women in Trade Unions*, London 1921, p 11.

dubious about women organising in unions. He said it was 'very natural for ladies to be impatient of restraint at any time', therefore the factory was an unsuitable place for them. 'Wives should be in their proper place at home'.[77]

By this time trade was depressed and unemployment increasing. The men tended to see protection as a means of eliminating competition. Mrs Paterson opposed the Factory and Workshops Act of 1877 because she feared it would place women at a disadvantage. She explained she was not for long hours, but until women got better pay any reduction in hours made their wages even lower. There were similar disputes in the 1880s. Later Mrs Paterson healed the breach somewhat by urging higher pay for women so they could not be used as cheap labour.

In the second half of the 1880s, and in the 1890s, workers who had been outside craft organisation started to enter the trade-union movement. They brought with them a new consciousness and a wider area of trade unionism. They affected the older societies' structure, and the attitude to the women's unions and participation in trades councils improved.

The action of working-class women at work also forced trade unionists to take their predicament and determination seriously. From 1888 to around 1892 there was a considerable amount of spontaneous industrial action not only by men but also by women who had never organised before. The matchgirls' strike is the best known because of the publicity the socialist Annie Besant gave it in papers and journals. However *Commonweal*, the paper of the Socialist League, reported several other incidents of female militancy in the same year. Blanket weavers in Heckmondwike, female cigarmakers in Nottingham, girls in a tin box manufactory in London, who pelted men who continued to work after they came out with red-ochre and flour, cotton workers, and jute workers in Dundee, took action spontaneously in 1888. The reasons for striking varied, from demands for increases to resistance to cuts, or opposition to fines. Again in 1889 mill girls in Kilmarnock came out over the bad quality of yarn they were being given. At Alverthorpe, near Wakefield, woollen weavers, women and girls, rejected a reduced rate and marched in procession headed by girls with concertinas. This was broken up by the police, and the girls with concertinas—obviously regarded as 'leaders' —were fined for obstruction. Even waiters and waitresses demonstrated at Hyde Park in October 1889—though unfortunately they saw foreign workers not their employers as their foes.

The socialist groups were often involved in these strikes, although radicals, liberals and Christians were also sometimes to be found helping women workers because of the moral outcry against sweated labour.

The Socialist League for instance, was helping cap-makers in Manchester form a union in August 1889, and an urgent appeal for help came from Bristol comrades for money for cotton workers on strike in November 1889.

In 1891 there was a long and desperate strike at Manningham mills in Bradford. Isabella Ford supported the mill girls because her parents had started one of the first evening schools for working class girls and she had grown up knowing the conditions in the mills. Although initially very afraid of speaking, she defended the girls on the platform and demonstrated in the streets with them. Isabella and her sister Bessie lived at Adel near Leeds and their house was a kind of informal centre where socialists, trade unionists and radicals would meet. Among the Leeds socialists was Tom Maguire, who organised the unskilled gas workers' strike and helped with the tailoring union. He was a poet as well as a political organiser and wrote some verses to women in the tailoring trade called 'Machine-Room Chants'. In one called 'The Duchess of Number Three', he was ironic about a very beautiful, proud girl who said she did not need to join the union as she was all right on her own.

In London too women workers were helped by the new unionists and by socialists. Laundresses tried to make a union. They were supported by 27 trades councils and held a joint demonstration with railway workers in July 1891 in Hyde Park. According to the records of the Women's Trade Union League this was the first demonstration of working women in the Park—presumably the waitresses were not counted. Evidently several thousand laundresses and other workers turned out, and there were three platforms with Miss Abrahams from the Women's Trade Union League on one, and Tom Mann and Clem Edwards, a docker, on the other two.

More male trade unionists were beginning to see the need to work with the women and sensing the wider implications of female industrial militancy. For example a representative of the Amalgamated Society of Tailors wished the Women's Union 'God Speed' at the annual meeting of the League in 1892. It was his 'opinion . . . that the women should be allowed to work out their own political and social questions for themselves just the same as men are doing now'.[78]

The publicity the strikes received was partly stimulated by middle-class guilt, but it also encouraged women to report and investigate the conditions of working class women's work. Beatrice Potter (later Webb) wrote *Pages from a Work Girl's Diary* in 1888 about East End tailoring. Annie Besant wrote up the conditions of the match girls in her paper *The Link*. Clementina Black exposed the conditions of home work as

78 Mr Flynn, Amalgamated Society of Tailors, Annual Meeting, *Women's Trade Union Quarterly Report and Review*, 18 January 1892, no 4, p 9.

well as helping women to organise in Glasgow. Middle-class women thus learned about the situation of working-class women and came to see them not as passive objects of pity but as people who had to organise. In many cases this experience radicalised the middle-class observers.

'Unless you have lived among oppression and injustice,' wrote Isabella Ford, 'it is most difficult to realise how full of it is our industrial system particularly when it touches women.'[79]

There are many questions about the relationship of middle-class women to the trade-union organisation of the working class which remain completely unstudied. It is not clear whether they simply imposed their own concerns for the unfortunate upon working class women, or whether they broke with 'rescue' work. Although this is partly a political question—the socialists were less likely to see trade unions in theoretical terms as an extension of 'rescue' than were the liberals—it is also a more complex question of personal class response. The same problem of course existed for the middle-class male radical and socialist.

It is certain however that there was some interconnection between the feminist movement and women involved with the organisation and conditions of working-class women. Also there was evidently an awareness in the 1890s among working class women of the wider implications of militancy. Margaret McMillan, a member of the ILP, writes in her biography of her sister Rachel, that although women were never equal in the trade union, within the labour movement

'A new feature . . . was the stir and murmur among women. Overworked mothers and wives, young girls too and older women who were unmarried, and living by their own labour, at factory or workshop, wakened as from sleep and began to conceive new hope and purpose.'[80]

It is very difficult to know how extensive this feeling was or what it involved in terms of organisation. We know very little about what working-class women discussed amongst themselves because they have only been considered worthy of history in exceptional instances. Thus it is not clear whether they were questioning their position as women, or demanding new rights like the vote. The responses of men are a little more accessible. Predictably there was both suspicion and enthusiasm among the leaders in the labour movement.

The TUC had been committed to adult suffrage as long as it had been in existence, and to votes for women since 1884, but in a pious rather than an active manner. Real doubts about giving the vote to women on the existing property terms, which weighed in favour of the

79 Isabella Ford, *Women as Factory Inspectors and Certifying Surgeons*, Women's Co-operative Guild, 1898.
80 Margaret McMillan, *The Life of Rachel McMillan*, London, 1927, p 137. For a different view, see Alexandra Kollontai, *Women Workers Struggle for Their Rights*, Bristol 1971, p 19. She says the English trade union movement 'bore a narrowly economic character'.

middle class, mingled with a straightforward feeling that women should stay in their place and let men decide on politics. The fear of women becoming active went beyond the vote. A member of the Women's Co-operative Guild, which was formed by Mrs Acland towards the end of the nineteenth century, remembered her husband's suspicions many years later. 'Sometimes my husband rather resented the teachings of the Guild. . . . The Guild he said was making women think too much of themselves.'[81]

There was at least some awareness of the connection between women's oppression at work and in the home among the 'new' unionists. Tom Mann, one of the leaders of the new unionism, wrote:

> 'Who would choose to be a workman's wife, with its washing every week, bed-making every day, meal-preparing every few hours, and for a change, to be up early on a bank holiday, wash and dress, and carry a number of youngsters to the station, look after them for a dozen hours, get jammed in half a dozen crowds, reach home ready to faint—lucky if no limbs are broken—and get up next day for the usual round?'[82]

He proposed that women should organise co-operative child care, shopping, cooking, eating, washing, and use gas instead of coal. There should be music and dancing for the children. He was careful to emphasise that the women should remain 'virtuous'. Co-operative housework did not imply 'free love' or 'mormonism'.

81 (ed) Margaret Llewellyn Davies, *Life as We Have Known It*, London, 1931, p 48.
82 Tom Mann, Leisure for Workmen's Wives, in *Halfpenny Short Cuts*, June 28, 1890, p 163.

13

Socialism, the Family and Sexuality

Behind middle-class anxiety lay not only pity for the weak but also fear of the strength of the working class and apprehension about the consequences of the new socialist groups which were breaking with the assumptions of liberalism. Out of this socialism came discussion of hitherto submerged questions. Like the utopian socialists earlier, revolutionaries in the 1880s and 1890s tried to connect sexual subordination to property ownership, and to discover the relationship between the oppression of women and the exploitation of workers.

The direct influence of Marx was not very great in England before the early twentieth century. Although his general ideas spread through works of popularisation, most of his early writings were only published later this century. In the *Economic and Philosophical Mss* of 1843-4 he had followed through Fourier's ideas about the position of women being an index of social development. The relation of man to woman was part of the whole relationship of human beings to the external natural world. 'The relationship of man to woman is the most natural relation of human being to human being. It indicates therefore how far man's natural behaviour has become human.'[83]

Shortly after, in *The German Ideology*, he described the division of labour between men and women in the family, and in the sexual act and the relationship of productive forces to human consciousness. The family was part of the productive forces. 'The production of life, both of one's own in labour and of fresh life in procreation, now appears as a double relationship: on the one hand as a natural, on the other as a social relationship.'[84]

The private ownership of property affected all social relations

83 Karl Marx, Economic and Philosophical Manuscripts of 1844, in (ed) T Bottomore, *Karl Marx: Early Writings*, London 1963.
84 Karl Marx, *The German Ideology*, London 1965, p 41.

including those between men and women. The worker's sale of labour power as a commodity was thus connected to the woman's sale of her body. 'Prostitution is only a specific expression of the universal prostitution of the worker.'[85]

In order to understand this connection historically both Marx and Engels studied pre-capitalist societies. At first Marx believed that the family was the original social relationship, and that the tribe followed. But he changed his mind later and came to the conclusion that the various forms of the family came out of the '. . . first incipient loosening of the tribal bonds'.[86] He believed he could see the same process within capitalist society, as the pre-industrial family disintegrated. Out of this disintegration came a new synthesis, the basis for relations between men and women, parents and children which were not distorted by property and ownership.

> 'However terrible and disgusting the dissolution, under the capitalist system, of the old family ties may appear, nevertheless, modern industry, by assigning as it does an important part in the process of production outside the domestic sphere to women, to young persons and to children of both sexes, creates a new economical foundation for a higher form of the family, and of the relations between the sexes.'[87]

Then he jumped into the future to say it was obvious that the 'collective working group' of people 'of both sexes and all ages' must, 'under suitable conditions', become a source of 'humane development', though its capitalist form was 'brutal', and the 'labourer exists for the process of production, and not the process of production for the labourer.'

However, this left the intervening period vague and mysterious. While capitalism continued, the collective working group meant the subordination of men, women and children to the expansion of capital. Nor did Marx take into account the consequences of the intervention of the state in the reproduction of labour power. He apparently presumed that the capitalist mode of production would completely erode all former kinds of property and production.

In fact their relationship proved more complex. Certain aspects of patriarchy continued to serve capital, by maintaining female subordination in the family and the state. The idea of the woman's body being the property of the man continued in cultural and sexual life even while the economic control of men over women's persons in the working class disintegrated. It had a useful economic function. Marx had observed how women were used as part of the reserve army of labour; they could be reabsorbed in the family when labour was plentiful and there they played their part in the reproduction of labour power.

85 Marx, Economic and Philosophic Manuscripts, op cit, p 156.
86 Engels's footnote in Marx, Capital, Vol I, p 344.
87 Capital, Vol I, p 496.

Marx saw communal domestic economy as presupposing the development of machinery and the use of natural forces, but, like Engels, he never envisaged the consequences of contraception. Capitalism was to create a technology which made control over production and over procreation technically but not socially possible. The family was streamlined but patriarchy did not disintegrate completely. The erosion of man's property in women, and of the ideology of man's superiority over women, occurred more slowly, too, than Marx imagined. The precise relationship between the continuation of patriarchal authority and the class system in capitalism was left unclear along with the more general problem of the connection between material and ideological structures.

In 1884 Engels' *Origin of the Family Private Property and the State* was published. This was an attempt to analyse the oppression of women in terms of the relationship between the mode of production and procreation and the connection between forms of the family and systems of property ownership. He stated his intention in the preface.

> 'According to the materialist conception the determining factor in history is, in the final instance, the production and reproduction of the immediate essentials of life. This again is of a two-fold character. On the one side, the production of the means of existence, articles of food and clothing, dwellings and of the tools necessary for that production; on the other side, the production of human beings themselves, the propagation of the species. The social organisation under which the people of a particular historical epoch and a particular community live is determined by both kinds of production, by the stage of development of labour on the one hand and of the family on the other.'[88]

The idea of production in the family being a factor in historical development was subsequently obscured in marxist thinking. But even in *The Origin of the Family* the specific form of the influence of 'the production of human beings' upon 'the production of the means of existence' is left unclear. Also human production is separated from human sensuous experience and feeling. Engels has here substituted a narrow conception of economic relations for a wider definition of material existence.

Nonetheless his argument is worth looking at in some detail. He saw the monogamous family as the result of the private ownership of property. The family was a microcosm of the contradictions and oppositions in society as a whole. Monogamy had meant the subordination of women. Men had appropriated individual women as property. Monogamy was based on the 'supremacy of the man', its 'purpose being to produce children of undisputed paternity',[89] who could inherit his property. The division of labour in the family regulated the division of property. Engels believed monogamy and private property were preceded by a period of primitive communism, in which this appropriation of women did not

88   F Engels, Preface to *The Origin of the Family*, London 1940, p 2.
89   *ibid*, p 65.

exist. Monogamy thus meant at one and the same time a great historical set-back for women, but also the necessary basis for a transformation of sexual relations. He thus saw monogamy as the equivalent of capitalism, and sex as the equivalent of class. The 'first class opposition that occurs in history coincides with the development of antagonism between man and woman in monogamous marriage'.[90]

He generalised the experience of middle-class women. Housework became a 'private service', the wife a 'head servant'.[91] In fact of course not all women were excluded from production. Engels believed that modern industry opened the possibility of ending the 'domestic slavery of the wife'. It absorbed women back into social production, and he thought it would make private domestic labour public. As it turned out capitalism did not need to make household labour public: instead women had to work both outside and at home. The reduction of family size made the continuation of the individual nucleus of the family possible while married women were absorbed into the labour force.

Engels saw individual sex love as a historical creation connected to monogamy. He believed that like monogamy and capitalism it was to be transcended. While reticent about making prophecies for the future he, like Marx, envisaged sexual relations in which economic dependence played no part. Capitalism had distorted the ways in which individuals experienced sexual love. Prostitution was the other side of monogamy, love was confused with possession, morality was bound by external codes, and not by the relationship between people. The evils of capitalist society were covered by the 'cloak of love and charity, to palliate them or to deny them'.[92] But in subsequent revolutionary movements it was to prove very hard to decide what elements in bourgeois romantic love should survive in socialism, and what aspects of sensuous individualism were antagonistic to the creation of communism.

Engels raised many questions which are still very relevant, though his analogy of female oppression with class exploitation does not really work. The notion of women as a class, as the proletarians in marriage, with the men as the bourgeois, means that only the economic aspects of woman's relations to man is discussed. The sexual difference between men and women is obscured by reducing the whole relationship to one of woman's capacity to work. This ignores that sexual relations are part of a whole human relationship to the external world, though in different communities these assume a variety of institutional and social forms. Moreover the family has a complicated connection to production and ownership of property. It does not always change neatly as they are transformed. Nor is sex the equivalent of class. Individuals in the past have

90   *ibid*, p 69.
91   *ibid*, p 79.
92   *ibid*, p 203.

been able to move from one class to the other. But women, except in very modern exceptional instances, cannot become men, any more than black people can become white. Also the victory of the proletariat means the abolition of class. The proletariat has no need for the capitalist. But the end of the subjection of women does not thus mean the abolition of men. The analogy of sex and class is confusing.

There are also problems about the type of anthropological material that was available to Engels when he and Marx studied these questions. He used the work of an anthropologist called Morgan, who was part of the evolutionary school. Evolutionary anthropologists were concerned with tracing back the origins of human society: there was much debate about the earliest forms of property and sexuality, and whether there had been a universal early stage of promiscuity and communal owner-ship. The belief that primitive communism might have existed, suggested that capitalism and monogamy also might be superseded, and shocked conservatives. Engels felt that Morgan's work related to his own and to Marx's study of capitalism.

However, because they were talking about a pre-historical period there was very little evidence, except for myths and existing primitive societies. It is very doubtful whether myths are literal descriptions of actual societies or historical happenings. They have been seen as the attempt to know a reality that remains hidden, as a means of bolstering the claims of one group against another, to express concealed fears of one group against another. The assumption that the existence of myths about an age in which women were not subordinate proves that such an era actually existed is thus almost certainly an over-simplification.[93] Also there is no necessary connection between a system of inheritance which passes through the woman in the family (matrilineal) and the political, social and economic dominance of women (matriarchy). The main diffi-culty though about the evolutionists' assumption that there was a univer-sal stage of society which preceded private ownership, is that they were forced to use *existing* primitive societies as evidence. They regarded the development of human society as a kind of biological childhood in which the 'children' always grew up in the same way. Yet one cannot with any certainty recreate the earliest societies from abstractions about existing ones. It would seem that the idea of a single universal stage must remain an hypothesis which can never be proved either way.

Nonetheless Engels's attempt to synthesise existing anthropology with marxism stimulated other revolutionary socialists in the last quarter of the nineteenth century and early twentieth century to study this whole area. When the evolutionary method was attacked by subsequent anthro-

---

93   See for example Maurice Godelier, The Origins of Mythical Thought, *New Left Review*, 69, Sept-Oct 1971. On Engels see Sara Delmont, Fallen Engels, *New Edinburgh Review* no 18, 1972.

pologists they neglected to ask the kind of questions Engels had felt were important about the ownership of the means of production and the position of women in society. Since the 1920s Marxists, too, have neglected the role of the family in historical development, and have contented themselves with a defensive return to Engels's system of categorisation. Only recently has a marxist anthropology conscious of the oppression of women begun to emerge.

* * *

Some of these more general questions were taken up by others in the socialist movement in Britain in the late nineteenth century. Eleanor Marx, Marx's daughter, with Edward Aveling, reviewed Bebel's book *Women in the Past, Present and Future* in the *Westminster Review* in 1885, in an article 'The Woman Question from a Socialist Point of View'. They were very sympathetic to Bebel's study and also referred to Engels's work. They were aware of contemporary feminist agitation for higher education, the vote, and against the forced inspection of prostitutes. They believed these reforms were important but did not strike at the structure of female oppression, which they believed, like Engels, was of an economic origin.

> 'Women are the creatures of an organised tyranny of men, as the workers are the creatures of an organised tyranny of idlers . . . no solution of the difficulties and problems that present themselves is really possible in the present condition of society.'[94]

They used the idea of women being the equivalent of the proletariat, and returned to the early radicals' insistence that women could not be freed by men. Women, like workers, had to recognise 'that their emancipation will come from themselves'. They would find allies among men, just as the workers found allies among the philosophers, artists and poets, but they had nothing more to hope from men as a whole, than the workers had from the middle class. Eleanor was very interested in Shelley and Ibsen and it is possible that her belief that marriage and morality were based on the economic organisation of society, her support for easier divorce, and her feeling that the 'sex instinct' was repressed in modern society, came from them as well as from her own relations with Aveling.

Edward Carpenter's *Love's Coming of Age* appeared about ten years later, in 1896. This was a collection of pamphlets originally published by the Manchester Labour Press, which had sold well in socialist and 'forward' circles. The willingness of the Labour Press to publish pamphlets on 'Sex Love' and 'Women' in the 1890s is itself an indication

94   Eleanor Marx, Edward Aveling, *Westminster Review*, 1885, vi, 25, p 211.

of the connection between Northern socialism and interest in sexual and psychological matters. Carpenter was an ex-clergyman who became a university extension lecturer in the North and then became involved in the socialist movement and developed an interest in Indian mysticism. Carpenter's whole life was a personal attempt to bridge the separation of man from nature, as well as the class and sex divide. He lived on a small farm near Sheffield in great simplicity and gave his private income to socialist causes. He was friendly with Havelock Ellis, an early sex psychologist.

In *Love's Coming of Age* he tried to connect existing anthropology and psychology to a vague rather mystical marxism. Like Engels he saw the family changing with different forms of society. He was enthusiastic about the contemporary feminist movement and not only supported the liberation of women, but questioned whether sexual differences were as fixed as people imagined. Homosexuality was even more taboo in the 1890s than discussion of heterosexuality. Carpenter published a pamphlet called 'Homogenic Love' through the Labour Press. Fisher Unwin panicked and turned down *Love's Coming of Age* at the last minute because Oscar Wilde had been convicted. So the courageous Labour Press brought the first edition out. In 1906 he added a chapter called 'The Intermediate Sex' in which he described the suffering of young people of 'the intermediate sex' whom he called 'Urnings'. Because 'a veil of complete silence' was 'drawn over the subject' they faced 'the most painful misunderstanding and perversions and confusions of mind'.[95]

Carpenter did not exactly 'come out' but his own homosexuality was not concealed from his socialist friends, including his working-class comrades in the Sheffield Socialist Society and in the Lancashire and Yorkshire movement. Carpenter belonged to a circle of intellectuals who broke very determinedly if self-consciously from their own class and sex supremacy. His attempt to think through the problem of sexual liberation was, however, restricted by the lack of any effective system of contraception. In 1909 he added the notes on Preventive Checks to Population. He believed women should not be a 'mere machine for perpetual reproduction'.[96] However he said:

> 'artificial preventatives . . . are for the most part very unsatisfactory, their uncertainty, their desperate matter-of-factness, so fatal to real feeling, the probability that they are in one way or another dangerous or harmful, and then their one-sidedness, since here—as so often in matters of sex—the man's satisfaction (is) at the expense of the woman.'

Despite the inadequacy of contraception he grasped the significance of non-procreative sex. When sexual pleasure was separated from conception, and when propagation was within human control, a new realm of

95   Edward Carpenter, *Love's Coming of Age*, London 1918, p 123.
96   *ibid*, p 172.

freedom became possible. He did not think though in terms of improving contraceptives. Instead he introduced into the English socialist movement the idea of 'prolonged bodily conjunction' without male orgasm. These ideas came from the theories of an American, J H Noyes, who had advocated free love and communal living based on male continence. It is possible too that Carpenter was influenced here by his study of Indian culture.

There was in the 1890s and early 1900s a good deal of discussion about sexuality, family, alternative ways of living, and an attempt to try and live something of the socialist society of the future in the here and now. This awareness of the connection between beliefs and practice did not only exist among middle-class people, who, like Carpenter, went off to live in cottages in the country and shared housework equally. Carpenter's influence was important in the North—many working-class socialists broke with Mrs Grundy along with liberalism. In East London anarchists like Rudolf Rocker and his wife defied existing conventions by living in a free union. In *Pioneering Days* Thomas Bell, later to become a communist, describes how class consciousness, the theory he learned in the Glasgow marxist economics study groups, and the attempt to live with his wife and children without giving in to the old world, came together in his political development.

Some marxists and socialists however were opposed to Engels's and Carpenter's books. H M Hyndman, the autocratic and sectarian leader of the marxist Social Democratic Federation, not only disliked Engels personally but regarded *The Origin of the Family* as 'a colossal piece of impudence . . . to garble Morgan's grand work'. The young rebels in the group, soon to split, got copies of Engels's book from America along with works by the industrial unionist Daniel de Leon.[97]

Engels argued generally against the SDF leaders who, he said, saw marxism as an orthodoxy that had 'to be forced down the throats of the workers'[98] and swallowed whole. Any participation in everyday union struggles was dismissed. Socialism was seen as being produced by a crisis, an objective process in which the consciousness and activity of men and women played a negligible part. They saw socialist 'education' as being not a learning through doing, organising and discussion in action, but as something which was brought from outside as received truth. This sectarianism reduced their effectiveness. It also meant that they displayed the same intolerance to the feminist agitation as they did to trade-union militancy.

There was also opposition later from the non-marxist socialists.

97 C Tsuzuki, The Impossibilist Revolt in Britain, in *International Review of Social History*, 1/3, 1956, p 377.

98 F Engels quoted in Walter Kendall, *The Revolutionary Movement in Britain: 1900-1921*, London 1969, p 11.

They were afraid discussion of the family and sexuality would give socialism a bad name and put people off. Robert Blatchford editor of *The Clarion*, a socialist newspaper, wrote to Carpenter after *Love's Coming of Age* was published, saying he was sure Carpenter realised the economic changes had to come first and wouldn't it be better to keep quiet about sex until after they had got socialism and change things then.

In fact the sacredness of the family was part of Blatchford's socialism. He believed in the rule of the 'efficient', the recreation of the Empire, and 'reverence for women'. He loved 'the common people', 'the women', and 'England'. Women were 'civilisers', 'angels'. 'It is when we need women that we learn their value. It is when we trust ourselves fearlessly to her protecting arms that we find the goodliness and loveliness of Mother England.'[99] Blatchford's idealisation of the woman as mother meant, not surprisingly, that he was wary of Carpenter's socialism.

In *Britain for the British* in 1902 he wrote, 'Socialists, it has been said, want to destroy home life, to abolish marriage, to take the children from their parents, and to establish "Free Love".'[100] Blatchford reassured everyone that free love was no more to do with socialists than it was with tories or liberals and he would never let his children be taken off by the state. Far from seeing the family as changing in different societies, he saw it historically and morally as the basis of the nation. 'I believe that the nation should be a family'. The nation 'family' had to be made safe, and protected against foreign competition. The 'family' had to be made healthy so the workers could control the Empire.[101]

Blatchford was a skilled propagandist and his ideas appealed to many of the existing attitudes in the working class. He was one of the 'non-ideological', 'practical', 'commonsense' socialists who believe in gradual reform and are convenient scarecrows decked out in the left-over rags of ruling class ideology and values. Other socialists, like Bruce Glasier in *The Meaning of Socialism* in 1919, waxed sentimental about the family. In its existing form in capitalism it was evidently '. . . a small socialist community' which should be extended into the nation as a whole.[102]

Thus while the Hyndman type of revolutionary socialist dismissed the family and sexuality as being irrelevant to marxism, the reformists saw the family as a moral absolute not as a changing social relationship, and idealised women as angels and mothers. Both these attitudes have had a curious longevity.

99 Robert Blatchford, *My Eighty Years*, London 1931, p 219, pp 68-69.
100 Robert Blatchford, *Britain for the British*, London 1902, p 78.
101 See Bernard Semmell, *Imperialism and Social Reform*, London 1960.
102 J Bruce Glasier, *The Meaning of Socialism*, 1st edition 1919, 6th impression Leicester 1923, p 1939.

14

The Struggle for Birth Control at the End of the Nineteenth Century

The old debate about population control continued in the second half of the nineteenth century. It was still within the framework of support or opposition to Malthus's ideas that there was a law making population increase faster than economic resources. Marx and Engels were firmly opposed to the 'contemptible Malthus'. They pointed out again and again that there were no abstract economic laws but historic laws which were valid only in particular forms of society. Though Engels wrote to Kautsky in 1881, that it was possible at some stage in communist society that the number of people would become so great that the society would 'regulate the production of human beings, just as it has already come to regulate the production of things', he stressed that this regulation would be under the control of the people themselves and not imposed upon them.

'. . . it is for the people in the communist society themselves to decide whether, when, and how this is to be done, and what means they wish to employ for the purpose.'[103]

However he seems to have been thinking of 'moral restraint' not of contraception. He thought in terms of the 'production of human beings' not in terms of the political consequences of separating sex from reproduction. Right-wing opponents of contraception were quicker to see these implications. When the secularists, Charles Bradlaugh and Annie Besant, were arrested in 1877 for republishing Knowlton's *Fruits of Philosophy* with medical notes by Dr George Drysdale, a supporter of Bradlaugh's Malthusian League, the Solicitor General declared it 'a dirty, filthy book . . . the object of it is to enable persons to have sexual intercourse, and not to have that which in the order of Providence is the natural result of that sexual intercourse'.[104]

103 Engels to Kautsky, 1 Feb 1881, in (ed) Ronald L Meek, Marx and Engels *On Malthus*, London 1953, p 109.
104 Quoted in Fryer, *The Birth Controllers*, p. 181.

Fear about the separation of sexual pleasure from procreation was entangled with male authority over women, and class power over the working class. Annie Besant was charged with publishing an obscene work that might suggest to the young and unmarried 'that they might gratify their passion'.[105]

She pointed out in her defence that a cheap edition of Knowlton's pamphlet meant working-class women could purchase for 6d what richer women were already buying at W H Smith's for a few shillings. Besant and Bradlaugh were found guilty but let off on a technical point on appeal (although Annie Besant lost the custody of her child because the judge thought her daughter might follow in her mother's footsteps). Mrs Besant wrote a new book on population control in 1877 and dedicated it to 'the poor in great cities and agricultural districts . . . in the hope that it may point out a path from poverty, and may make easier the life of British workers'.[106]

Although Bradlaugh and Besant were not prosecuted again, other advocates of population control were. In the 1890s there were several cases, and a 67 year old Newcastle phrenologist was sentenced to a term in prison with hard labour.

Opposition came not only from followers of Marx and Engels, from the church and the conservative upper class but also from the groups concerned to protect the purity of young girls. There was thus an uneasy relation between a section of the feminist movement in the nineteenth century and the Malthusian League though when Margaret Sanger came to England in 1915, Alice Vickery, an old woman by then, told her of the Malthusian pioneers, and Sanger says that Vickery 'had been one of the first to welcome the militant suffragettes'.[107]

The Malthusians found the going hard in the nineteenth century, because not only was there widespread opposition but the methods of contraception they advocated were either awkward and clumsy or difficult to obtain; coitus interruptus, injections of alum and water, the vaginal sponge soaked in quinine, the French letter, and quinine pessaries. The most important innovation was the Mensinga diaphragm, which had been invented by a Dutch doctor in the 1870s, and thus became known as the Dutch cap. However the more effective methods were beyond the reach of most working-class women, though the idea of birth control certainly spread through scurrilous verse, and by word of mouth.

When the Great Depression in the 1870s caused unemployment, there was an added incentive to regulate families. There was evidently some support in London amongst politically conscious workers. Tom Mann describes how he became involved in Malthusianism, trade union-

105 Quoted in Banks, *Feminism and Family Planning*, p 117.
106 Fryer, *The Birth Controllers*, p 183.
107 Margaret Sanger, *An Autobiography*, London, 1939, p 163.

ism and teetotalism, when he was working in Kings Cross during 1879-1880. Then he went to work in Chiswick where 'on top of Trade Unionism and curtailing the output of families, they laid considerable stress on the necessity for co-operation'. He was later to become a land nationaliser, and then a socialist and 'see the limitations of Malthusianism'.[108]

By the turn of the century some of the middle and upper classes, the new white-collar workers and the more skilled and politically conscious working people were already practising some form of family limitation, though these were probably still coitus interruptus, the sheath, or vaginal syringes. The birth rate began to fall in the late 1870s and though the precise connection between birth control propaganda and population size is hard to prove, surveys and enquiries done in the early 1900s indicate a definite correlation between the two.

Although feminist suspicion of birth control was to be gradually overcome in the twentieth century, the marxist opposition to Malthus spilt over into opposition to contraception and meant that controversy continued between socialists and birth controllers well into the twentieth century.

108   Tom Mann, How I Became a Socialist, 1896, quoted in (ed) E J Hobsbawm *Labour's Turning Point 1880-1900*, London 1948, p 35.

15

The Vote

Emmeline Pankhurst married into a family with a history of radical and suffrage agitation. Like many other middle-class radicals in the 1880s and 1890s she and her husband moved towards socialism. They joined the ILP in 1894 and Emmeline began her public political career by standing for the School Board and marching with the unemployed to the Poor Law Office when they demanded the right to work. She was active on the Board of Guardians, which administered poor relief, and she campaigned for better conditions for people in the workhouse. Despite her nervousness about speaking she began to give talks at socialist meetings, supporting her husband as an ILP candidate and fighting with him against the attempt to stop public meetings in Boggart Hole, Clough. She was to be seen doing outdoor speaking with her penetrating voice and her pink straw hat bobbing in the crowd. After the death of her husband she continued to be politically active. Women could not be elected to the School Board which controlled education locally, but they could be co-opted onto the Education Committee.

Emmeline Pankhurst, like many other socialists in the 1890s, thus received an education in practical politics by agitation over the poor law, and attempts to improve on the 1870 Education Act. The Independent Labour Party was theoretically vague and confused but practically flexible and the more rigid and sectarian revolutionary socialism of the Social Democratic Federation lost ground in the 1890s.

When the 1901 Taff Vale judgement made trade unions liable for damages claimed against their members on strike, trade unionists became concerned with political activity because this seemed the only way to get the law off the statute books. The rise of the Labour Party after Taff Vale was a result of this new sense of political urgency in the trade-union movement, backed by active ILP preparation.

There appeared again to be a chance of getting parliamentary backing for women's suffrage. It seemed possible that the Independent Labour Party and the Labour Representation Committee would commit themselves to the vote in a way the Liberal Party would not. Emmeline and her daughter, Sylvia, were friendly with Keir Hardie, who gave the cause of women's suffrage his complete support, though Christabel, the other daughter, was inclined to doubt the socialists' commitment.

In 1903 a small group of women in the ILP met at Mrs Pankhurst's home and formed the Women's Social and Political Union, with the slogan 'Votes for Women' and the intention of getting the new Labour Representation Committee to make the vote a party question. At the 1904 ILP conference Mrs Pankhurst got official party backing to sponsor the Women's Enfranchisement Bill. The new movement for the vote thus came out of the ILP and had natural links with working-class organisations like the Women's Co-operative Guild.

. On 12 May 1904 the Women's Social and Political Union (WSPU) along with other supporters of the suffrage and with a group of Lancashire textile workers and four hundred women from the Women's Guild assembled outside Parliament, only to see the Bill talked out to the amusement of their masculine legislators. Mrs Pankhurst tried to call a meeting but they were hustled away. Bedraggled and defeated they clustered around some distance away from the House of Commons. Keir Hardie came out to join them.

Out of this defeat they turned to direct action. Their heckling of political meetings began, and with it the legal confrontation with the state.

Christabel and Annie Kenny, an Oldham cotton worker, went to a meeting in the Free Trade Hall in Manchester and asked what was to become a familiar question, 'Will the Liberal Government give women the vote?' The girls were thrown out and arrested after a struggle in the hall and an attempt to speak in the street outside. The Liberal, Grey, said Women's Suffrage was not 'a Party question'. Both Christabel and Annie refused to pay their fines and were imprisoned for short periods. At this stage Mrs Pankhurst had no strategy of direct confrontation. Sylvia said that she '. . . hurried to the cells with proud congratulations, pleading with motherly solicitude: " You have carried it far enough: now I think you ought to let me pay your fines and take you home." "If you pay my fine I will never go home again," her daughter answered hotly.'[109]

Other suffrage supporters were embarrassed but Keir Hardie telegrammed his support. Christabel was threatened with expulsion from Manchester University but the crowd gave her an enthusiastic welcome when she was released. This imprisonment was the first taste of martyrdom and glory. Mrs Pankhurst admired her daughter's

109 E Sylvia Pankhurst, *The Suffragette Movement*, London 1931, pp 52-53.

determination and told Sylvia, 'Christabel is not like other women; not like you and me, she will never be led away by her affections'.[110]

Faced with an unenthusiastic ILP, a Labour Party which would not put votes for women on their programme, and the indifference of the Liberals, the WSPU began an independent election campaign. At the 1907 conference Keir Hardie told the ILP they would have to choose between Votes for Women or losing some of their 'most valuable women members'.[111]

Mrs Pankhurst said that until women were enfranchised she would not abandon her independent election policy. She pleaded she had been 'loyal to Socialism on every point', but would reluctantly surrender her ILP card if forced to choose. Even allowing for Sylvia's obvious interest in emphasising her mother's socialism, there was a close connection between feminism and socialism in the early years of this century and the divorce between the two was long, painful and protracted.

It was not a simple question of reactionary middle-class feminists versus enlightened working-class socialists. The political reality of the suffragette movement was both more fluid and more confused than the conventional stereotype.

Subsequent accounts of the suffagette movement have tended to concentrate on the Pankhursts as personalities. This means the actual social composition of the movement remains unclear. Very probably many suffragette supporters came from the same social strata as many of the members of the Fabian Society—disaffiliated intellectuals, and the new lower middle class, especially teachers and clerical or shop workers. The movement for the vote was undoubtedly mainly middle class but support from working-class women certainly existed, despite the policy of courting upper-class women after 1907. The original inspiration for the forming of the WSPU had probably come from a petition signed by women in the textile industry in Lancashire, Cheshire and Yorkshire. Annie Kenny, of the Lancashire textile workers, was an exception, in becoming involved on a national full-time basis. But there was certainly sympathy from other Northern working women. There was also some sporadic organisation in Yorkshire. Sylvia says that in South Leeds 'textile mill hands, mothers and wage workers demonstrated with Mrs Pankhurst in a torch-light procession to Hunslet Moor where 100,000 assembled'.[112]

In Leeds the connections between the suffrage movement, the socialists and the industrial organisation of the tailoresses were close and had been made through a decade of organising together. Isabella Ford and Mary Gawthorpe in Leeds were active in both the feminist and

110   ibid, p 47.
111   ibid, p 65.
112   ibid, p 74.

socialist movement locally. In Southampton Florence Exten, a young clerk and member of the WSPU spent many early mornings chalking on the pavements 'Votes for Women'. Her father was a member of the SDF and she had helped him canvass in the back streets of Southampton's dockland. She was in the Clarion Cycling Club and in the women's section of the shopworkers' union. The local history of the suffrage movement has yet to be written. When it is we will be better able to trace the political origins of the agitators for the vote and understand the experiences which brought women to the suffragette cause.

It must have been difficult for most working-class women to travel around on delegations or go to meetings. The middle-class women were more mobile. It would be interesting to find out the extent to which the suffragettes could rely on local support when they held meetings. In 1908, for example, they were pursuing candidates at by-elections and would appear to have had considerable impact. The Manchester Guardian carried this report in January 1908 of the Newton Abbot by-election.

'I think there can be no doubt that the suffragists did influence voters. Their activity, the interest shown in their meetings, the success of their persuasive methods in enlisting popular sympathy, the large numbers of working women who acted with them as volunteers—these are features of the election which although strangely ignored by most of the newspapers, must have struck visitors to the constituency.'[113]

They were also able to get support from men. A manufacturer in Newcastle in September 1908 reported to Asquith, the Prime Minister, that the suffragettes were influencing the waverers, including the engineers.

'I have been present at several meetings addressed by various branches of the Engineers' Society by members of the Women's Social and Political Union, and in many cases spontaneous resolutions were put forward in their favour and enthusiastically adopted, and also what is more important, pledges were given to support the Women's Franchise cause by voting against the Government.'[114]

When the campaign intensified and the militant tactics of the WSPU led to jail sentences it must have been even harder for working-class women to take part—though some did go to jail for 'the Cause'. An ex-suffragette in Greenwich said for instance that the ladies broke windows while the working-class women like herself stayed at the back.

As the WSPU leaders, Emmeline and Christabel, moved further away from the Left, and as feelings hardened on both sides, many working class women socialists who had been initially attracted to the WSPU must have felt torn in several ways. In her biography, *The Hard Way Up*,

113   F W Pethick Lawrence, *The Bye Election Policy of the Women's Social and Political Union*, 1908, p 6.
114   *ibid*, p 14.

Hannah Mitchell describes how she developed feminist and socialist ideas together but gradually came to the conclusion 'that socialists are not necessarily feminists'.[115] In arguments with her socialist friends she decided that although they talked about social and economic equality they were less keen on sexual equality. Nor was it only the men who were insensitive to the liberation of women. Hannah Mitchell fumed silently when a woman socialist speaker from the middle classes ate the tea Hannah had prepared for her without bothering to speak to her, but became animated while talking to her husband. She was caustic in her criticism of women like this, '. . . who made this fatal mistake of treating their less gifted sisters with intellectual contempt. The average woman can sense this attitude a mile off'.[116] Thus a combination of factors, both personal and political, led her into the feminist movement. 'I realised that if women did not bestir themselves the Socialists would be quite content to accept Manhood Suffrage in spite of all their talk about equality.'

Apparently other women in the ILP felt the same way because, according to Hannah, one of the original sources of hostility was Mrs Pankhurst's success in recruiting women from the ILP for the WSPU.

In 1906 she went off to interrupt Winston Churchill's meeting in Deansgate, Manchester, with 'Will the Liberal government give the vote to women?' She was immediately attacked physically but defended herself vigorously and managed to get her question in again. She was sent to jail for her activity in 1906 and was disgusted when her husband came to get her out.

'He knew that we did not wish our fines to be paid and was quite in sympathy with the militant campaign, but men are not so single-minded as women are; they are too much given to talking about their ideas, rather than working for them. Even as Socialists they seldom translate their faith into words, being still conservatives at heart, especially where women are concerned. Most of us who were married found that 'Votes for Women' were of less interest to our husbands than their own dinners. They simply could not understand why we made such a fuss about it.'[117]

Many working-class men who were not socialists took a dim view of women organising, regardless of class. In Ashton market there was a market man who drowned their street meetings with a thunderous 'Go whoam an' mind yer babbies'.[118] In Victoria Park in London it was 'Wot about the old man's kippers?'[119]

When the suffragettes took violent action, Hannah Mitchell did not blame them for destroying letter boxes and burning churches, because she knew how long they had struggled and what they went through in

115 Hannah Mitchell, *The Hard Way Up*, London 1968, p 99.
116 *ibid*, p 119.
117 *ibid*, p 149.
118 *ibid*, p 155.
119 *ibid*, p 159.

prison. But she did not agree with their attacks on even the socialist men who supported them, and she also came to dislike Emmeline and Christabel's organisational ruthlessness. Finally when the suffragette leaders supported World War I, Hannah broke with them and became a pacifist.

The issue of the vote formed a means of uniting women of very different political views—though this single-issue unity was not without its tensions. It is curious that at a time when increasing sections of the labour movement were becoming disillusioned with parliament, the women were ready to risk and suffer so much for the vote.

Of course it was not just the vote they wanted, but the power they believed they would have when they got it. Here there were divergent hopes. A suffragette in the Conservative and Unionist Party said it would be a means of ending the White Slave traffic and reducing prostitution. Mrs Pethick Lawrence thought women would be able to reform prisons, improve wardresses' conditions, and transform the economic helplessness of the unsupported mother. Mrs Pankhurst said it would help to end sweated work and improve the training of midwives. Other supporters of women's suffrage echoed Lloyd George's prophecy of doom, that the vote would see women on the road to equal pay! It proved to be a very long road.

Most of the suffragettes thought change would come out of reforms they would achieve in Parliament. They were still in the tradition of earlier radical movements, although a revolutionary socialist minority saw the vote as merely a necessary reform on the way to the social ownership and control of the means of production. The range of the hopes of the suffragettes, however, was as nothing to the variety of reasons for opposition.

From 1906 the Labour Party was divided on what should be the tactics of getting women's suffrage. Though in the abstract most Labour Party members thought it just for women to have the vote, they could not decide whether they should support a limited measure like that proposed by the WSPU which would enfranchise women householders or adult manhood suffrage which would give the vote to the men who were still excluded, soldiers, household servants and the sons of house-owners, or go all out for a comprehensive change in all the anomalies in the franchise system. Labour Party supporters argued against the WSPU that if propertied women got the vote they would strengthen the conservatives. On the other hand a limited measure of manhood suffrage would also benefit the sons of property owners, and was not therefore a clear class issue either.

In order to prove that votes for women on the existing property terms would not necessarily benefit only the 'ladies', Keir Hardie organised a survey which showed that a significant proportion of working-class women would come under the existing categories of occupiers or tenants of single dwellings or as occupiers of unfurnished lodgings valued at £10 per annum. Forty ILP branches surveyed 59,920 potential women voters and found that 82.45% of the women who would get the vote under the proposed Bill were working class. This survey was criticised however, both on the grounds that most ILP branches were in working-class areas and consequently did not reflect the much higher overall proportion of middle-class women in these categories in the country as a whole, and also for its very vague definition of 'working class'.

However there was another survey in the North of England in which three women's organisations, the Lancashire & Cheshire Women Textile and Other Workers Labour Representation Committee, the Manchester and Salford Women's Trade and Labour Council, and the Women's Co-operative Guild, found that in 1904 the proportion of working women voters, in Nelson, Bolton, Barnsley, Horsforth and Leeds for example, would be well over the 82% of the ILP sample. Even in Kirkby Lonsdale Mrs Llewellyn Davies, supporter of the Women's Co-operative Guild and an advocate of Adult Suffrage not just votes for women, reported 49 trades and working women who would qualify and only 8 rich women.

Given this kind of evidence it is impossible not to feel that behind the Labour Party suspicion of the 'Ladies Bill' lurked other more general suspicions of women having the vote.

The Liberal Party was similarly divided. The majority of the party believed in the principle of votes for women, though Lloyd George maintained that there must be a Bill to give working men's wives the vote as well as spinsters and widows. However, in the Cabinet there was a determined lobby including Asquith and Lewis Harcourt who were virulently opposed to the vote for women on any terms at all. Commenting on Harcourt's attitude in 1913 Lord Hugh Cecil said it was not just his antagonism to votes for women but,

> 'the extraordinary quarrel he appears to have with the female sex in general. He might have been recently spanked, and he feels so deeply and bitterly as never to have got over the indignity of having been born of a woman.'[120]

If their opponents were determined, many of the women's liberal supporters were lukewarm and wavering and not united about the tactics of getting the measure through.

In the Conservative and Unionist Party the majority of the party were opposed, but the leaders, Balfour and Bonar Law, were sympathetic to women's suffrage. J L Maxse, a conservative journalist, put Balfour's support down to 'cranky female relatives' who undermined his capacity

120   Hansard 24 January 1913, quoted in Neal Blewett, 'The Franchise in the United Kingdom, *Past and Present*, No 32, December 1965, p 54.

to take 'a manly and statesmanlike position' like Asquith. He was also afraid that the 'pernicious movement' . . . 'one of the most factitious agitations that has ever been organised', could, if it continued, 'split the Party from top to bottom'.[121]

Of course this kind of response was exactly what Christabel hoped for and what her mother was increasingly brought to believe might happen too. The Tories, Christabel, argued, would give the women the vote just as they had enfranchised a privileged section of the working class in 1867 to scotch the Liberals.

The militant tactics of the WSPU were born of despair after years of patient constitutionalism. They were defended with appeals to the tradition of physical resistance in the struggle for political freedom in Britain. Mary Gawthorpe in her pamphlet *Votes for Women* reminded working-class men of their own past and the opposition they encountered when they tried to get the vote or form trade unions. On trial for conspiracy to break the shop windows of tradesmen Mr Pethick Lawrence said in court that he stood with Hampden—the Civil War rebel—and warned that if men were not willing to suffer in the women's cause a situation of outright sex war would ensue. He was never a member of the WSPU because only women were admitted, but he campaigned energetically in the women's cause.

The question of the relationship of men to the suffrage movement was evidently problematical. Many men, like Mr Pethick Lawrence, did support them and demonstrated and were convicted with them. But there was a strong emphasis in the WSPU on women depending on themselves, of learning their own power, and a very deep resentment at the vacillation of some of the men who said they were for the vote, but would risk nothing for it. There would appear to have been a division between the suffragettes who wanted to work with the men who would support them, and those who did not want to place any reliance on men, because it reminded them too poignantly of their old humiliation. There was, too, a sexual suspicion of men, that came partly from the older tradition of feminism and moral purity, and the incongruity of intense feminist involvement and the everyday apparently unchanging sexual assumptions of men. The slogan 'Votes for Women and Purity for Men' in 1913 summed up this feeling that men were congenitally inclined towards debauchery. The feminists were turning the Victorian male image of woman's nature inside out. If celibacy was the only choice open to women, men had to adopt it as their programme too.

In a more general sense the women were forced in conflict with the state to see through the myth of the impartiality of the law. They were tried and judged by men. They had no part in making the laws. They were protected only by the bounds of masculine authority, appendages

121   Maxse to Sanders, 5 July 1910, Balfour Papers, quoted in *ibid*, p 54.

of father or husband. Once beyond the pale they were without any rights at all. As the agitation intensified the remnants of Victorian chivalry towards middle-class women wore increasingly thin. In 1906 Theresa Billington Greig an elementary school teacher was hit on the back by a policeman and charged with assault: she denounced the court and its man-made laws.

Some of the women went further. The state and the laws were not only controlled and created by men in their own interest: they also represented the coercive power of a class.

When the suffragettes went to prison they were not given the privileges of political prisoners. They were the first group of middle-class people to go into prison in any numbers and, with the exception of the socialists, the first to clash violently with the police. When they came out they not only exposed the conditions in Holloway, but their experience in prison was more broadly educative. Mrs Pethick Lawrence in *The Faith That Is In Us* describes the first time she heard a baby cry in Holloway and reflected on the hypocrisy of the society which said a woman's place was in the home but would allow her to leave home for jail, but not to make the laws. Poverty and economic dependence on a man who had gone were the main crimes of the women inside. Sylvia Pankhurst wrote, 'Writ on Cold Slate', verses about women in prison with her: an old woman convicted as a prostitute, a woman whose baby died in jail, and the cleaners. She said in one 'we're declassed'. They were the victims of a state in which they had no say and no control. In different ways they were all political prisoners.

Prominent and upper-class women received preferential treatment in jail on the grounds of ill-health. To avoid this Lady Constance Lytton dressed up as a seamstress and led a demonstration through Liverpool in 1910. When she was arrested she went on hunger strike and was forcibly fed without a heart test. She was violently sick and the prison doctor hit her. She was permanently injured and remained paralysed for the rest of her life. If she had really been a seamstress she might have passed unnoticed but when her identity was discovered there was a public outcry. Lord Lytton introduced a Bill for Women's Suffrage and hope began to build up again. However in November 1910 a demonstration to Parliament ended in a clash between the suffragettes and the police and a watching crowd. The fight went on for several hours, many women were injured and two died. The following day Mrs Pankhurst returned with an avenging deputation and caught the police off-guard in Downing Street. Mr Asquith had a narrow escape, Mr Augustine Birrell was so nervous he slipped and broke his ankle, and Mr Churchill, the conquering hero, turned up when the street was emptied and found one exhausted suffragette leaning against the wall.

'Mr Churchill as usual was unable to resist the dramatic gesture. He beck-
oned a policeman. "Drive that woman away", he said, though he knew her
perfectly well to be a Mrs Cobden-Sanderson, his hostess on several occasions, and an intimate friend of his wife's family.'[122]

It seemed in 1911 as though Asquith might compromise and accept
a bill which excluded the £10 lodgers clause. However in November 1911
he told an organisation for People's Suffrage he would accept a measure
for universal manhood suffrage but still exclude women. The militancy
began again, but this time the women carefully and systematically
attacked property. Windows were smashed all over the West End, including those of Number 10. The insurance companies began to get worried.
The government retaliated with the charge of conspiracy which carried
more severe penalties.

The escalation of militancy from heckling meetings, to confrontation with the police, to the destruction of property does not appear to
have been part of a long-term strategy. New tactics would seem to have
been introduced on the initiative of individual women and then adopted
by the WSPU. The first hunger strike for instance was started by a suffragette called Marion Walker after she had painted a slogan on St Stephen's
Hall and refused to stop until she was taken off to jail. The women
seemed capable of continuous demonstrative sacrifice. They also picked
their targets. For instance on 13 June 1911 two women were found
crouched outside the house of the hated Lewis Harcourt, with inflam-
mable oil, pick-locks and glass-cutters. Their targets were not only
chosen because of personal hatred but because of their symbolic significance. There were no sacred male preserves safe from their attack. 'Votes
for Women' even appeared burned in acid on golf courses.

The period 1910-1914 was a trying time for the government facing
industrial militancy, and an Irish crisis, besides the suffragettes. It is
possible that the Liberals might have been forced to secure the loyalty
of upper and middle-class women before 1918 if ever the forces of extra-
parliamentary opposition had coalesced. In 1912 the Labour Party conference committed the Party to the vote for women. In the same year a
bill before Parliament was lost by only 14 votes.

However in 1912 on Christabel's instructions there was a change
in the policy of the WSPU. The suffragettes deliberately isolated themselves, cutting the last links with their supporters in the labour movement
with the decision to attack Irish and Labour MPs as much as Liberals and
Conservatives. Not only did this put stalwarts like Lansbury out on a
limb, it forced women like Hannah Mitchell to declare for one side or
the other. Also the onslaught on property reached a new phase as the

122   George Dangerfield, *The Strange Death of Liberal England 1910-1914*, New
York 1961, p 162: see also Antonia Raeburn, 'What Emily Did', *Spare
Rib*, July 1972.

suffragettes moved from defacing buildings and smashing windows to arson. They no longer sought arrest and martyrdom. Instead they tried to do as much damage as they could, apparently believing that the pressure from insurance companies would be so great that the government would give in. From 1912 the WSPU was virtually an illegal organisation, with its 'headquarters' in Paris, and its activists working underground.

The tactics of the WSPU had thus turned full circle: from being a movement to persuade the new Labour Party to support the vote, it had become an underground organisation committed to propaganda by deed, not like the anarchists imagining that the masses would be roused by example, but aiming their actions solely at dividing the male ruling class.

The luke-warm supporters of the suffrage, Lloyd George and Ramsay Macdonald, were thus provided with an ideal excuse to dissociate themselves from even lip-service support. Men like this were obviously relieved to be let off the hook and remain self-righteous. For instance Macdonald said in 1914, with predictable sanctimony: 'The violent methods . . . are wrong, and in their nature reactionary and antisocial, quite irrespective of vote or no vote.'[123]

George Lansbury and Keir Hardie, however, whatever their views of 'violent methods', continued to defend the suffragette movement.

In fact, regardless of what Ramsay Macdonald might have thought, the women's actions were within a very old radical tradition. The middle class in the Reform Bill crisis earlier were by no means non-violent. The women were using violence against property for a constitutional end. Parliament had blocked them so they were taking direct action outside—in order to be received within. The women in the WSPU who set fire to pillar boxes, flooded the organ in the Albert Hall and destroyed Scottish castles were taking extreme action for an apparently moderate reform. But if their action was traditional, the context and consequences were not.

The leadership of the WSPU depended on publicity. They were trying to shock and divide male ruling class opinion into conceding the vote. The movement had lurched on from sensation to sensation, they had packed meetings in the centre of London, they had demonstrated, and they had attacked property. The choice of tactics increasingly came to define the structure of the organisation. Emmeline Pankhurst was no democrat and ruled from on top. The members did not even have a vote in their own movement. Theresa Billington Greig, an elementary school teacher, had already split off to join the Women's Freedom League in 1908 on this issue. The League has never received the attention and publicity of the WSPU because it quietly organised tax and census resist-

123 Quoted in Ralph Miliband, *Parliamentary Socialism*, London 1961, p. 25.

ance. The faithful Pethick Lawrences were to follow, and finally Sylvia and the East London Federation.

When the movement was forced underground and 'headquarters' —Emmeline and Christabel—were sending instructions from Paris, the possibility of democratic decision-making became more remote. Also the tactics of illegality made secrecy and a para-military discipline in response to orders, necessary.

Behind both tactics and structure was a political choice. Thus, while the use of violent tactics progressively isolated the WSPU and changed the nature of the suffrage campaign from a mass organisation to an élite corps trained in urban sabotage, both became comprehensible when seen in terms of the people they were trying to influence. The WSPU for all its militant flurry was a pressure group, albeit a heroic and defiant one. Emmeline and Christabel did not think in terms of building a mass organisation or of mobilising women workers to strike, but of making ever more dramatic gestures.

Once they had begun to adopt militant tactics, the choices closed in on them. They could spread resistance and impose their own sanctions but this was difficult because the mass of women were by no means united behind them. Or they could seek alliances with other insurgents but Emmeline and Christabel knew that this would make the 'respectable' politicians close ranks against them. So when Sylvia supported a meeting in the Albert Hall to free the Irish revolutionary, Jim Larkin, Christabel and Emmeline decided that she and the East London Federation must go. The only alternatives were to escalate the attacks on property and to suffer more martyrdoms, or to give in.

On all these points Sylvia was at variance with her mother and sister. Before she was expelled she was already searching round for some way of breaking out of the impasse of isolationism—apart from her activity in the socialist movement she was also trying to base the East London Federation on community groups, not on much publicised actions, and to organise within the area rather than in central London. She thought it would be possible to organise a rent strike for the vote.

The issues which were discussed when the East London Federation of Suffragettes (ELFS) split reflect those differences. Sylvia reported on 27 January 1914 that 'headquarters' had told her they 'had most faith in what could be done for the vote by people of means and influence', whereas the ELFS was working from 'the bottom up'. The WSPU Pankhursts had also ventured to suggest they had a higher fighting standard, but afterwards that was withdrawn. The ELFS had been trying to organise a rent strike for the vote.

'Headquarters said it was impossible to work it through their organisation because their people are widely scattered and because it is only in working-class homes that the woman pays the rent. They said a deputation to the

Labour Party was all very well for us, but one to the king was better for them. They do not have men in their bodyguard, but I pointed out that our People's Army was not part of the Federation.'[124]

The split was obviously very painful to Sylvia. The details of organisational separation—red included in their colours, a weekly news-sheet, 'they said we might have the band instruments'—were the outward and visible political signs of her personal estrangement from her mother and sister.

Sylvia sought to ally the women's movement with socialism and the labour movement. In 1915 for example the ELFS was campaigning against the conditions of sweated work with the Herald League, the British Socialist Party (formerly the SDF), the Dockers Union, some ILP branches, and union branches as well as the Women Writers Suffrage Union. In January there was a demonstration in Trafalgar Square supported by the East London women, the Women's Freedom League and the Northern Men's Federation for Women's Suffrage. By 1915 the ELFS had nine branches outside London. However the suffragette movement had been further weakened by the war. A section of the WSPU split off when Christabel and Emmeline supported World War I. The feminists were thus divided on the question of tactics, by political loyalties, by commitment to persuading the upper class or building a base among workers, and finally on the issue of the war. Given the extent of their disagreements, the tremendous effect they had on people's consciousness before World War I is some indication of the power of feminist ideas in the early twentieth century.

124   27 Jan 1914 Minutes East London Federation of the Suffragettes, Institute of Social History, Amsterdam.

16

Some Responses to Feminism in the Socialist Movement before 1914

The struggle for the vote focused a much wider feminist consciousness. Between the end of the nineteenth century and the immediate postwar era, both the position and the self-image of women changed radically. Mothers who had held 'advanced' opinions in the 1890s looked with horror at their daughters' bobbed hair, short skirts and casual 'spooning'. The young women of the twenties took for granted the issues and ideas for which their mothers and grandmothers had suffered and struggled.

Feminism in this period was diffuse, inchoate and contradictory. It was not a clearly worked out ideology, but was rather a rebellion against the norms of bourgeois Victorian femininity. It extended into every area of cultural life and it had an international impact. The newly emerging socialist organisations were no exception.[125] Their responses to the feminist movement were varied and complex. They had no universally held position on either the 'woman question' or on the feminist movement and the reaction to the latter was somewhat different from a theoretical analysis of the origins of women's oppression. Formal commitment to the emancipation of women was one thing. A practical and personal response to feminism as an autonomous movement was another.

General political emphases within the socialist movement affected the nature of the response to feminism. The question of the vote for instance was inseparable from the arguments between the various tendencies on the left over the relationship between democratic reforms

125 This is an aspect of the history of the socialist movement which is being rediscovered by socialist women now: see for example—Alice Waters, 'Feminism and the Marxist Movement', *International Socialist Review*, October 1972. Mari Jo Buhle, 'Women and the Socialist Party 1901-1914', *Radical America*, February 1970.
For a contemporary account see Alexandra Kollontai, *Women Workers Struggle for their Rights*, and *Sexual Relations and the Class Struggle*, Bristol, 1971 and 1972.

within capitalism and the achievement of socialism, and about the role of parliament. The connection between a socialist party and a feminist movement was part of another contemporary controversy; what was the role of the party? Was it merely to propagandise for a socialist revolution or should it be involved in day-to-day activity.

Feminism raised many personal questions about how men and women should behave. There was a very strong current in the socialist movement to make politics relate to every aspect of living. Socialism was not seen only as public ownership, or the control of the worker over the produce of his or her labour, it was also the search for a new ethic, a new culture, a new life. This connection between the 'new life' and the class struggle tended to be implicit in personal practice. It was not however made explicit as part of socialist theory. The feminist movement was activist and relatively unconcerned with analysis—this is reflected within the socialist movement. It does not seem that women who were both socialists and feminists felt a strong need to work out theoretically the implications of their dual loyalties. Instead they referred back to Bebel and Engels as a sufficient explanation. *Women and Socialism* and *The Origin of the Family* formed the basis for socialist thinking on the position of women. Both were being read in Britain in the early 1900s. Carpenter's *Love's Coming of Age* was also popular. All three had aroused a storm of controversy when they were published and were considered daring, indeed almost obscene. Even amongst socialists they never acquired the stamp of popular orthodoxy of texts like Blatchford's *Merrie England* or Morris's *News from Nowhere*. Granted that Marxism was anyway a minority tendency in the socialist movement, Bebel and Engels were never completely accepted even within the marxist Social Democratic Federation.

The WSPU came, as we have seen, out of the Independent Labour Party which campaigned for Labour Representation in Parliament. The ILP had already a tradition of prominent women members in the 1890s. But although these women obviously played an important role in the party, the position of a rank-and-file working-class woman was more difficult. In the daily life of the working-class family the woman found herself doing housework—regardless of her husband's political principles. Hannah Mitchell for one resented this. In her autobiography *The Hard Way Up* she describes her early life on a Derbyshire farm. She became a feminist before she ever knew the meaning of the word, she loved reading but had to do endless household chores. The final sexual indignity was darning her brothers' socks. Why couldn't they darn their own, thought Hannah. 'My mother honestly thought me lazy because I didn't like housework.' She went off to work in a shop, became aware of the agitation for shorter working hours, and a weekly half-holiday, met socialists, read Robert Blatchford's *The Clarion*, and attended meetings where she heard Katherine St John Conway, the wife of Bruce Glasier, speak. Her first political intervention was at a meeting on 'Women and Politics.' She jumped up in a rage when she heard 'a callow youth' quote Milton against women, and quoted Tennyson back at him.[126]

Her own home had been unhappy and she had seen her mother crushed by hard work so she was cautious about marriage. However she finally married a shop assistant who shared her socialist views.

> 'Probably I should have hesitated even then, but for the newer ideas which were being propounded by the socialists. Men and women were talking of marriage as a comradeship, rather than a state where the woman was sub-servient to and dependent on the man.'[127]

But marriage meant looking after a home and working at the same time—not the useless leisure of middle-class women.

> 'Even my Sunday leisure was gone for I soon found that a lot of the socialist talk about freedom was only talk and these socialist young men expected Sunday dinners and huge teas with home-made cakes, potted meat and pies, exactly like their reactionary fellows.'[128]

Then, to her despair, she got pregnant. The birth of her child was painful and difficult and she resolved never to have another child. Because of her own experience she was in favour of contraception, not because it would cure all social problems, but because so many working-class women became worn out with child bearing and hard work.

It was very hard to convince people in the socialist movement that these details of domestic life were part of politics. The men who domin-ated the organisations were not affected by them and middle class women still had servants. The leaders of the ILP were also reluctant to accept that women had distinct interests and had to organise for them. Sylvia says both Ramsay Macdonald and Philip Snowden were against the femin-ists and most men shared Bruce Glasier's view that it was not essential for everyone to have the vote as long as possession of the vote was not on class lines.

Although some women left the ILP for the feminist movement the women who stayed in were by no means necessarily all hostile to the suffragettes. In 1908 an article in *The Labour Leader* by 'Iona', explained some of their attitudes. She said ILP women were busy with their party work and could not play a full part in the suffragette agitation but that every member believed in votes for women. She was aware of the effect on the consciousness of middle class women who became feminists. She reports on a 'gossamer lady' who had lived a sheltered life in the country-side, who told her of the new experience of sisterhood.

126 Mitchell, *The Hard Way Up*, p 54.
127 *ibid*, p 88.
128 *ibid*, p 96.

'I used to think women could hardly do anything, that it all depended on men. Now it seems to me that there is nothing brave women cannot do if they are only given the chance. Only look at the women who are taking the chair at our Hyde Park demonstrations.'[129]

At a local level there was probably a considerable interconnection between feminists and local branches of the ILP. Mary Gawthorpe in Leeds for instance managed to combine being on the National Committee of the WSPU, and being Vice-President of Leeds ILP.

Another Leeds socialist feminist Isabella Ford wrote a pamphlet in 1904 arguing that the emancipation of women and of labour were 'different aspects of the same great force'. She said,

'. . . these two movements have had in the past, as now, the same object, and have therefore been largely interdependent, in that both have fallen and risen together, and the same events have affected each, more or less in the same manner. Also that the same powers have been and are still hostile to both.'[130]

However both sides were unconscious of that 'kinship'. Indeed 'it even seems at times as if each mistrusted the other a little. . . .'

'In the Labour Party a prejudice one finds exists against the woman's party because it owes its origin and its growth to middle class women mostly, if not entirely. On that account it is branded by many as a middle class affair, possessing no fundamental connection with the Labour movement save what it is now acquiring through the awakening of the working woman to an understanding of her need for economic and therefore political enfranchisement.'

She thought this an 'anti-socialistic' attitude and pointed out that many of the earlier socialists like William Morris had been middle class. Isabella Ford believed too that middle-class 'suffragists' were becoming more aware of the connection between their situation and that of the 'industrial' woman, and were determined not to gain political emancipation only for 'middle class purposes'.[131] She admitted though that the feminists were suspicious of 'labour', because they had seen their claims pushed aside time after time in order to safeguard bills to enfranchise the workers.

Isabella Ford saw the vote as a means of securing wider social change. She believed that parliament could be used by the labour movement and by women. But the emphasis in her writing was not upon parliament as a remote place where legislators changed society for other people. The representation of women, like that of labour, was for her the political expression of a rank-and-file movement. She was also concerned about making connections between an autonomous feminist movement and the socialists.

129   Iona, The Women's Outlook, *Labour Leader*, June 5, 1908.
130   Isabella Ford, *Women and Socialism*, 1904, p 3.
131   *ibid*, p 7.

The Independent Labour Party created its own organisation in 1906 called the Women's Labour League under the auspices of Margaret Macdonald. She explained that as trade unionists came in to the Labour Party in great numbers, 'the wives and sweethearts were being left outside'. So they decided,

> 'a special effort must be made to reach the women and enlist their support. We do not want to organise ourselves separately from the men but we have found that the best way to co-operate with them is to educate ourselves; to teach ourselves to discuss and understand and take responsibility in our own meetings, and thus to increase our power and at the same time our powers for the right.'

They wanted 'direct Labour Representation of women in Parliament and on all local bodies'.[132]

The executive committee included the ubiquitous Miss Gawthorpe, Mrs Despard from the Women's Freedom League and representatives of the Postal Telegraph Clerks and the Women's Trade Union League. It had close links to the Women's Co-operative Guild, and the Socialist Sunday Schools and was affiliated to the Workers' Education Association, the Women's Suffrage Campaign and Joint Committee and the Labour Party.

The 'Women's Labour League' was cautious and defensive—a far cry from the consciousness of sisterhood of even the gossamer lady in 'Iona's' article. The League reacted towards the feminist consciousness which was growing outside, they were not concerned with themselves developing a socialist feminism, though there was an understanding of the personal and practical predicament of the working-class mother.

> 'Very often a married woman is forced to give up meetings for a time because she has a young baby to look after and cannot get about. In such cases it is of the utmost importance for members to show their comradeship with her and not to let her drop her connection with the movement altogether.'[133]

The strength of the ILP was its flexibility to movements and campaigns, which meant that on the level of isolated women's issues it could respond to feminism. The kind of socialism it stood for was a confusing mixture of humane reformism and revolutionary rhetoric. There was in the ILP a sentimental vagueness about the realities of class power and a hopeful and naive faith in the goodwill and basic English decency of the ruling class. Among the middle-class leaders who were to play an important role in the Labour Party there was also a tendency to see change as something fixed from on top by enlightened people in the 'know'. They were reluctant to accept that capitalism would only be overthrown by organised force from below.

At the same time though, many of the women members were deeply

132   Margaret Macdonald, 'Women Workers', Souvenir Pamphlet of Women's Labour Day, 17 July 1909, quoted in Suzie Fleming in notes on Kollontai, *Women Workers Struggle for their Rights*, 1971, p 34.
133   Marion Phillips, *How to do the work of the League*, nd.

involved in the suffrage agitation, Margaret says of her sister Rachel McMillan that though she never joined the raids, she was aware that the suffragettes 'quickened the pace' and 'the iron entered her soul'[134] when the police charged, knocking over a frail old woman, and hurting Margaret. In 1913 she tried to prevent the police using violence against peaceful demonstrations and opposed the Cat and Mouse Act. Fred Jowett and the Bradford ILP supported her. The ILP tended to oscillate between wariness and enthusiasm.

However, with all its limitations, the socialism of the ILP was wider and more alive than that of the so-called 'marxist' leaders of the revolutionary Social Democratic Federation. The founding group of marxist socialism in England was influenced greatly by the personal quirks and hobby-horses of its leadership. Tragically, revolutionary ideas and politics were poisoned at source in Britain. Anti-semitism, jingoism, chauvinism, and the eugenic superman went with a pedantic acceptance of Marx's economic theory. It was not therefore surprising that the leaders of the SDF dismissed feminism. Hyndman was as hostile to feminism as he was to Engels's *Origin of the Family*. He met Sylvia Pankhurst one day outside the home of Dora Montefiore, a member of the SDF who was a feminist, and exploded, 'Women should learn to have influence as they have in France instead of trying to get votes'. Sylvia commented that 'He always seemed to me like an old-fashioned china mantle-piece ornament.'[135]

Belfort Bax, another leading member of the SDF, was actually a member of the Men's Anti-Suffrage League. He was not just anti-feminist, but anti-woman as a whole. In his *Essays in Socialism* he argued that women were not oppressed because they were shielded legally in certain cases and did not have the responsibility of supporting families. If women had the vote men would be n an unequal position because there were more women than men. Along with a remarkable gift for missing the point Belfort Bax took up a kind of sexual determinism, arguing that women were originally inferior because they had smaller brains.[136]

But the group around Hyndman did not reflect the attitudes of the SDF at branch level. There were also revolutionary socialists, both male and female, in the SDF who were deeply committed to the liberation of women.

Quite different views were being expressed by a young dissident in the London SDF called Guy Aldred. On 7 January 1906 he spoke to

134   McMillan, *The Life of Rachel McMillan*, p 138.
135   Pankhurst, *The Suffragette Movement*, p 120.
136   See E Belfort Bax, *'The Monstrous Regiment of Womanhood'* etc, in his *Essays in Socialism*, London 1907. (Guy Aldred commented that, 'Bax was a strong anti-feminist which no Socialist should be'. Guy Aldred. *No Traitor's Gait*, Strickland Press, Glasgow, 1955-6, no 6 p 136).

Southwark Socialist Club (SDF) on 'Secularism and Women'. He took his listeners back to an earlier tradition of sexual radicalism, quoting from a letter by Robert Dale Owen saying men and women should not live together when they were unhappy. He also referred to Annie Besant's *Marriage as it was, as it is and as it should be* published in 1882. He pointed out too how capitalism had a contradictory effect on the role of women. She still 'bears even more surely the chains of the past and earns very often the means of her male colleague's existence, whilst being regarded as his inferior'. She had not only her special subordination but exploitation too as a wage-earner. He pointed out that the double exploitation of women under capitalism was synonymous with her 'intellectual awakening'.[137]

The uneasiness characteristic of the revolutionary left at the time over the question of how immediate reforms connected to socialist revolution, is reflected in Guy Aldred's approach to the position of women and to feminism. On the one hand there was the attitude of economic determinism. The objective change was going to come anyway so the job of socialists was only to prepare people ideologically. This could produce a sectarian passivity towards day-to-day agitation, or a millenarianism which simply waited for the crisis. Guy Aldred, with millenarian zeal, advocated celibacy for socialists, not on Malthusian grounds, but because 'comradeship' was preferable to sexual passion. He did not believe socialists should be opposed to the suffragettes because they campaigned for a vote which implied property qualification. If women got the vote on the present terms as men it merely meant equality between 'parasites'. He thought logically the female parasites should be entitled to the same privileges as the males. But he pointed out that universal adult suffrage was also a 'palliative' and therefore socialists had as much grounds for supporting votes for women as adult suffrage.

'In other words, as a disciple of Bakunin who, nevertheless, understands the Marxian position, I realise the fallacy underlying the palliative propaganda and the futility of striving for anything short of Socialism. So long as the workers are dominated by the capitalist class, so long as they remain the slaves of society, economically the lowest class, so long will they lack that industrial liberty without which "adult suffrage" is a farce. Economic determinism, the slow but sure awakening of the masses to their real position are the factors governing the nature of capitalistic concessions; so that the nearer the people come to the realisation of their condition, the more advanced will be the nature of the palliatives we shall secure. Hence there is no necessity to concentrate our energies upon the securing of palliatives.'[138]

Presumably the tension inherent in this revolutionary Calvinism, meant that Aldred's doctrinal purity kept cracking under the pressure of

137   Guy Aldred, The Religion and Economics of Sex Oppression. Pamphlets for the Proletarian, no 2, 1907, from a lecture to Southwark Socialist Club SDF, 7 January 1906, p 41.
138   *ibid*, p 41.

his activist sympathies. He says in his autobiography that the pamphlet was 'marred' by his 'youth'. He describes himself as an 'enthusiastic feminist and therefore strongly in favour of women's suffrage.' And he quotes from a letter from himself in July 1906 to *The Women's Tribune*, a feminist paper, in which he attacked the 'inanities' of a leading member of the SDF, Herbert Burrows, and agreed with *The Women's Tribune* which had evidently taken a dim view of something Burrows had said about feminism. Aldred says,

> 'he has frequently fallen foul, both of his secularist and socialist comrades on the question of the social position of women. . . . It is with regret that I have noted the bigoted superstition maintained by the average member of the organisation to which I belong—the SDF—on this point: and with pleasure that I note the persistence shown by women suffragists in fighting for a right that has too long been denied them.'

He preferred to work for the wider measure of adult suffrage. 'But I do think it is ridiculous to regard the passing of a measure extending the franchise, even on the property basis, to women as a retrograde measure.' (Evidently Burrows did.) Aldred added that he was 'not so sure that it is not necessary in order to shock male supremacy.'[139] Aldred was soon to leave the SDF and form the 'Industrial Union of Direct Actionists', with its own amalgam of marxism, anarchism and syndicalism. But the debate continued in the SDF.

In 1909 controversy broke out in the group's journal *The Social Democrat*. Dora Montefiore in the April issue attacked Belfort Bax and said women who were socialists demanded the socialisation of industry *and* the vote. Women had a special oppression which they had to struggle against themselves. Bax replied in May. Someone with the pseudonym 'Fair Play' joined in in August—Fair Play was apparently a woman. Male authority in the family was attacked, Ibsen's *Doll's House* quoted, women should be able to choose whether to get married, and marriage should not be the only future for women. H B Samuels responded angrily in October with 'Women's Rights and the State', arguing that 'Woman's place is in the home.' Capitalism had destroyed the home, but once the means of production were 'conquered and controlled by the people', woman would be restored to her 'true sphere'. [140] In other words Socialism was to put women in the place the SDF male leaders thought was suitable to them. The debate went on through 1910, arousing considerable passion on both sides, and even touched on the question of sexuality. A man called E A Phipson wrote an article on 'Feminine Idiosyncrasies' which provoked a 'numerously signed protest' to the editors. The protest claimed his article was 'an extreme expression of the dregs of

---

139   Aldred, *No Traitor's Gait*, p 163.
140   H B Samuels, 'Women's Rights and the State', *The Social Democrat*, October 1909.

sensualism stirred by sex animosities' and 'an insult to women'.[141]

Dora Montefiore was in the WSPU and later in the Adult Suffrage League as well as the SDF. She had been imprisoned for suffragette activity, and indignant at Bax's suggestion that all the feminists were pampered in jail. In 1907 she went to the conference of the Second International as a representative of the SDF and to the women's section of the conference as a delegate from the Adult Suffrage Society. The Stuttgart conference resulted in a clear declaration of commitment to the principle of equal rights for women. An attempt by Austrian socialists to prevent the International declaring for women's suffrage was defeated. The Stuttgart conference also resolved that women workers should campaign for the vote not with the liberal supporters of women's rights but with the class parties of the proletariat.

In the English context this meant either the Women's Labour League, or as the SDF had walked out of the meetings of the Labour Representation Committee, women's SDF circles. A women's committee had existed since 1906. By 1910 there were 5,000 in the League and ten SDF circles. A British section of the Women's International was set up. Thus although they were on principle separated from the liberal feminists, the definition of socialism was very wide. The British section included women members of the Fabian Society, the Adult Suffrage Society, the Socialist Teachers' Association, and the Clarion women. The second International Women's Socialist Conference was held in Copenhagen in August 1910.

In 1909 the SDF had formed a separate committee for propaganda and 'members of the Party, predominantly women, raised the campaign for universal franchise, to counterbalance the demands the suffragettes were making for electoral qualification'.[142]

Thus between 1906 and 1910 the divergence between the feminists in the WSPU and the socialist women who supported equal rights for women was formalised in distinct organisation. However the advantage of clarity and unity in the socialist forces was not gained by separate organisation. The old division between the ILP and the SDF was perpetuated. Also the women in the organisations were not all suffrage campaigners, and there was hostility from some of the male leaders.

Matters were further complicated by divisions not only between the marxist SDF and the Labour Party, but also by splits and divisions within revolutionary socialism. In 1903 some Scottish members of the SDF broke off to form the Socialist Labour Party. The SLP was opposed to using the vote and parliament. They were influenced by the American socialist de Leon, who advocated the organisation of industrial unions

141 *The Social Democrat*, February 1910, p 72.
142 Kollontai, *Women Workers Struggle for their Rights*, p 31. See also pp 18-19, 25.

and the General Strike. The SLP were intensely involved in theoretical debate and very concerned to distinguish themselves from other socialists. During 1910-1911 they were having some success in recruiting Singer Sewing Machine workers in Clydebank to the SLP union, the Industrial Workers of Great Britain, including some women workers, though a strike in 1911 was broken.

Impatience with Parliament meant that the SLP was not concerned with the suffrage movement, although they did believe in the social freedom of women. A woman called Lily Gair Wilkinson wrote a pamphlet on *Revolutionary Socialism and the Woman's Movement* around 1910 which was published by the SLP. She pointed out that it was important to define not only the relationship of socialism to 'the woman question' but also to the actual feminist movement. This was made all the more urgent 'because the bourgeois feminists have received great support in their campaign from many reformists calling themselves Socialists, who pretending to serve the cause of women, serve that of the enemy instead'.[143]

She says that the opponents of feminists and socialists are the same, that socialists must be committed to equality between men and women. She was not opposed to the 'militant tactics' of the feminists, but she believed they were misdirected because the only significant struggle was against class exploitation. All attempts to reform capitalism were useless. Therefore the degradation of women was inseparable from the capitalist robbery of surplus value from the working class. Sex antagonism affected only middle-class women. She denied that the franchise on the present conditions would include working-class women. Lily Gair Wilkinson was also distrustful of the demand for complete Adult Suffrage, although she recognised that such an extension of the franchise would develop the possibilities for political action. 'The vote is useless to the workers while it is not backed up by an organised economic power sufficient to ensure the introduction of socialism'.[144]

This was consistent with the SLP dismissal of parliamentary agitation and with their faith in industrial unionism. Their political perspective defined all struggles for reforms as 'reformist'. This gained them the nickname of 'impossibilists', 'imps' for short. They retaliated by calling the Hyndmanites 'kangaroos', people who believed one could achieve socialism in jumps. There was thus no common strategy among socialists either about their attitude to Parliament nor about how the question of immediate reforms inside capitalism could connect to the creation of a socialist society. While the ILP women like Isabella Ford saw the vote as a means of bringing about broader social change, Dora Montefiore

143   Lily Gair Wilkinson, *Revolutionary Socialism and the Women's Movement,* SLP c. 1910, p 2.
144   *ibid,* p 9.

in the SDF, wanted the vote and the social ownership of production, and Lily Gair Wilkinson was scornful about struggling for the vote at all. The response to the suffragette movement is then inseparable from the general contemporary debate about the role of reforms in capitalism.

The anarchist women would seem to have shared the SLP's dismissal of 'palliatives' like the franchise. Lilian Wolfe for example worked for the GPO and was a member of the Civil Service Socialist Society. She became disillusioned with Parliament while she was on a suffragette lobby and was attracted by the anarchist movement, though she never lost her commitment to the liberation of women.[145] She started a paper called *The Voice of Labour* with some anarchist friends.

Before World War I the East End was the meeting place for diverse strands of radical and revolutionary ideas. Besides the Clarion vans and the speakers on Mile End Waste, there were many exiles, many from persecution abroad, many of them Jews, bearers of anarchist thinking. The anarchists met in a pub called 'The Sugar Loaf' which used to be in Hanbury Street, Whitechapel, and in a club which opened in 1906 in Jubilee Street. The presses of *Arbeiter Fraint* (Workers' Front) were in an adjoining building. Although this was a Jewish political paper, it had a Gentile editor, a German anarcho-syndicalist called Rudolf Rocker.

In February 1907 a benefit was held at the Jubilee Street club for *The Voice of Labour*. The young dissident marxist, Guy Aldred, went along and met a Jewish girl there, Rose Witcop. Rose came from an orthodox family and her sister Milly had come from the Ukraine, worked in a sweat shop and managed to get the whole family over. Milly had become involved in the anarchist movement and was a member of the *Arbeiter Fraint* group. She also, to her parents' great distress, lived in a free union with Rudolf Rocker.[146] She must have influenced Rose, her younger sister, who was not quite seventeen when Guy Aldred met her but was already involved in anarchist politics and thinking about the feminist movement. Guy Aldred, involved in his own arguments with the SDF and soon to break away to form his own group, the Industrial Union Direct Actionists, was interested to read a letter Rose Witcop wrote to *The Voice of Labour* in March 1907, commenting on the suffrage and Parliament.

It started off by recognising the effect of feminism on women's consciousness. ' It is true that this movement shows us that women who so far have been so submissive to their masters, the men, are beginning

145   Information from an interview with Lilian Wolfe, 'Lifetime Resistance', *Shrew*, vol 4 no 4, 1972, pp 6-7.
146   For information about Rocker, the Jubilee Street Club, Milly Witcop and Lilian Wolfe, see Rudolf Rocker, *The London Years*, London 1956, and William Fishman, 'Rudolf Rocker', in *This is Whitechapel*, Whitechapel Art Gallery 1972, reprinted from *History Today* January 1966.

to wake up at last to the fact that they are not inferior to these masters.'
But she said the most oppressed women had no time for 'such trifles as
voting'. She was more generous towards the feminists than Lily Gair
Wilkinson. 'I sincerely hope that these brave women will in time realise
the fact that no Parliament ever can or will do anything towards better-
ing the conditions of the working man or woman.'

But she agreed with the SLP that parliament had done nothing
and that 'Anything that has been gained has been solely gained by force'.
Woman was not subordinated because she did not have the vote, but
because she was a slave at work and in the home. Women could not be
freed by votes in parliament but 'by their own strength'.[147]

The emphasis in Rose Witcop's letter is more on independent self-
activity from below than it is in Lily Gair Wilkinson's pamphlet. However they shared a mutual rejection of parliamentary politics.

Dismissal of the suffrage was not of course synonymous with
opposition to the liberation of women. The anarchists believed very
strongly in a harmony between their revolution and their everyday life.
They tried to live in freedom in an unfree world. This meant they took
questions like marriage and how people lived together very seriously.
Young anarchist women round the Jubilee Street Club were thus proud
of being 'free women'. They were against the State and believed relations
between men and women should be decided only by the individuals concerned. This did not mean that all personal problems were solved, but
the women were conscious of the responsibility of equality and dignity.
They faced unhappiness and sexual jealousy with the pride of being free
women. Rocker describes the difficulty Milly's parents had in understanding her actions when she lived with him without being married.
When Rose and Guy Aldred decided to live together, not only Mrs
Witcop but also her sister objected on the grounds that Rose was still
very young.

Anarchist free unions were affairs of principle not in Aldred's words
'harum-scarum irresponsibility'.[148] Indeed by Aldred's account their
early years together were intensely ascetic. There was no time for 'kiss-
ing' because they had so much to discuss—though it sounds as if Guy
Aldred did most of the talking, telling Rose about Eleanor Marx and
Edward Aveling, and addressing meetings where she circulated the
literature.

However the women still had to face contempt and derision. Rose
was accused of being a prostitute by the police. When Lilian Wolfe
became pregnant she was refused admission into Queen Charlotte's Hospital, not because she was an unmarried mother, but because she was an

147 Rose Witcop, The Voice of Labour, 2 March 1907 quoted in Aldred, No
     Traitor's Gait, Vol 1 no 12, 1957, p 315.
148 ibid, p 329.

unrepentent sinner who continued to live with the child's father. The anarchist emphasis on heroic acts of defiance necessarily placed the greatest strain on the people who were already socially vulnerable. The new morality was so completely at variance with the standard of the time that it necessarily was restricted to a minority even within the left.

The anarchist movement, like the socialist and the feminist, split on the question of the war. While Kropotkin supported it, others became active pacifists. Lilian was living in a communal house with Tom Keell of Freedom Press. Some of the men tried to avoid the call-up by hiding in the Scottish mountains. She and Tom were watched by the police and arrested for printing and distributing an anti-conscription leaflet. Subsequently the emphasis on the connection between ideas and living in the anarchist movement became divorced from any political struggle and tended to become an end in itself. But before World War I the relationship was maintained, and the insistence on making a new culture before the revolution created a degree of sympathy for the liberation of women from the family and for a new concept of sex equality.

Anarchist women were hostile to the suspicion of men which prevailed in the feminist movement. They were concerned to emphasise the unity of interests between men and women. In about 1914 Lily Gair Wilkinson wrote a pamphlet called *Women's Freedom* for the Freedom Press; the basis of her argument had completely changed from the SLP pamphlet, but there were certain consistent themes. For example, she is opposed to what she feels is a feminist idealisation of women as a group, the 'angelic sisterhood'. She is also still contemptuous of the struggle for the vote. But the grounds for her dismissal of the suffragettes have become more clearly anarchist. She mentions the women in the French Revolution and in the Commune, especially Louise Michel, also the American anarchist-communist, Emma Goldman, and the Russian Marie Spiridonova as examples of women who had fought for real freedom.

> ' "Votes for Women!" there is a cracked and treble sound about that. The call for "votes" can never be a call to freedom. For what is it to vote? To vote is to register assent to being ruled by one legislator or another.' (She went on to say that the suffragettes) 'although many of them suffer bravely for their illusions, are but a travesty of true rebel women. Rebel women struggle to be free from bondage and they struggle not against the men who share their interests in life, but side by side with these men.'[149]

She believed the liberation of women was inseparable from the creation of a society in which there was no longer 'possession by the few' of the 'means of life' and thus no longer the economic dependence of women on men. Men and women could then give themselves in love

149 Lily Gair Wilkinson, *Women's Freedom*, Freedom Press, c. 1914, pp 8-9.

freely. She thought this society would be based on small autonomous agricultural communes.

Men would not have to go out to work and the women stay at home. There would be a return to handicrafts and the men and women would work at home. The man's sphere was the home just as much as the woman's was. She opposed the feminists' attempt to get middle class women into the professions, and the entrance of working class women into the factories.

> '. . . in free communal life it will be found, not that women are to be emancipated by becoming lawyers and doctors and whatnot, but that men are to be emancipated by withdrawing from such abnormal occupations and returning to home and garden and field as the true sphere of human life.'[150]

The influence of William Morris is very clear here. It is possible that some of these ideas came from Kropotkin too but they were probably simply in circulation. Although especially associated with the anarchists they were also held by other left-wingers. The enthusiasm for country cottages had been very much a feature of the Carpenter circle. Carpenter himself was a link between the anarchists and the socialists. In fact, the connection between personal life-style and left-wing politics persisted from the socialist revival in the 1880s. Though there was always a tension between the search for a new life and the practical day-to-day agitation, and there was never any clear idea how personal cultural transformation related to a political strategy.

Distinctions which appear clear to us now were at the time obscured by personal contact and friendship. Interest in a new consciousness among men and women was much wider in range than most historians of either the feminist or the socialist and labour movement have indicated. For instance some women in socialist groups noticed the personal attitude of superiority men had towards women. Reviewing Carpenter's *Love's Coming Of Age* in *The Labour Leader* in 1896 Lily Bell said he was one of the few men who could write about women and sexuality:

> 'Most men write with such an air of superiority, such an assumption of masculine authority and right to lay down the law as to what women may or may not do, what may or may not be her proper "sphere" in life, that I usually take up their articles merely to lay them down again with a feeling of impatience and irritation.'[151]

Carpenter noted the response from the men. He scribbled in some 'Notes on Women's Suffrage' in 1908 that the women were 'full of go and originality'. As a result, 'Males getting alarmed for their supremacy. And sometimes I think a good thing. They *should* be alarmed—stir them up a bit'.[152]

150 *ibid*, p 15.
151 Lily Bell, 'Matrons and Maidens', *Labour Leader*, 27 June 1896.
152 Carpenter Collection. Sheffield Public Library. Mss 165 1908.

Amongst the 'alarmed' no doubt was the young D H Lawrence. Clara, in *Sons and Lovers*, is modelled on a socialist and suffragette called Alice Dax and Miriam on Jessie Chambers. Alice lent Jessie, Carpenter's *Love's Coming of Age* around 1909-1910. Alice was also a friend of Sallie Hopkin, wife of a cobbler in Eastwood who knew Carpenter well. Sallie Hopkin's daughter, Enid, says Alice Dax was 'years ahead of (her) time', 'widely read', 'advanced' in dress, thought and house-decoration, trying to live according to Carpenter's notions of 'simplification of life'[153] which meant cutting down on material needs. She was in reaction against Victorian formality and hypocrisy. She was also antagonistic to men, and her marriage was a form of revenge. The 'advanced' circle in Eastwood were in touch not only with Carpenter but with other socialists and feminists. Philip Snowden, Ramsay Macdonald, Charlotte Despard, Annie Kenny, Beatrice and Sidney Webb, Keir Hardie, and Margaret Bondfield all visited them.

Lawrence was to look for personal moral solutions to the new free relations between men and women, not towards formal politics. In 1912 he told Sallie Hopkin 'I shall do a novel about Love Triumphant one day. I shall do my work for women better than the Suffrage'.[154] In January 1915 he wanted to found a 'colony' of 'some twenty souls' away from the world at war.

There are certain similarities between Carpenter and the early Lawrence. They both stress feeling against the intellect, nature against civilisation. They are both concerned to find harmony between the conscious and unconscious and want the area of politics to be much wider. Lawrence too shared Carpenter's reaction against Christian asceticism and his interest in love between people of the same sex. It is almost certain that Lawrence had read Carpenter and heard his idea discussed in the socialist feminist circle at Eastwood. However their politics subsequently diverge. Carpenter's eros was still progressive, middle class and optimistic. It could be reconciled with rationalism and pre-war marxism. Lawrence's dwelt in darker regions of the psyche and could not reconcile itself with either the feminism or the marxism of the post-war world, though in the earlier period his rebellion against industrialisation and all its works could still locate itself with the left.

Before 1914 the delineations between personal and political revolt were not clearly defined. There was no agreed route to revolution and the tension is evident not merely between the 'new life' and day-to-day struggle, but between the less definable personal implications of the new feminist consciousness and the official face of socialism. Feminism touched upon extremely delicate taboos. It threatened socialists precisely

153 Quoted in Emile Delavenay, *D H Lawrence and Edward Carpenter, A Study in Edwardian Transition*, London 1971, p 22.
154 *ibid*, p 26.

where conscious reason had the covers down. It would have been surprising if many men in the socialist movement had not recoiled somewhat, especially as there was nothing in their theory which could explain the relationship between present half-conscious feelings and the ideal future society.

Both anarchist and socialist women were obviously afraid of antagonism between the sexes because they felt it would have a destructive effect on the movement. However the feminist consciousness did create a strain in sexual relations because women became aware of their own subservience and passivity. They hoped that in comradeship they would find a new sexual equality. But the hope and aspirations of women were still at variance with their actual predicament. Ethel Snowden in 1906 in *The Woman Socialist* quotes an anonymous poem which she says reveals 'the heart-ache and echoes the heart-cries of ten thousand women, who still sit at the feet of Fate even whilst their spirits rebel,

Oh, to be alone!
To escape from the work, the play,
The talking every day;
To escape from all I have done,
And all that remains to do!
To escape—yes, even from you,
My only love, and be
Alone and free.

Could I only stand
Between gray moor and gray sky,
Where the winds and the plovers cry,
And no man is at hand;
And feel the free wind slow
On my rain-wet face and know
I am free—not yours, but my own—
Free and alone!

For the soft firelight
And the home of your heart, my dear,
They hurt, being always here.
I want to stand upright,
And to cool my eyes in the air,
And to see how my back can bear
Burdens—to try, to know
To learn, to grow!

I am only you!
I am yours, part of you, your wife!
And I have no other life.
I cannot think, cannot do;
I cannot breathe, cannot see;
There is "us", but there is not me:—
And worst at your kiss I grow
Contented so.[155]

It was very hard to work out how sexual feelings connected to political consciousness, especially when the inner being was opposed to the external conscious world.

155 Quoted in Ethel Snowden, *The Woman Socialist*, London 1907, pp 64-65.

Similarly the problems of sexuality and reproduction presented great difficulties for the socialist movement. The question of human control over sex and procreation became inextricably confused with state regulation of breeding, motherhood and childcare. Ideas of race supremacy and the extension of state control into the most intimate aspects of life did not have the sinister connotations which fascism was to bring later. It is evident that theories about breeding efficiently which were argued by eugenicists had an appeal not only on the right but in the socialist movement as well. Karl Pearson for instance argued for class unity, imperialism and the survival of the fittest but he called himself a socialist. Eugenic arguments influenced not only members of the Fabian Society but were quite favourably regarded by other socialists who were further to the left.

There was too a curious overlap between eugenics and feminism, because the eugenicists were interested in the conditions of motherhood and in control over reproduction. There was also considerable anxiety about a 'birth strike' before and after World War I. Anti-feminist eugenicists both in Germany and England pointed out that high fertility and healthy motherhood were essential for the superior race. In Britain the Fabians argued for social reform in order to improve the physique of the working class who would have to be the defenders of the Empire.[156]

The same issues were taken over by pro-feminists to insist that unless the women were granted their demands for a new social order their refusal to have children would result in racial decline. A book called *The Sexual Crisis* by a German woman, Grete Meisel-Hess, published in 1909 argued that the ablest and most intelligent women were increasingly unwilling to marry because of the growth of feminist consciousness. Unless there were very extensive changes in society's treatment of motherhood only 'inferior' women would give birth.[157] These arguments were repeated quite uncritically by Maurice Eden Paul in a talk to Poole and Branksome ILP in June 1911. He was concerned to connect socialism and eugenics and denied scare stories of 'stud farms'. He wanted *voluntary* sterilisation of the feeble-minded and habitually criminal and thought that under socialism the only reason for anti-social behaviour would be inherited deficiency.[158]

156   See Semmel, *Imperialism and Social Reform*, pp 35-82, and Ludwig Quessel, 'A Spectre Haunts Europe—the spectre of the birth strike', (eds) Maurice Eden and Cedar Paul, *Population and Birth Control, a symposium*, New York 1917, p 149.

157   Kollontai in *Sexual Relations and the Class Struggle, Love and the New Morality* (first edition Russia 1919), refers uncritically to Meisel-Hess while arguing for a materialist approach to sex.

158   See Maurice Eden Paul, *Socialism and Eugenics*, London 1911, and Eugenics, Birth-Control and Socialism, in (eds) Eden and Cedar Paul, *Population and Birth Control*.

The confusion between socialism and social engineering, between workers' control and state control, which existed in the socialist movement at the time, thus appears also in the debate on the woman's control over her reproductive capacity. As there was no marxist orthodoxy, no accepted approach to sexuality, only a few hints from the marxist fathers, it was by no means a revision of marxism. It was rather an attempt to fill an absence in marxism. It was not only that theories about the political significance for women of control over procreation, over their own persons, remained underdeveloped, but more seriously that these notions had origins which came to seem very sinister after the fascists had begun to utilise them in a new political context.

17

The War

The period immediately before World War I saw not only the suffragette movement, conflict in Ireland, and intense socialist propaganda, but was also a time of great industrial unrest. Workers who had never taken action before began to unionise.

The problems of unionising women workers were far from solved. The Women's Trade Union League had become the National Federation of Women Workers. But it operated on a shoe string. When Mary MacArthur became its secretary in 1903 she inherited two office rooms, which did not even have a telephone or typewriter; but it had acquired a sizeable debt. She began to build the Federation on her own indomitable determination. She needed to be enthusiastic—but found it backfired sometimes.

> 'About the first time I started an open air meeting I got a number of girls around me on a street corner and I told them about unionism. I was very enthusiastic and perhaps I gave it to them in too glowing terms. They believed me and gave me their names to join the Union. Ten days afterwards the girls looked more inclined to mob me than anything else and I asked them what was the matter. "Oh, we've been ten days in the Union and our wages haven't gone up".'[159]

In 1906 the average wage of the male worker in Britain was around 30s a week. Women's rates were well below this. Textile workers were amongst the best-paid women, and had a long tradition of unionisation. They earned about 18s 8d in this period. But women in the linen and silk trades, in glass making and in printing earned only half this amount. Below these came the home-workers. A woman carding hooks and eyes at home could earn 5s a week if she worked eighteen hours a day.

An enquiry in 1906 into women's work by Edward Cadbury showed

159 Quoted in Gladys Bourne, *The Women's Trade Union League*, New York 1942, p 30.

that the women themselves believed that it was right for their wages to be much lower than a man's. They accepted inferior status and inferior payment as part of the order of things. Masculine dominance and authority seemed equally natural. Women were not 'free' to sell their labour on the same terms as men. Indeed in domestic service and shopwork the employers' relationship was still paternalistic. Employers expected to control the moral and spiritual lives of their employees. Women workers had all the strengths and weaknesses of a labour force that has not been broken in to capitalism. They were erratic in their commitment to the union but capable, once they began to move, of an infectious militancy which spread rapidly beyond the confines of economic issues. When the women resisted they turned strikes into festivals.

In 1910 for example the transport workers were on strike, everything started to close down, food piled up in the docks, vegetables grew scarce and butter rancid. Suddenly some women workers in a confectionery factory in Bermondsey left work. They went through the streets singing and shouting, and other women poured out of factories and workshops. Jam, pickle, and biscuit workers followed along with bottle washers, tin-box makers, cocoa workers, rag-pickers and women in the distillery trade. Their average wage was 7s-9s a week for women, 3s for girls. They wanted more pay. There were tales of a fat woman who had called them out on strike, though nobody had actually seen her, but they all knew people who had.

Though the fat woman never materialised, Mary Macarthur did. She opened a strike headquarters and feeding centre in Bermondsey. Within a week she had four thousand recruits and within twenty days the employers had given in to eighteen of the twenty strikes. The women dressed up in their best clothes, feather boas and fur tippets, 'as though the strike were some holiday of the soul, long overdue'.[160] It was this quality in women's action at work which made the most unlikely people support them. Susan Lawrence was a convinced Tory before Mary MacArthur showed her the conditions of the London County Council charwomen who had begun to unionise and were demanding a minimum wage of 14s a week, full pay during holidays and direct employment by the Council. Susan Lawrence not only became their zealous supporter but was transformed into a socialist and campaigned in East End street meetings—much to the mirth of bystanders—with a monocle and a high class falsetto accent.

However, spontaneity and enthusiasm have their limitations and the women were far from having the organised industrial strength of the men.

The outbreak of war in 1914 not only divided all the radical political groupings into supporters and opponents, including of course the women;

160 Dangerfield, *The Strange Death of Liberal England, 1910-1914*, p 265.

it also transformed the whole context of industrial activity. For the first time outside the traditional area of women's work like Lancashire, large numbers of women were concentrated together in industry. Women represented a crucial pool of labour power which the war economy had to use.

On the eve of World War I there were around 15 million women in Britain. About 7½ million of these were either married or widowed and looking after their homes and families. It was quite common for daughters to stay at home and care for younger brothers and sisters and there were about 1½ million single women who worked only as housewives. There was also still a great demand for domestic servants and service accounted for another 1½ million women's jobs. This leaves just under 4 million women, a quarter of the female population, employed outside the family.

> 'Even this figure overstates the number of women who actually worked outside a family environment since some of the women included in this category were engaged in helping husbands or other male relatives run a family business. The remaining women were either studying, retired or living from private means. To most people living in these circumstances it must have seemed a fact of nature that a woman's work was in the home.'[161]

In 1911 there were about 1,400,000 women in private domestic service. During the war about 400,000 of these women left to do other work. Between 1914-1918 a total of 792,000 women entered industry.[162]

It was necessary in the exceptional circumstances of the war economy to overcome social ideas about women's place because of military and economic necessity. Women worked as nurses, munitions workers and supplied clerical labour power for the war effort. It was not simply a matter of helping the war machine, they had to replace men at work who had gone off to fight. The dependence on female labour meant that the notion of men's and women's work was no longer inviolable. Women left domestic service, outwork and the despised women's trades. Married women and widows, including middle class women who would have never dreamed of working before, went into clerical work. Working-class women replaced youths or semi-skilled men in the metal trades. Sometimes a group of women did jobs which had previously been done by a smaller number of men. In other instances, machinery broke down the work process so untrained women could substitute for men.

These changes were the result of the military needs of an imperialist war. The price for doing men's work was harsh indeed and it would be naive to see the work itself as emancipating for women workers. The integration of women into the labour force was accompanied by and in

---

161 Jean Gardiner, *The Structure of Women's Work in the 20th Century*, unpublished paper.
162 See 'The Position of Women after the War', *Report of the Standing Joint Committee of Industrial Women's Organisations*, London 1918, p. 3-4.

part a result of dilution of labour and production speed-ups. All protective legislation was put aside, and women were exposed to dangerous and heavy trades, with disastrous effects on health. In some cases too women did work which had previously been jealously guarded. They became bus and tram conductresses, for instance. Outside London they even drove the buses. When women were substituted they generally took home less pay than the men though in some trades union agreement secured them equivalent pay for equivalent work. Women on the railways in grades where they were not employed before the war started at the men's rate. Women dockers in West Hartlepool got 7d an hour. But in the depressed women's trades the only increases came because of longer hours. Health and child care suffered too, even though for some women pay was higher.

The war hastened and made more definite, trends in the structure of women's employment, which were already emerging before 1914. Capitalism was beginning to need an increasing number of workers who were not directly involved in production but who were essential in servicing the production of goods. The expansion of administrative and clerical work and the use of women's labour persisted after the war.

The office was more attractive than the factory and the more privileged women went into clerical work both to replace men and to deal with the mounting paper work required to run the war machine. The social status of the clerk was temporarily elevated, when the typewriter had already transformed the role of male secretary and clerk into a mechanical task suitable for women. In *This Freedom* in 1922, the popular novelist A S M Hutchinson described his young upper-class heroine, Doda, impatient with school and knitting scarves for soldiers. Aged 16 in 1917 she longed to go out to work.

'She didn't much want to go into a hospital or into any of those women's corps. They were a jolly sight too cooped up in those things from what she'd heard. She wanted to go into one of the Government offices and do clerical work. Several of the school old girls who had been there with her were doing that, and it was the most ripping rag.'[103]

The conditions of war work for the less privileged were far less 'ripping'. However there were significant changes in all women's attitudes to work. The war broke down many of the assumptions which had persisted throughout the industrial revolution. Young women like Doda from the upper middle classes came to assume that they had a right to work. Working-class women who experienced their capacity to do a man's job began to question female subordination at work. The numbers of women in trade unions went up during the war. This meant that for the first time, outside textiles, women workers were organised on a

163   A S M Hutchinson, *This Freedom*, London 1922, p 293.

sustained and continuing basis. This was to have a very important effect on women's attitudes towards unionisation.

The men were caught in a dilemma. Although they resented the dilutees, male or female, they had to insist that they belonged to a union. They could no longer ignore the unionisation of women. However the whole position of the union had changed. The official machinery of the trade unions was incorporated directly into the state. Union leaders now sat on government committees. Mary Macarthur became part of this new officialdom in contrast to her pre-war position.

As male militants became increasingly disillusioned with this process of integration they began to create new bargaining structures. The shop steward, originally merely a collector of dues, began to assume a new importance as a representative of skilled engineers threatened by dilution in wartime production. Despite its craft origins, the context of its emergence transformed the shop stewards' movement.

Out of the political and economic unrest of wartime Clydeside came a struggle in which direct action at work spread beyond the skilled men, and out into the community.

The women on Clydeside became involved through a tenants' movement against rent increases, led by a working-class housewife, Mrs Barbour from Goven, Glasgow. Perhaps there was an earlier pre-industrial memory. Many older people in Glasgow must have heard of the Highland clearances from crofters who had been evicted. The brutality of that uprooting from the countryside still burned within the memory of the urban community. But there were more recent factors to explain the combination of community and industrial direct action. Clydeside had a tradition of intense revolutionary socialist agitation and working-class marxist education. Political consciousness and class solidarity were for a time strong enough to overcome the divisions fostered by capitalism.·

William Gallacher, in *Revolt on the Clyde*, describes how the women organised:

> 'Street-meetings, back-court meetings, drums, bells, trumpets—every method was used to bring the women out and organise them for the struggle. Notices were printed by the thousand and put up in the windows, wherever you went you could see them. In street after street scarcely a window without one. " WE ARE NOT PAYING INCREASED RENT".'[164]

Evictions were effectively resisted so the property owners tried to take them to court for debt and impound rent out of wages. The women were determined to prevent this. 'All day long, in the streets, in the halls,

---

164 Quoted in *Women's Voice*, No 1, 1971 p 8.
See also Walter Kendall, *The Revolutionary Movement in Britain 1900-21*, London 1969, Chapter 7, Clydeside in Wartime, and Bob Horne, '1915 The Great Rents Victory' in *Scottish Marxist*, No 2 Winter 1972.

in the houses, meetings were held, kitchen meetings, street-meetings, mass meetings, meetings of every kind.'[165] The organisation of the tenants began to cut across the division between work and home. Though the women at home did not have the support of the workers in the munitions factories, contingents did come from the shipyards and demonstrated with them. A massive and angry crowd gathered outside the Court where the trial for debt was to take place.

The law was helpless. The sheriff phoned Lloyd George, then Minister of Munitions, in a panic. 'Stop the case', he was told. 'A Rent Restriction Act will be introduced immediately'. Because of the war the need to produce arms was more important than the landlords' class interests. Victory celebrations went on all night. This combination of community and industrial action had achieved the first measure of rent control.

The Clydeside movement was contained by 1916. However the shop stewards' movement reappeared in Sheffield. This time it had broadened out and included every worker, skilled, semi-skilled, unskilled, men and women, trade-union members and non-unionists. It had ceased to be only an economic movement, but was now clearly a new form of working-class democratic organisation.[166] The extent to which women participated is, however, unclear.

J T Murphy, a socialist who played an important part in the Workers' Committee movement in Sheffield, wrote a pamphlet called *The Workers' Committee: An Outline of its Principles and Structure,* published by the Sheffield shop stewards in 1917. He described the men's attitude to the women in engineering and said they were 'tolerated with amused contempt as passengers for the war'. He foresaw the way in which women would be unemployed along with many men after the war ended. 'Domestic service cannot absorb all women, as some suggest, nor is it possible, as others remark, for them to go back to what they were doing before the war.' He understood the basis for antagonism between men and women at work, the fact that women were used as cheap labour and were slower to organise than men and also how the subordination of women to men made the divisions capitalism had created between workers of different sexes even more difficult to overcome. 'We men and women of today have now to pay the price of man's economic dominance over women which has existed for centuries, Content to treat women as subjects instead of equals, men are now faced with problems not to their liking.'[167] With the end of the wartime pro-

165 *Women's Voice*, No 1 p 8.
166 Bill Moore, 'Sheffield Shop Stewards in the First World War', in Munby (ed), *The Luddites and other essays*, p 246.
167 J T Murphy, *The Workers Committee. An Outline of its Principles and Structure,* first published by the Sheffield Workers Committee 1917, reprinted Pluto Press 1973, p 18.

duction the shop stewards' movement collapsed and the militants found themselves outside the factories. However, the ideas about workers' councils and direct action continued after the war, and were greatly stimulated by the success of the factory councils and soviets in the Russian Revolution.

There was also apparently some mobilisation of soldiers' and sailors' wives, for in Walthamstow in March 1918 they had formed a League of Rights for higher allowances and pensions.

Immediately after the revolution in Russia in 1917, the dream of soldiers and workers, men and women, skilled and unskilled, coming together to make a new peace and a new world seemed almost a reality. There were though very real antagonisms and divisions between men and women during the war, partly because of conflict over dilution, but also because women who did not work were not touched by the shop stewards' or workers' councils' movements.[168]

Working-class militancy at work during the war was high. But the conditions of the war made any form of revolutionary political organisation very difficult. Syndicalism, which concentrated on grassroots organising at work contributed to the failure to connect to political action. This had obvious implications for the organisation of women. Women's oppression cut across home and work. Industrial economic militancy did not include the family and the community. These weaknesses were never overcome though there were instances of struggles in the community in which women were prominent, and which succeeded in partially overcoming the separation between work and home which had been the legacy of the industrial revolution.

An example of sustained community organising is the work of Sylvia Pankhurst and the Federation of the Suffragettes who campaigned against a whole series of hardships and discrimination, not just for the vote. The women left at home in World War I faced many problems. Interfering officials made it difficult for them to collect their allowances as soldiers' dependents. Working-class women walking alone were harassed as prostitutes by the police. In June 1915 the Board of Trade

---

See also J T Murphy *Preparing for Power*, Pluto Press 1972 for a reference to the Convention held at Leeds in 1917 which passed a resolution condemning discrimination against women workers. However this Convention had little rank-and-file base and though various women's organisations were represented no real power to change the conditions of either men's or women's work.

168 In their pamphlet *Direct Action* in 1919, William Gallacher and J R Campbell tried to overcome this by the supplementation of industrial organisation by social organisations. 'In other words it will be found necessary to organise the workers in the place where they live as well as in the place where they work.' They saw this as a means of involving working class housewives. (Pluto Press edition 1972, p 27).

sent an appeal to families to cut down on meat. As many poor families only had meat once a week this was virtually an instruction to eat none at all. The East London Federation defended women over allowances and against police harassment. They tried to take action over high prices by a boycott of shops with expensive items, and thought of simply walking in and taking food.

Sylvia Pankhurst exposed the conditions of women's work in her paper *The Dreadnought*. In one Limehouse food factory women worked in a steaming basement, with food in a state of decomposition. Ironically they were supplying turtle soup for the royal household! Melvina Walker, a docker's wife, and Charlotte Drake, a former barmaid, went to the Board of Trade and demanded that the men's trade unions should be urged to admit women, that when women were drafted for war work they should get the same wages as men who worked in the jobs before, that no woman should get less than male union rates, that women should receive industrial training at government training schools, and that the government should be responsible for all workers displaced by the war. *The Dreadnought* defended the rights of unsupported mothers and revealed the abysmal pay and conditions of home workers.

Probably because it was frustrating to keep on agitating with little positive results they started to run their own alternatives. A toy factory was started for women who needed the work; they had equal pay and it was run under workers' control. A crèche was started for the children, in the factory. Appealing for money Sylvia Pankhurst explained 'working mothers can leave their babies for the day at a charge of 3d a head. For this the children receive three meals and the loan of suitable clothes, and are properly cared for in every way.'[169] The children learned drawing and painting with a girl who had been an art student with Sylvia and the nursery education was on 'Tolstoyan'—later Montessori—principles.

The crèche was a success and had to move to a larger place. They collected money and bought a pub, 'The Gunmakers Arms', at 485 Old Ford Road, and renamed it 'The Mothers Arms'. The bar-room was the reception centre. Long cupboards contained medicines and invalid foods, including fresh eggs from the country. Most of the mothers and babies were undernourished. There were maternity outfits, baby weighing, specially designed toys, weekly hygiene and domestic science lectures and a nurse who kept records of the children's and mothers' health.

There was a basic contradiction, though, despite the success. Sylvia was forced to scrounge from her mother's rich friends and connections in the West End. Community care was in fact thinly-disguised charity. Inevitably too the East London Federation became mixed up in the

169 Sylvia Pankhurst, letter to The Times, 11 December 1914, in Sylvia Pankhurst Collection ELFS, Institute of Social History Amsterdam.

internal tangles of administering their own services. In 1917 this came to a head with the woman who supervised the factory. Not only was she inefficient and kept the wages down, but she tried to slip in a capitalist friend of hers as manager, while the Federation wanted it to be run by a democratically elected committee. There was trouble too with the nurse at 'The Mothers Arms'. She was discovered to be buying Nestlé's milk and selling it to the mothers at a profit, arguing about the price of milk with them, and to be generally on the fiddle. When a mysterious wave of pilfering started she was suspected.

Because the Federation got involved in providing community services rather than agitating for the council to do something they absorbed a great deal of their members' energy in these administrative problems. On the other hand by providing their own alternatives they could feel they were achieving something. The factory and crèche provided a means of making contact with women in the area, because when the suffragettes arrived they were very much outsiders. These early private welfare schemes had an important influence as models for wider scale measures later although this was little consolation at the time.

Immediately before the war they had thought of organising a rent strike for the vote. The housing shortage during the war though made action over housing itself urgent. They got the idea of squatting from the Russian revolution, which they had greeted with enthusiasm. In Russia people took over houses for the poor and homeless. Norah Smythe went along to Poplar Trades Council and the Labour Party and suggested that the Russian example should be followed by people in the workhouses who had lost their homes in air raids. Some other delegates supported her and Bow Council agreed to meet a deputation.

The Workers' Dreadnought in January 1918 was advocating the socialisation of the food supply, the production of food under the control of workers' committees appointed by the TUC and the local Trades Council. They also insisted that half the members on the committees should be women. Food was very scarce and so they also wanted rationing and free food supplied off the rates.

But although agitation was sustained throughout the war and although the attempt was made to overcome the split between home and work, consumption and production, women and men, feminists and socialists, the divisions went very deep and the ELFS was powerless to overcome them. The feminist organisations had divided over the war. Christabel became one of the most fervent opponents of Germany. *The Suffragette* changed its name in 1915 to *Britannia* and supported military conscription for men, industrial conscription for women. The WSPU suffragettes were among the first women to give men in civilian clothes white feathers of cowardice. They campaigned to get women into the munition factories and marched against the men who were trying to protect skilled workers. The government obliged by paying the suffragettes' expenses for the march. They were greeted by their old enemies, Lloyd George and Winston Churchill. At a meeting in the Albert Hall in October 1916 Mrs Pankhurst spoke in favour of servicemen having a vote and denounced 'conscientious objectors, passive resisters and shirkers'.[170]

In fact among the conscientious objectors were her old allies, the Pethick Lawrences, and a substantial section of the suffrage movement. Her daughter Sylvia never ceased to attack 'this capitalist war'. The split between mother and daughter was now complete. Sylvia Pankhurst said that the WSPU had 'entirely departed from the Suffrage Movement. Giving its energies solely to the prosecution of the war, it rushed to a furious extreme, its chauvinism unexampled amongst all other women's societies.'[171]

The Russian Revolution and the triumph of the Bolsheviks made this separation impossible to overcome. Sylvia's future was with revolutionary socialism; her mother's with the Conservative Party.

The conflict of interest between men and women workers was approached by the feminist movement in several ways. Emmeline and Christabel demanded that the dilutees be taken on without any safeguards for the male trade unionists, Sylvia and the East London Federation struggled for equal pay and better conditions for working-class women.

However, the problem remained. What was to happen when the men returned?

The women's position in industry was the exceptional product of wartime. While the war continued people talked politely about 'readjustment' not unemployment. Women's organisations had tried hard to prevent a return to pre-war conditions. The Women's Trade Union League, the National Federation of Women Workers, the Women's Labour League, and the Women's Co-operative Guild had demanded equal pay for equal work, regulation of wages in low paid trades, a 48-hour week, abolition of fines and truck, more women factory inspectors, protection in the dangerous trades, maternity provision, co-operative homes for working girls, reforms in technical education and of course the vote.

The war had brought a new urgency to the discussion about mixed or separate unions. In the report of the Joint Committee of Industrial Women's Organisations the women said they wanted all trade unions to be open to women workers. But they were aware of the danger of women being swamped by more confident male trade unionists. Their proposals were clear and to the point:

170   Ramelson, *Petticoat Rebellion*, p 168.
171   *ibid*, p 169.

'Special provision should be made in the rules for the representation of women on the governing bodies of the unions, and there should be inside each Trade Union special machinery for dealing with the organisation of women in the trade and with their special needs and grievances.'[172]

They suggested a Women's Council, or a sub-committee of the Executive and the appointment of women organisers and officials. The general trend was towards the amalgamation of small unions for greater strength. Though in favour of this they thought women's 'autonomy' must be safeguarded. They believed in 'the closest possible co-operation between the men and women trade unionists', but felt 'it is idle to deny that there are industrial problems which affect women specially and which require special treatment'. They also stressed the effect of trade-union membership on the women's sense of their capabilities.

'We are convinced that no form of Trade Union organisation amongst women can be satisfactory or permanent if it does not aim at encouraging women to take a large part in the management of their own affairs. . . . There is no stability in a merely paper membership from which the educational value of Trade Unionism is largely absent.'[173]

Some of the men were extremely dubious about the women's terms. Thomas Shaw, for instance, a weaver, said at Ruskin College in 1916: 'I think there is a danger that existed even before the war of a feeling growing up amongst the women that unless they are organised, officered and managed separately their interests cannot be attended to.'[174] Women in an organisation with men could get better wages than they could on their own. 'I deprecate the tendency of so many people to think that unless a woman represents a woman the woman worker cannot get representation at all.'[175]

He completely by-passed the problem of women's interests sometimes being different from men's and the difficulty of women organising within the male-dominated union for their special point of view. Mary MacArthur was of the opinion that the attitude of the Engineers, who kept women out of their own union but helped the National Federation of Women Workers to organise women in engineering was better than that of trade unionists who admitted women, took their contributions, and used the organisation without consultation to exclude women from jobs after the war. She said that even before the war women had got rather fed up of hearing their place was at home. 'They had begun to realise that those who talked of the home really meant the kitchen.'[176]

The popular press was quick to forget the women's war effort. They

172   The Position of Women after the War. *Report*, p 13.
173   *ibid*, p 16.
174   Conference on the Reorganisation of Industry, Ruskin College 1916, p 39.
175   *ibid*, p 39.
176   Mary MacArthur, 'The Women Trade Unionists' Point of View', in Dr Marion Phillips (ed), *Women and the Labour Party*, London 1918, p 18.

were full of the extravagance of the munitionettes, *The Daily Graphic* for example being indignant that women should presume a right to work.

'The idea that because the State called for women to help the nation, the State must continue to employ them is too absurd for serious women to entertain. As a matter of grace, notice should be at least a fortnight and if possible a month. As for young women formerly in domestic service, they at least should have no difficulty in finding vacancies.'[177]

Despite unemployment though the women wanted any job but domestic service.

But the war had not only transformed women's attitudes to work. The young VADs or WAAC privates saw their friends go down in hospital ships, saw other nurses buried with 'Killed in action' on the crosses after the bombing of Étaples. They became self-conscious about class. Middle-class girls from private boarding schools met working-class women on equal terms. They rejected middle-class morality. There was no time for the legal niceties of bourgeois marriage. As Vera Brittain says, 'For the younger generation life had grown short, and death was always imminent; the postponement of love to a legal occasion might mean its frustration for ever.'[178]

There were tiny gestures of this new impatient sexual independence everywhere. When Margaret Sanger came to London she saw the women knitting socks but 'was more impressed by the fact they were smoking in hotel lobbies—a new indication of emancipation for me—and even rolling their own cigarettes'.[179]

The problems of the men in readjusting to civilian life was a common theme of the literature of the post-war era. But the psychological experience of the women found very little serious expression. Vera Brittain, whose *Testament of Youth* was one of the rare exceptions, complained that male writers either ignored women completely or produced a stereotyped Andromeda 'smiling through her tears' or an equally stereotyped time server 'battening upon the sufferings and savings of the fighting soldier.'[180]

True, Robert Graves mentions his wife Nancy at the end of *Goodbye to All That*. She was a socialist but for her, 'Socialism was a means to a simple end: namely judicial equality between the sexes.' He says,

'She ascribed all the wrong in the world to male domination and narrowness, and would not see my experiences in the war as anything comparable with the sufferings that millions of working-class women went through without complaint.'[181]

177 Quoted in David Mitchell, *Women on the Warpath*, London 1966, p 266.
178 Vera Brittain, *Lady into Woman*, London 1953, p 186.
179 Sanger, *An Autobiography*, p 127.
180 Brittain, *Lady into Woman*, p 188.
181 Robert Graves, *Goodbye to All That*, London, 1st ed 1929, Penguin 1966, p 237.

However this inarticulate suffering, the gnawing hardship, the shattered dreams of millions of working-class women remained obscure and thus were easy to ignore.

With the war over, the ruling class wanted a return to business as usual. At first they had to proceed cautiously. They were faced with bitter heroes in arms and women who had tasted a fleeting independence and had begun to shed the illusions of sexual subordination. Demobilisation was carried out very slowly. The troops were promised a new world and homes fit for heroes, promises which were never kept though initially there was a burst of legislation introducing rent control, council housing, and the extension of insurance and education. These immediate post-war reforms were passed in an atmosphere which was very near to insurrection, in which mutinies and riot were erupting spontaneously and industrial militancy so widespread that even the police went on strike.

Although the feminist organisations had been divided by the war, feminist consciousness was still very strong. Indeed it had gained a new cultural confidence because of the social consequences of the war. The government successfully followed a policy of divide and rule. The antagonism between men and women workers was exploited. The differences between classes and between old and young women were also used. In the period 1918-1920 there were a series of legislative reforms which tended to benefit the older, more privileged women. In 1918 women over 30 got the vote, but it was not until 1928 that women got the vote on the same terms as men. Dora Russell in *Hypatia* in 1925 wrote bitterly,

'In 1918 they bestowed the vote, just as they dropped about a few Dames and MBEs as a reward for our services in helping the destruction of our offspring. . . . They gave the vote to the older women who were deemed less rebellious.'[182]

Women were also allowed to sit on juries although because there was a property qualification this only applied to householders. It was still felt that women were not qualified to make decisions on certain kinds of crime. The Judge would cough when a sex crime came up and the jury woman would be expected to leave. In 1919 the Sex Disqualification Removal Act was passed. This declared that no one should be disqualified from holding any public office or civil and judicial post by sex or marriage. Women could thus become JPs—providing they had the time and leisure of course.

More significant in its effect was the Maternity and Child Welfare Act of 1918 by which welfare clinics could be set up. This Act was undoubtedly a great victory for the women's organisations, especially the Women's Co-operative Guild which had campaigned for better maternity conditions. However there was another aspect of it as well—a recognition

182   Dora Russell, *Hypatia*, London 1925, pp 3-4.

that women had to be somehow persuaded to give birth to children in order to make up for the lives which had been sacrificed to international capital during the war.

The embryonic welfare provision which related very much to women and the family had from its origins a dual character. On the one hand it was the result of pressure from the working class and from women for social reforms. At the other it indicated structural changes in capitalism which required a different relationship between the state and the nurture and education of the labour force. Such tendencies, barely visible in 1918, were to have a significant effect on the longer term position of women and the functions of the family.

Feminists, both outside the labour movement and within it, were in general unaware of this shift in capitalist society. The predominant feeling in 1918 was a conviction that the vote was only the beginning. They saw a continuous progression in women's position, a steady movement towards full emancipation, even if they differed in their political alignments. Isabella Ford, for instance, wrote to her old comrade Alf Mattison in 1918,

'And now, the great tasks that lie before us, Peace, Reform and all the rest, will be so much easier to work at. We shall have a weapon in our hands, and hitherto we have had none.'[183]

The vote was not a useless weapon, and women were to achieve a good deal by legislation. However, there are limits to the kind of change which can be effected by law while the structure of society remains the same.

It was evident to only a few observers at the time that the need to make profits and maintain the sexual division of labour in industry and in the family was capable of withstanding much reform and that patriarchy still served that need.

Stella Browne, described by Margaret Sanger, when she met her in 1915, as 'an ardent feminist',[184] active in the birth control movement, struck a more pessimistic note in a book on population edited by the socialists, Eden and Cedar Paul, and published in 1917. It included essays by various German and English socialists and supporters and opponents of contraception. Stella Browne predicted that Maternity Insurance would be introduced after the war. But she thought this would be accompanied by a more merciless and systematic exploitation of women's capacity to labour and to reproduce. She prophesied an ideological reaction against feminism, birth control, and the economic and social advances women had managed to secure during the war. There would be, she thought,

183   Isabella Ford to Alf Mattison 1 February 1918, Alf Mattison's Letter Book.
184   Sanger, *An Autobiography*, p 119.

'. . . a specialised education for girls, concentrating on the sentimental and the domestic, and a fevered propaganda in favour of what some reactionaries already term "the normal family", a propaganda in which the licensed imbecilities of the pulpit are backed up by the venal and impertinent irrelevancies of the press and the pomposities of the debating platforms and stiffened by determined efforts to penalise (or at least to restrict) the sale of contraceptives to the poor.'[185]

The counter-attack did come though its effects were not felt immediately and the feminists were for some time strong enough to withstand it.

185 F W Stella Browne, Women and Birth Control in Paul (eds), *Population and Birth Control*, p 248.

18

Anti-feminism

'It's 1919, they've caught the rising generation, the flag of liberty that the war flamed across the world; licence the curmudgeons call it, liberty the young set free.'[186]

Hutchinson in *This Freedom* described Doda's rebellion against her family, her search for sexual pleasure, and the independence she found with her wage as a clerk in the barracks-like Government Department. A contemporary song complained about masculine women and feminine men—Sister Susie stopped sewing soldiers' shirts and was said to be learning to shave. A bevy of American 'Red hot mommas' and 'Hard-hearted Hannahs' invaded popular music.

The cultural signs of sexual unrest had been evident before the war. In the atmosphere of release, anti-climax, and bitter recognition that the years of the war were lost and wasted, they asserted themselves more powerfully. There were more divorces in 1918 than ever before, and the divorce rate continued to rise. The Matrimonial Causes Act of 1923 meant that adultery was grounds for divorce for the wife as well as the husband—an important equalisation in moral standards. Official upper-class morality was shifting too. Divorcées were becoming respectable. The notion of what was sexually acceptable had changed. Subjects like lesbianism and homosexuality which had previously been taboo were openly discussed among the young middle-class intelligentsia.

Moralists deplored these changes. Clergymen complained that new dances like the shimmy made the morals of a pig-sty respectable by comparison. Many older feminists must have wondered at the ease with which young women who could not remember the pre-war era seemed to take to a style of sexual emancipation which would have been inconceivable to the earnest progressives of the early 1900s.

186   Hutchinson, *This Freedom*, p 298.

But in fact the sexual liberation of the early twenties was extremely superficial. The term 'flapper' was not originally a term of abuse. It was used in a derogatory way by Punch in 1927 but in 1919 when a film appeared called 'Irresistible Flapper', it simply described a tomboyish young woman. A flapper was a 'good brick', a 'daring old thing', who rode pillion on the flapper bracket of a motor-cycle. She was a chum, a comradely, sporting, active asexual girl, quite different from the languishing beguiling vamp.

The young women who shocked their elders, with their no-nonsense approach to sex, were also in fact extremely vulnerable to quite traditional sexual reprisals. A S M Hutchinson satisfies middle class morality in *This Freedom* by killing off Doda, in a backstreet abortion. 'She lay . . . upon the altar of her gods of self, of what is vain, of liberty undisciplined, of restless itch for pleasure.'[187]

The emancipation of female sexuality was restricted by the inadequacy of existing methods of contraception and by the ignorance of the majority of young women about birth control. The 'new freedom' belonged to the middle-class young. It never included older married women, and barely affected working-class girls. There were the usual grumbles of course in the twenties about the younger generation's sexual habits. Working class girls were accused of jumping from boy to boy in order to get more presents from them. The dreariness of cramped living conditions and poverty made love the only escape. The young girl's idea of romance came from the novelettes and new pop songs, her sexual encounters were furtive and brief. Girls and boys with no money for dancing met one another strolling on the streets in the so-called 'monkey parade'. In *The Woman in the Little House*, written in 1922, Leonora Eyles pointed out how the short period of courtship provided the only glimpse of freedom many working class women ever saw.

> 'Girls nowadays are "on the make" where boys are concerned. A girl who has not got a boy has to stay in the miserable home, helping with ironing or washing up, listening to a constant stream of complaints from father and mother, putting up with the noise of the younger children.'[188]

In the 1920s sexual defiance was a style, a fashionable cultural stance, and although it struck horror into the patriarchal soul, it ignored many of the real problems most women had to face. It glossed the surface of things. It was a release for a privileged minority, not a new way of living for the majority. Ray Strachey says in *The Cause* that the sexual revolt was a reaction after the war strain, but believed that the passive doll-like heroine of the old era had gone for ever.

In fact change in the leisure industry meant that cosmetics, cheaper clothes, and the film industry expanded along with the earning power

---

187   *ibid*, p 314.
188   Leonora Eyles, *The Woman in the Little House*, London 1922, p 67.

of young women white-collar workers. Although the depression was to restrict these developments, in the more prosperous South-east the beginnings of a mass market for leisure items was there.

In 1923 they bobbed their hair, in 1926 they had Eton crops. The hairdressers enjoyed a new prosperity. Fashion changed too. Although post-war fashion papers had prophesied that grandmamma's ways were coming back, the transformation in women's clothes was dramatic and made a new wardrobe imperative. From 1924 clothes assumed a tubular shape. They were predominantly beige—it was said the manufacturers were still using up wartime khaki supplies. Skirts became shorter. Silk stockings were introduced in 1924, and expenditure on stockings went up. So did the skirts. Clothes became much lighter and it was easier to move. In 1925 they weighed one-tenth as much as in the mid-Victorian period. This meant women could be more active but going out to work in short skirts and fragile shoes was a problem. Russian boots reaching up to the top of the calf were popular in 1924-5 but they didn't last long among the fashionable middle class because they showed you were a pedestrian. Only the poorer working girls continued to wear them. Short skirts persisted until just after the General Strike when fringes and frills appeared and in 1928 the hem-line started to come down.

Although these changes meant that women were much physically freer than the Victorian women, weighed down with long, heavy skirts, other fashion changes proved less liberating. Cosmetics were no longer applied secretly. In the 1920s they were meant to show. It was as if women were being forced to make their own mask to face the strange new masculine world they were invading. Britain followed America in the manufacture of beauty. The beauty-makers, often women, were evangelical. Every woman, no matter how plain, could emulate the heroines of the screen. The image of feminity was projected back to millions of women, and served the interests of capital well. Not only were profits made directly in the film and cosmetics industry, but glamour became accessible on the market, disguising the economic and sexual misery which lurked behind the millions spent and the weariness and frustration which continued in the real world outside the picture palace.

Despite its superficiality and escapism the post-war sexual rebellion still contained a very real antagonism to the traditional role of Victorian women. By the end of the twenties there was a restraint even upon this limited revolt. In the popular songs of the time Sister Susie and Hardhearted Hannah wound up in 'The Little White House in Honeymoon Lane' with butterflies flirting round the kitchen curtains. 'Glad Rag Doll' was 'just a girl that men forgot'. If she refused to learn her place, she would end up as 'The Lonesomest Girl in Town'. She would never share Gene Austin's 'Blue Heaven' where 'Molly and me and the baby makes three'. By 1930 when Noel Coward was writing about his 'model maid' in 'The Island of Ballumazoo', 'the ladies' had become 'dusky, domestic and fair'. They did not care for the suffragette movement. Indeed 'they'd think "Votes for Women" were something to wear'.

The cultural attitudes of the twenties and thirties were remote from those of the Victorian era. It was not so much a reaction; it was rather that anti-feminism took on new social and cultural forms. Instead of political opposition to feminism as a movement, the new defenders of patriarchy told women that their sexual needs could only be met by a man who humiliated them. The cult of the 'Mean Man' proved remarkably resilient, and used as its stalking horse the rhetoric of sexual liberation.

In 1926 W L George published *Gifts of Sheba*. Hallam, the hero, murders the feminist heroine's invalid husband and arouses her interest because he is forbidden and repellent. Hallam looks at her contentedly in the last chapter. 'By jove, life has made something of her. Taken the sociology out of her, smashed up a few of her ideas and made her what she ought to be—a woman to be enjoyed by the connoisseur.' The Hallam-type hero always presented himself as doing women an inestimable favour. Women were told that feminism had made them unhappy, intellectual and frustrated. The 'Mean Man'. brought sexual satisfaction —but at the price of submission. Hallam tells Isabel,

> 'You're a modern woman. You can't love properly as the beasts do, and they're the only creatures that know. You can't live with strong men, because you're damned if you're going to be ruled; and you can't live with weak men because you're damned if you're going to be bothered to manage them. . . . The only kind of man the modern woman can live with is the kind that doesn't care a damn for them.'[189]

While Isabel falls into his arms, Hallam yawns his indifference to her.

Writing in the early 1930s, the liberal feminist Winifred Holtby said, 'cropped hair and serviceable shoes is waging a defensive war against this powerful movement to reclothe the female form in swathing trails and frills and flounces to emphasise the difference between men and women'.[190]

She observed some of the developments Betty Friedan noted later in the US in the fifties. Baby-faced blonde film stars established a new image of beauty. In intellectual circles there was a reaction against liberal rationality which was the ideological basis of middle class feminism. The feminists were powerless to deal with Lawrentian emotion and 'natural' women.

At a much more sinister level fascism too played on feelings which

189 W L George, *Gifts of Sheba*, quoted in Robert Graves and Alan Hodge, *The Long Weekend*, Penguin, 1971, p 124.
190 Winifred Holtby, *Women in a Changing Civilisation*, London 1934, p 119.

had been hidden by reasonable liberal men. In Germany a book by Otto Weininger was frequently republished declaring the emancipation of women to be a Jewish plot. The Nazis made a big fuss about women being in their proper sphere, though the demands of their war economy tended to undermine the return to the kitchen. In *The Greater Britain* Mosley wrote in 1932 in the section on 'Women's Work', 'The part of women in our future organisation will be important, but different than that of men, we want men who are men and women who are women.'[191]

This 'equal but different' argument was to filter imperceptibly into other political circles later. The emphasis in Hitler's Germany on women's place being at home received a favourable reception among some British industrialists. In autumn 1933, for instance, Sir Herbert Austin quoted Hitler's example and said he would like to turn all women out of his employment.

These ideas were extreme, but were a manifestation of the much more general shift in attitudes and ideas as the earlier feminist consciousness was steadily eroded in the inter-war years. It was a part of, and inseparable from, the general decline of a revolutionary working-class awareness.

191   Quoted in Holtby, *Women in a Changing Civilisation*, p 161.

19

Work, Trade Unions and the Unemployed after World War 1

Despite male antagonism the capitalist economy continued to need women's labour power, especially in Britain, because there was no alternative supply of cheap, unskilled, non-unionised workers. The employers were facing increasing international competition and were seeking to reduce wages and 'rationalise' production by whatever methods they could use. In the Midlands and South-East where new industries, light engineering and chemicals, were developing there was an increase in the female labour force. The old divisions between craftsmen and labourers were being broken down. Skilled turners and fitters were being replaced by semi-skilled assembly workers who were quite often women. A similar process was taking place in the trades where women were traditionally employed. For example in clothing the employers introduced a conveyor belt system, which transported the partially made garments round the workshop. The management adjusted the speed of the belt and tried to make the rhythm of work faster. Ironically productivity did not increase in the clothing trade, though the workers felt they were working harder and bitterly resented the belt. In 1933 the Labour Research Department produced a report on Wages and Profits in the Clothing Trade which stated,

> 'The employers are attempting to get a large supply of cheap labour, women who will be forced into the industry at 12s per week by the possible threat of losing their labour exchange benefit, which will result in throwing many skilled workers now in the factories out of work.'[192]

The twenties saw the emergence of the office girl. Earnings were low and class difference was perpetuated in the stratification between 'secretary' and general typists. The lower-class girls inherited the saucy image of the shop girls and servants who had provided light entertain-

192 Quoted in Shirley W Lerner, *Breakaway Unions and the Small Trade Union*, London 1961, pp 95-96.

ment for upper-class respectable men. The typists were not the girls one married. Even this limited economic and sexual independence, however, affected the outlook of girls who went into offices. Arnold Bennett wrote of 'Salary-Earning Girls' in 1920 that they had become 'money grubbers' and valued their new economic bargaining power.[193]

The reality of office work was more mundane. Young girls who had managed to learn shorthand and typing travelled into London and other large cities from the suburbs. The early workmen's train was cheap but left them with an hour to spend with a cup of tea and a bun. Relations with the 'chief' were generally remote. He was an austere figure who rarely spoke personally to the typists and clerks even when he dictated a letter. The offices still tended to be mainly small, the typing pool only a handful of girls. The girls faced considerable antagonism from male clerks, afraid for their jobs. Girls employed in offices and banks were expected to be grateful for work which was more genteel than shop or factory work.

As unemployment mounted, resistance or unionisation became impossible. The typists and clerks who were kept on knew they were the lucky ones. Outside was the abyss of poverty and unrespectability. In the thirties typists sat all day with blank paper in their typewriters, simulating a clack-clack of activity when the 'chief' emerged, furtively reading magazines in the desk drawer where they kept forbidden sandwiches. Coffee breaks were rare privileges. There was lunch at Lyons, or perhaps in a special part of a restaurant which did cheap lunches for women only. Married women were only occasionally allowed to stay on. The office workers faced spinsterhood, or the loss of their wage packets on marriage.

'Rationalisation', wage cuts, the substitution of women for men, speed up and the reduction in the power of trade unions through unemployment meant that there were objective reasons for antagonism between men and women workers. Women were obvious scapegoats. There was a widespread belief that the employment of women had actually caused unemployment. Because the slump weakened the bargaining power of all workers, the question of equal pay was postponed indefinitely. Government Commissions paid lip service to it, the House of Commons received resolutions on it. But its realisation was no nearer in the 1930s than it had been in 1914.

In November 1933 there was a big meeting in Central Hall, Westminster, which 'echoed, faintly but unmistakably, the spirit of pre-war suffrage meetings'.[194] This was followed by an Equal Pay for Equal Work meeting in March 1934. But 1933 was the year when unemployment was at its height.

193 Arnold Bennett, *Our Women*, London 1920, pp 124-147.
194 Holtby, *Women in a Changing Civilisation*, p 113.

The slump came after a long period of defensive strikes, in which the working class was forced into retreat. The defeat of the General Strike in 1926 and the lock-out which followed it in the mining industry had also contributed to the demoralisation which was to become a feature of the depression and reduced the possibility of extending or even holding the gains of the immediate post-war era.

Women began to re-enter domestic service again from about 1921 onwards because they could not find other work. The numbers of women in domestic service between 1921 and 1931 actually went up by 200,000. In some areas in the thirties, men too, in desperation, tried to become servants again. However it was a reluctant return and the result of harsh necessity. The hatred of domestic service which made some girls prefer even factory work was not merely an affair of the hard work and low pay because these factors applied to both types of job. Young girls resented very bitterly the lack of freedom and the employers' supervision of their morals. Margaret Powell in her autobiography *Below Stairs* tells how her friend told her to pretend she worked in a factory, since young men had no time for servant girls because they had so little time off.

The attitude of trade unions to women workers was still ambiguous. The women who were inside trade unions faced the same problems as the women had earlier. But the whole tendency in the 1920s was towards the amalgamation of small unions and the women's trade unions joined the larger unions with men. The big unions were much stronger and could pay out strike money. The small unions, friendly societies, women's trade unions or left political unions tended to disintegrate when they had a strike on their hands. The women's trade unions had had an important educational role, but were not able to defend their members on strike. On the other hand, the big unions tended to be both male dominated and bureaucratic. Barbara Drake in *Women in Trade Unions* in 1921 repeated the warnings and suggestions of the women's organisations' Report in World War I, of the danger of the women being controlled by the men. She pointed out that this was not solved by an all women branch because this too could be controlled by men. For this reason she recommended women's advisory councils in trade unions. The council's job was to help women members with their special problems and encourage them to take part in union business. But the council could only be really effective though when the women were conscious of discrimination. It could not solve the problems of women in trade unions for, without continuous pressure from the rank and file, the women's advisory council became a meaningless token.

It was still difficult to keep women involved on a sustained basis. Women would act in exceptional circumstances but they tended to expect rather more of unions than the men. During the General Strike, for example, many women in a printing works in Harrow joined the union while there was picketing for the miners. The activity 'made our trade unionism real to us'. The disillusionment felt with the decision to return to work and leave the miners isolated was particularly acute among women.

> 'When the strike was called off, there was bewilderment and indignation. Where was the sense?' they asked. The position was simple to the girls. We were fighting the bosses. Things were going well: we ought to keep on and win. And there was victimisation. Was trade unionism really a fraud after all.'

In fact in this case they were persuaded that, 'Trade unionism has not failed, only the leaders were afraid to use the strength we put in their hands'.[195]

However the women were still capable of spontaneous eruption and of heroic defiance which made their struggles go far beyond economic issues. For example in 1928 young women workers took on their employers, Rego Clothiers, although it officially meant breaking the existing union agreement. The girls were aged between 16 and 21 and their spirit began to influence the whole community. They had not only union branches but shop keepers and the general public behind them along with Edmonton Labour Party and Urban District Council. Even Ramsay Macdonald sent £1 donation. They were given the Co-op Cinema for a mass meeting, the National Unemployed Workers Movement Band played for them. After picketing hundreds of girls flocked to Edmonton Town Hall where they sang and heard speeches. When the London Committee extended the strike to Rego's eighty retail shops, the girls paraded through the city singing songs and carrying banners with their strike slogan, 'Stick it'. The dockers and transport workers helped them when they arrived at bus depots and the docks. Finally defeated after a long struggle, the Rego girls had shown again that women were not unable to act and organise for themselves at work.

However, the difficulties remained. The whole conditioning of women made it difficult for them to participate in union organisation. They had to confront not only the bureaucratic apparatus of the union structure which was dominated by men, but also blatant prejudice.

There were not only problems of participation when women were in trade unions. The majority of women at work were non-unionised. Arthur Pugh, President of the TUC, estimated in 1926 that out of 5,750,000 women working only about one-sixth were in unions. Beth Turner, writing in *The Communist* in 1927, felt that male trade-union officials were as much to blame as the women. After the war women had been thrust out of many of the jobs they had done in the war, and the much-heralded return to 'normal' had meant only 'cut-throat com-

195   G T, Letter, The Girls Talk It Over, *The Woman Worker*, June 1926, p 3.

petition and ever-increasing exploitation.' The response of the trade unions had been very negative.

'Trade unions in the past have thought to remedy this evil by ignoring it, or by attempting to drive women out of industry altogether. Agreements between unions and employers have been made to ensure that women shall be employed on certain operations only—these operations being invariably the worst paid.'

'There are still trade union leaders, some of whom are regarded as left wingers, who oppose strenuously the principle of equal pay for equal work.'[196]

She showed how so many of the jobs women did were hard to organise. The conditions in domestic service for example made unionisation wellnigh impossible, although there had been repeated attempts. When women were refused unemployment pay it made them ready to accept low wages of £1 and 25s a week. Women were cut off from benefit if they did not accept the first jobs offered to them. Married women were barred from many jobs and were thus in an even weaker position.

The following year in the same journal, Marjorie Pollitt took up a similar theme. She was reviewing *The Woman Worker and the Trade Unions* by Theresa Wolfson. Wolfson argued that in America the failure to recruit women workers was partly caused by a narrow craft outlook in the unions, and ignorance about the real problems of women workers. Marjorie Pollitt observed, 'In England we are equally familiar with the cry of the trade union official that we spent so-and-so in organising women, and if we managed to get them in we couldn't hold them.' She believed that 'if there is persistent and sincere purpose in the organiser',[197] these problems could be overcome.

Marjorie Pollitt was among the women members of the Communist Party who were arrested on charges of sedition during the General Strike. She was fined £50 at Bow Street for publishing 'The Workers Bulletin', a newsletter issued by the Communists. Her fine was paid but she lost her job as a schoolteacher and later was in danger of having her teaching certificate withdrawn. Other women were arrested for 'seditious' speeches or for giving out leaflets to the troops, or for printing leaflets or even for possessing copies of 'The Workers Bulletin'.

During the miners' lock-out there was agitation in the coalfields for relief to be paid to single men and women. A miner's wife sent a description of a demonstration in the Mansfield area against a Mr Fulwood who had gone to see Baldwin to ask if the miners could go back to work for an 8-hour day which the miners were opposing. The

196 Beth Turner, Women in the Labour Market, *The Communist*, November 1927, vol 2, no 10, p 223.
197 Marjorie Pollitt, Review of Theresa Wolfson, The Woman Worker and the Trade Unions, *The Communist*, January 1928, vol 3, no 1, p 115.

women made him a wreath and sent it off to his home. The wreath began to fall to pieces and a young miner mended it with flowers and ferns. They were told that Mr Fulwood was under police protection but they continued on their way to his house.

'The women then sang the "Red Flag", afterwards booing the Fulwoods family, calling out "Baldwin's Pup". They then gave three cheers for A J Cook. The demonstration then started on its return; while on the road home the women were stopped by Mr Sam Garner, the Clipstow miners' union official who told them to mind their own business as they could look after their own affairs constitutionally. Well, they got over him alright and proceeded home after doing a good day's work.'[198]

In South Wales community disapproval of blacklegs or would-be blacklegs took a more extreme form. Miners' wives tarred and feathered men who broke the strike. They also met their share of repression. In Mansfield the miners' wives held a mass picket during the lock-out. One woman who was pregnant

'. . . was dragged a considerable distance along the road by the police. Her boot toes were worn through by friction from the road surface, her knees were badly bruised and bleeding, her arms were terribly bruised and her neck scratched both sides by the fingers of the police. On top of this her face was smacked and she had been punched in the chest.'[199]

The mining communities retained the closeness of a workforce who lived near their work and shared a common experience. When the women took action they had a community solidarity more characteristic of small semi-urban environment than of twentieth century capitalism. In the desperate necessity of the lock-out an extension of this communal feeling was created in the ad hoc schemes of community kitchens which sprang up. Men and women alike worked in these. Scarcity and the threat of starvation thus broke down some of the patterns of work which in normal times were accepted as natural.

In exceptional periods of class conflict many of the divisions between men and women, work and home, industry and community could be overcome. During the General Strike for instance the idea of Councils of Action which would include factory workers and housewives appeared again. But it was in the everyday times that the results of these antagonisms were most destructive, because they weakened the capacity of men and women to connect resistance and move from defending particular interests to a concerted offensive against the whole structure of capitalist society.

It is one of the most bitter and terrible ironies of capitalism that dreadful and soul-destroying as it is to work, it is even worse to be forcibly prevented from labour. The exploited are the lucky ones. The

198 Letter from Mansfield miner's wife, *The Woman Worker*, July 1926 no 4, p 4.
199 *The Woman Worker*, September 1926, p 3.

others are worn out and scrap because they are not even needed to make profits. The organisation of the unemployed was thus imperative as the rate of unemployment mounted after 1920. The unemployed servicemen had banded together after they were demobbed but tended to concentrate on relieving the distress rather than calling on the Government to take action to prevent unemployment. Many of them did not see that unemployment was a political question and a matter of class power.

In October 1920 a demonstration of 40,000 unemployed workers was attacked by the police, trapped in Whitehall and beaten by truncheons. The medals of the ex-heroes provided little protection. This confrontation was the first of many. The unemployed started a 'Go to the Guardians' demonstration, demanding outdoor relief for all people who were out of work. Wal Hannington who was active in the organisation of the unemployed throughout the 1920s and 30s, writes:

> 'We had no inhibitions about constitutionalism or legalism. We had no treasured banking accounts to conserve, and as money was raised by the penny a week contributions of the unemployed it was spent in organising activity. We were desperate in our poverty and in the hopeless prospect of employment and we used desperate methods to call attention to our plight and compel a remedy. On a mass scale we became "disturbers of the peace" and battles with the police became a daily occurrence. We had hundreds of men and women who in their indignation found their voice and became public speakers for our movement.'[200]

The very poor travelled light and had nothing left to lose. Direct action had a more obvious appeal than the constitutionalism of the trade union leadership. People who are no longer useful to capital are after all beyond the constitution. The unemployed occupied baths, church halls and libraries for their meetings. In Islington the police ejected them from a disused library, so they marched in thousands from all over London on the town hall and were charged by the police on horseback.

The unemployed organisation was pledged to assist workers who came out on strike in every way. But this was not enough to eliminate the suspicion of employed workers and the trade union leadership were always luke warm in their support for the unemployed.

Evidently the women were not much involved in the very early years. In 1922 a letter appeared in the paper *Out of Work* appealing to women to organise. According to one woman writing in the paper, 'We must realise that in the past we have been a mill-stone around the necks of our fellow workers.'

At first the suggestions for involving women were extremely cautious. Women were to help with banner making and look after the children on the marches. However, Lily Webb was elected organiser for the Manchester district and reported that the men had completely

200   Wal Hannington, *Never on our Knees*, London 1967, p 93.

ignored the question of conditions in food centres, clinics and maternity homes. She also revealed that contempt and antagonism existed towards the women. She said, 'I think it will need a great amount of "persuasion" to make the men see that it is essential that women become class-conscious and fully understand the position, so it is up to us to do that "persuading".'

The men were scornful of the women's unfamiliarity with formal committee procedure. They had separate committees and barred the women from joining the men's committees. However all decisions had to be ratified by the men and the women appear to have been in a minority so they were virtually powerless. Lily Webb argued against separate committees, though the women continued to have separate meetings in the morning, but those who could attended the men's committee.

> 'If you disagree with any of my points I am open for criticism, because I am working this entirely on my own and should be glad of good suggestions. If we find that we cannot develop in any way whilst merged into the men's committee it will be necessary to remain affiliated *but* to also have our separate meetings, when we could develop a psychology which would be beneficial to the movement. Men take so long over *their own* committee work that anything peculiar to women is left over. Therefore it is necessary that while assisting the men directly, we launch out on branches of activity where opportunity offers.'[201]

The women's movement of the unemployed thus encountered precisely the same organisational dilemmas as the women in unions. If they were separate from the men they could build up confidence but their capacity for effective action was reduced. If they united with the men their specific problems could often be shelved as not of 'general' importance. The men felt their interest was the general interest and the women's concerns a diversion. Poor mill-stones!

Evidently the women did launch out on their own. London women from Camberwell and Deptford wrote to Sir Alfred Mond about the inadequate supply of milk to expectant mothers, and for equal relief for single women living at home whose parents were expected to support them and who were often forced onto the streets to survive. They were met after much delay by an official who treated them as a joke and said if they got their milk at home they would probably use it to make puddings for the children.

But the women refused just to go home and paraded with children and placards in Whitehall and Fleet Street. Their slogans show they took the government's propaganda seriously. After all the rhetoric about motherhood and the need for a healthy imperial nation, real mothers and children were neglected and ignored. The women were not asking for much. 'You may kill us, but don't kill the babies.' 'In the

201   See *Out of Work*, 1922, nos 29-36.

land of full and plenty the children's stomachs are empty.' 'Milk we need, the child to feed, to make an A1 nation.' 'Homes for heroes. See the conquering heroes come.'

Out of Work added its own slogan, 'All power to working women. Follow Camberwell and Deptford'.[202]

Apparently other London women did organise. In the same year there are reports of activity in Bethnal Green, Eltham, St Pancras, Erith, Lewisham and Stepney. And when militant workers were sacked from a Deptford tin-box works, including their chief steward, Mrs Page, the women's section of the unemployed held meetings, picketed and managed to reorganise the factory again.

The National Unemployed Workers Movement gathered strength in the Depression later and is remembered for the Hunger Marches. However the organisation of the unemployed has a history which goes back much further, and there was obviously a sustained commitment, not only from people like Hannington who achieved national fame, but also from local organisers who are less well known. Lily Webb for instance was still active ten years after she had gone up to become organiser in Manchester. In 1932 while the Irish unemployed fought police and armoured vehicles in Belfast, Scottish, Welsh and English marched to London against the Means Test. There was a separate women's contingent on this march led by Lily Webb and Maud Brown. It assembled in Burnley, Lancashire, for a three weeks' march and included women from all the large industrial northern towns. They arrived in Burton-on-Trent to find there was no accommodation for them except the workhouse. They refused to accept the 'casual' regulations and marched to the centre of the town to protest. They gained a lot of support from working-class people in the town and at 11 o'clock marched back to the workhouse with thousands of supporters. The town worthies were obviously in a quandary. They finally gave way at one in the morning. The women entered the workhouse in triumph 'to the cheers of their supporters, with all the regulations withdrawn'.[203]

Other Hunger Marchers were less successful and the confrontations and attacks from the police, which had been a feature of the earlier movement continued, so too did the coldness of the official trade union leaders and the Labour Party. But very often local trades councils and Labour Party branches ignored their leaders and welcomed and fed the unemployed. It would be wrong to see all working-class women in the 1920s and 1930s as completely crushed by poverty and unemployment. But it is true that the position of women in capitalism made it even harder for them to resist than it was for the men.

202 *Out of Work*, 1922, no 37.
203 Hannington, *Never on our Knees*, p 259.

20

The Family and Sexual Radicalism

Women's role in the family, bearing children and caring for them and the husband meant that working women carried a double load. Married women who worked were exhausted by the time they were thirty.

Leonora Eyles describes how the family restricted women's capacity to unionise.

> 'Many times last year I went to meetings organised by Trade Union officials to ask women to join various unions; these women came in small numbers to the meeting place; sat down on a seat in weariness so profound that no propaganda could get into their heads; and all the time children played about the door calling, "Mum, aren't you coming home? I want my tea" . . . They were utterly worn out.'[204]

Even if women did not work married life when it came was exhausting and monotonous. Leonora Eyles describes the typical working-class diet in the twenties as boiled meat and stewed fruit on Sunday, cold meat on Monday, followed by stew on Tuesday, and a crisis in mid-week, solved by some combination of sausages, corned beef and pickles, or just bread and margarine. Working-class women still spent a large proportion of their life pregnant and nursing and continued to wear uncomfortable cheap corsets long after middle-class women had discarded them altogether.

Treats were rare. For some women their wedding day was the last day they ever dressed up. Women seldom went out, except for shopping. They did not even go into the Lyons tea shops, where shop and office girls met after work. Occasionally women went to the pictures, because they were accessible there and it was possible to keep the children quiet.

204 Leonora Eyles, *Women's Problems of Today*, The Labour Publishing Co, 1926.

In 1922 Cedar Paul in the paper *The Communist* criticised those socialists who considered that housework was not really work in capitalism.

> 'To be "nurse and housewife" as Nature had designed for women—to cook, clean, to scrub and mend, to cook and wash up, to dress children in the morning and put them to bed at night after tending them throughout the livelong day in the sort of "home" capitalist society provides for workers' wives—these things were merely *play* and comprised woman's "true sphere in life".'[205]

Although bad housing affected the whole family, the woman was particularly affected as she did the cleaning. If the man was unemployed, the family income went down and rent was impossible. In the depressed areas the housing was old and poverty cumulative. In London there was acute land shortage and rents were particularly high. In Finsbury, Bethnal Green and Stepney in the early 1930s families who lived on the bottom floor at pavement level dwelt in a perpetual twilight. A survey in 1933 in Bethnal Green, Hackney and Poplar found it was quite common to have five or more people living in one room, and chronicled a grim list of the amenities of slum dwellings, including rats in the basement and bugs upstairs. Hackney had its own special drawbacks, the underground river and reclaimed marsh making it extremely damp. A report in 1930 echoed the complaints of the medical officer of health in 1901 about the area.

The homeless faced either the workhouse, with its poor law tradition of punishing the poor by separating men and women, or the streets. Squatting was the only other way out. But squatting in the eyes of the law, and the class who made the law, was an offence against property and order. In December 1922 for example four homeless families moved into a house which had been empty for a year. The men had come back from the war and found their wives and children destitute. The Recorder pontificated:

> 'You have broken two old statutes. They are old, but they are founded on strict common sense. The rights of property must be respected. Everyone must know it, it is time that they were taught. If I found you were working with persons who were undermining the law of the land, to replace it by direct action, I should have given you considerable terms of imprisonment. I understand you found yourselves under the compulsion of need, and seeing an empty house, you went in. People must be taught that this kind of action is not permissible.'[206]

The Recorder presumably was not familiar with 'the compulsion of need'.

Although labour-saving devices like hoovers and washing machines

205   Cedar Paul, 'Women and Communism', *The Communist*, 11 March 1922, p 6.
206   The Case of Four Homeless Families, *The Workers' Dreadnought*, 2 December 1922, p 2.

were on the market and were being bought in the thirties by middle-class women, the depression meant that the mass market for consumer durables which could potentially reduce housework was not there. It had to wait until the 'affluence' which was based on the wife working as well as the husband.

It was evident that the woman at home *was* in fact working, but housework did not come within the accepted category of 'work'. Writing in *The Communist* in 1922, Peggy Rothwell said she believed there would be revolt, not only among the unemployed, but among 'thousands of unpaid never unemployed—the wives and mothers'.[207]

It was not clear how this potential for revolt was to be organised in the immediate future, though in the long term communist women predicted communal laundries and kitchens, labour-saving devices, holiday and convalescent homes.

During the First World War separation allowances were paid to the women and were important, according to Peggy Rothwell, in giving 'the woman a different idea of the value of her labour in the home.'[208] This kind of argument was to become increasingly common in the 1920s and 1930s because women realised that the feminist case for equal education and equal job opportunity was restricted to the single woman. Marriage and a family meant that working-class women could not benefit from this limited kind of emancipation.

The Women's Co-operative Guild had a strong tradition of defending the interests of the woman at home, having already campaigned for improved maternity conditions during World War I. When the executors of the Prince of Wales Fund decided not to give relief to unmarried mothers because the clergymen on the board thought it would outrage married women, the Women's Co-operative Guild sent an indignant deputation. Their representative, Mrs Layton, said later,

'I explained that I represented the Women's Co-operative Guild, an organisation 30,000 strong, chiefly composed of respectable married women, and that the Guild entirely repudiated the statement that married women would be resentful' (and) 'asked them to remember that every time a woman fell a man fell also.'[209]

However there was a certain amount of controversy in the Guild about whether the economic position of women could be helped most by improving conditions and pay in industry or by extending allowances paid to the woman in the family. If they concentrated on the former they neglected the problems of women at home. But there was the opposite danger of simply reinforcing woman's traditional role by

207 Peggy Rothwell, Mainly about Women, *The Communist*, 4 March 1922, p 6.
208 *ibid*, p 6.
209 Mrs Layton, Memories of Seventy Years, Margaret Llewellyn Davies (ed), *Life as we have known it*, by Co-operative Working Women, London 1931, p 51.

emphasising the importance of the housewife and mother. The same argument appeared again when Eleanor Rathbone pointed out the 'undervaluation of housework' while campaigning for Family Allowances in the 1930s.

This dilemma did not only affect women in Britain but in all the capitalist countries. It was part of a more general strategic problem, that of defending the specific position of women without capitulating to the idea of women as a sex having a separate feminine sphere. Women who were socialists were aware that the different nature of work in the home from work on the cash nexus was responsible for the idea of women as attachments to the men which still persisted in the legal structure of marriage, and also for the assumption that women should be paid less than men in industry. At an international meeting of women from various gradualist socialist organisation, including the British Labour Party and the Women's Co-operative Guild and the ILP in Vienna in July 1931, the Belgian delegate argued that 'misunderstanding' about 'the real value of a woman's work at home in her household' led to disdain for 'women's work'. She said there was very little investigation of housework, but in order to prove to 'working-class women that we do not reject them', it was necessary to 'attribute a professional value to household work'.

'By underlining constantly the fact that the emancipation of woman can be brought about only by paid work, we have excluded from our ranks women who were ready and willing to come to us.'[210]

The confusion of emancipation with work in capitalism was obviously a distorted conception of freedom. But the trouble was that within capitalism the only kind of value which could possibly be put on work which was not directly part of the wage-labour system, was doubly distorted, because work in the family was inseparable from the conditions of exploitation and alienation which were predominant in the social relations of commodity production.

The Belgian delegate had unconsciously echoed ideas which were used to elevate motherhood when unemployment made it necessary to keep women at home. For instance the British Board of Education in 1926 published *The Education of the Adolescent* and made the same points arguing for housecraft to be taught to working-class girls:

'They should also be shown that on efficient care and management of the home depend the health, happiness and prosperity of the nation. Distaste for the work of the home has arisen, in great measure, from the fact that housecraft has not been generally regarded as a skilled occupation for which definite training is essential, and it has too often been practised by those who, through lack of training or through undeveloped intelligence,

210 Fourth International Women's Conference 1931, *Labour and Socialist International, Reports & Proceedings* 1932.

have been incapable of performing it efficiently and of commanding the respect of their fellows.'[211]

Rather than demanding that housework be reduced to a minimum and divided between the sexes, both the Belgian delegate and the English education report considered that if women approached housework with an improved sense of status it would become more meaningful. They missed completely the changes which capitalist production had made in the whole organisation of labour, inside as well as outside the home. They were concerned with changing attitudes not with transforming the structure of capitalist society and the relations between classes and groups within that structure.

There does not seem to have been any socialist feminist attempt to analyse the nature of female production and its effect on the predicament and consciousness of women, though some women in the revolutionary left in the very early twenties were touching on these questions. Nor did many people argue that the distribution of work between the sexes should be changed. Lily Gair Wilkinson's earlier dream of involving men in the household never gained much support. The emphasis was more upon taking women out of the home into production, or upon increasing the welfare allowances for women, rather than on breaking down sex roles in the family. However, Alec Craig in Sex and Revolution did argue that: 'Persons of both sexes would continue to share the burdens of house-keeping and child production, maintenance and education.'[212]

Craig fails to distinguish between housework—much of which is cleaning and washing—and caring for children—which is a relationship between people. He reduces the relationship to a task of mere economic production with emotion and feeling somehow detached from the material needs of the child.

The ideas of Freud and his followers about the importance of the child's early development had an important influence upon English sexual radicals, replacing Havelock Ellis and Edward Carpenter in the post-war era.

The only immediate practical expression of the ideas of sexual reform and change in the family were the progressive schools in which parents participated, like Russell's school on the Hampshire downs, and the Caldecott community which was unusual in including working class parents. While it is true that the progressive schools and particularly the work of A S Neill have done much to alter ideas about children's education, their impact upon the structure of the family has been negligible.

The sexual reformers do not appear to have attempted, as Reich did in his early years, to connect sexual politics to the working-class revolutionary movement, or to understand theoretically the connections

211   *The Education of the Adolescent*, Board of Education, HMSO, 1926.
212   Alec Craig, *Sex and Revolution*, London 1934, p 91.

in society between biology and class exploitation, psychology and dialect-
ical materialism, though there were several attempts by marxists to
understand how Freudianism related to marxism.[213] Christopher
Caudwell in *Studies in a Dying Culture*, published in 1938 had struggled,
apparently in complete intellectual isolation, with questions which were
rarely discussed within the marxism of the period, including questions
of love and sexual relations.

The sexual radicals in Britain were not necessarily feminist. They
were inclined to argue by the thirties that they had gone beyond sex
antagonism and the reluctance of the feminists earlier to discuss sexuality
confirmed them in this view.

Writing in 1925, Dora Russell believed that feminism had neglected
the biological, sexual situation of women in their concern to capture
male strongholds.

> 'We went as far as we dared with an eye to male hostility. Young femin-
> ists today would be the first to admit that it would probably have paid us
> to go further. . . . To me the important task of modern feminism is to
> accept and proclaim sex; to bury for ever the lie that the body is a hind-
> rance to the mind, and sex a necessary evil to be endured for the perpetua-
> tion of our race.'[214]

But such an affirmation of sexuality was remote from the material
conditions of working-class life. Leonora Eyles found that many of the
women she spoke to regarded sex as a chore not a pleasure. She believed
that lack of sex education and old wives tales of storks and parsley beds
were responsible, along with 'nervous debility'[215] caused by bad housing,
poor food and hard work. The men were often as confused as the
women. It was not their unkindness or insensitivity but sheer ignorance
which prevented them from understanding the women's attitudes to sex.
It was the same with contraception. Women were consequently paralysed
with fear about the economic and physical danger of pregnancy. As
remedies Leonora Eyles stressed sex instruction at school, propaganda
against the male idea of sex as the husband's right, and state allowances
for mothers.

Sexual emancipation in the twenties and thirties remained con-
fined to a narrow, privileged section of society. Consequently the conflict
within feminism over sexuality and the biological situation of women
could never be fully thought out, because they found a very limited
practical expression. The struggle for birth control, for instance, as a
necessary first step was still in its early stages. Just as there was no clear
feminist strategy about the problems of women in the family and its
relationship to production, so too the specific female biological situation

213 See for example R Osborn, *Freud and Marx*, London 1937.
214 Dora Russell, *Hypatia*, London 1925, pp 23-25.
215 Eyles, *The Woman in the Little House*, p 133.

still tended to be dismissed by sexual radicals and elevated into anatomic destiny by sexual conservatives. It seemed impossible to distinguish between biology and history, nature and society.

21

Motherhood and the Family

The 1920s saw a fall in the birth rate and declining family size. In the mid-Victorian period the average family had about six or more children. By the 1920s it was more like two. This trend continued in the thirties. In 1933 when unemployment was at its height, the birth rate was at its lowest point. Some contemporaries saw the decline in family size as a feature of the depression. But although people in all social classes were having fewer children it was most marked in the middle and lower middle classes, not in the working class. The agitation for birth control had still not really got through.

The low birth rate produced an 'underpopulation' scare. Behind this was the fear that the middle classes would be swamped by the higher birthrate among the poor and unemployed. The poor were making themselves visible in the national hunger marches which started in 1932. The birth rate panic was part of a more explicit concentration of state repression. There was also the fear that the white races would be over-run by the blacks. Nationalist movements in the British colonies made politicians afraid for the safety of the Empire. In 1935 Neville Chamberlain was muttering about the time when 'The British Empire will be crying out for more citizens of the right breed, and when we in this country shall not be able to supply the demand'.[216] All this gave added force to the back-to-the-kitchenites and the supporters of women's 'natural' role who, Winifred Holtby noted, had the feminists on the defensive in the thirties. They were joined by psychological 'experts' who used the new IQ tests to prove that the national intelligence quota was bound to fall with the birth-controlled breeding habits of the upper classes.

Noreen Branson and Margot Heinemann detect an 'implied

216 Quoted in Noreen Branson and Margot Heinemann, *Britain in the Nineteen Thirties*, London 1971, p 165.

reproach' that young middle-class women did not revert to the child bearing habits of the Victorians,[217] but apart from a small increase in income tax relief nothing practical was done in the thirties to make it easier for women to have more children if they chose. Women were left feeling guilty, without any significant improvements in maternity provision or in child care facilities. In fact although infant mortality declined, maternal mortality did not. In the period 1922-33 it actually grew. Between 1920 and 1930 about 39,000 women died in childbirth in England and Wales. Improvement in the maternal mortality rate did not occur until the early 1940s.

The campaign for better care for mothers during childbirth had been a longstanding concern for the Women's Co-operative Guild. Their publication of accounts by working-class women of pregnancy and childbirth described the conditions of maternity in working-class homes and had helped agitation. It also showed that working-class women before World War I had been desperately improvising their own system of birth control. 'There is a kind of strike against large families.'[218] The Co-operative Guild wanted maternity benefit to be included in the Insurance Act and to be counted as the wife's property. They also wanted welfare clinics in which maternity care would be combined with birth control. The 1919 Maternity and Child Welfare Act provided for advice, treatment and social assistance for pregnant women. But health visitors were not allowed to give advice about contraception.

It was soon apparent that improving maternity conditions alone was not enough. The long term health situation of working-class women affected the maternal death rate. In 1924 Dame Janet Campbell published her report on 'Maternal Mortality' which showed that 3,000 women died every year in childbirth. Many more were permanently injured. Not only could most of these deaths have easily been avoided with better care, but there were obvious connections to poverty. Mothers with larger families were at greater risk—and the poor had larger families.

In times of particular crisis, motherhood was especially dangerous, because the pregnancies of working class women were already hazardous and the margin between survival and acute poverty narrow. During the 1926 lock-out miners' wives suffered terribly. Support came from many women's organisations. The Labour Party women's section set out to find who was pregnant so they could give them extra food. The following application for relief came from Northumberland in August 1926 and describes the predicament of women who had just given birth.

'This is my fifth baby and I am hours awake at night without a wink of sleep waiting for another day so that my mind can be occupied with my

217   ibid, p 166.
218   Quoted in Fryer, *The Birth Controllers*, p 287.

housework and kiddies, as I dare hardly think about this little one. I have nothing for it and cannot get anything. I cannot turn to my own people as they are just pit folks in a sorry plight. I hope you will understand what this means to me, for it is not our fault we are as we are today. . . . The poverty among the miners is pitiful, and we cannot make ends meet when they are working, so how can we do now?'[219]

In the areas affected by the depression later the women's health deteriorated very quickly. They went without food themselves in order to have something to give husbands and children. Dr Andrew Laird, for example, in charge of maternity and child welfare in Newport, reported on new cases of rickets, and diet deficiency in breast-fed babies. The children were increasingly badly shod and clothed. The women were disheartened and 'careless' because of 'out of work conditions'.[220] The final report of the Department Committee on Maternal Mortality and Morbidity was published in 1932, and the Womens Health Enquiry Committee was set up in 1933. Investigation kept campaigners quiet. The results of interviews and surveys of 1250 married women were published as a Pelican book in 1938 written by Margery Spring Rice and called *Working Class Wives* with a foreword by Dame Janet Campbell. Its emphasis was very much on the women's overall health. The list of almost permanent minor ailments spoke eloquently of poverty, bad housing, overcrowding, bad diet and sheer exhaustion. Anaemia was the most common complaint, followed by headaches, constipation, rheumatism, gynaecological troubles, bad teeth, indigestion, and many more. The depression had its psychological effects too. Women said the hopeless struggle against poverty made them 'nervy', an understatement that covered the whole complex of psychological pressure, exhaustion from noise, sexual troubles, the wearying monotony of life on the dole, the humiliation of the means test. Very few of them were working so they had no health insurance.

A woman from Blackburn, aged 35 had six children, of whom the first one had died. She was anaemic, with varicose veins, and described how she hardly ever left her home which was 'damp and dark'. 'Never go to Market or Cinema. Sister used to come and look after the children and let me go out, but has now removed from the town.'[221]

People were forced to accept bad housing because they could not afford anything better. One woman in Battersea, London, had a family of eight and was living in two rooms, sharing a lavatory with sixteen others. The place was leaking and damp. The rent was 7s 6d. She couldn't afford council rents at 19s 7d per week plus 2d for electric light, because when her husband was out of work they only had an income of 33s 3d

219 Quoted in Marion Phillips, *The Miners Lock Out*, London 1927, p 69.
220 Allen Hutt, *The Condition of the Working Classes in Britain*, London 1933, p 43.
221 Margery Spring Rice, *Working Class Wives*, London 1938, p 109.

per week. Bad living conditions made housework an exhausting and continuous routine. She said:

'I expect some people think living in two rooms one didn't have much work to do. I would rather clean a house down than clean my two rooms every day. I had a bed in the back for the two girls, a bed for the boy, which I take down every day and put up at night to make more room. We have our food in this room. I do all my cooking here; in the other room is my bed, a bed I make up for the other little boy on the settee and the pram the baby sleeps in.'[222]

The report advocated increased wages, more communal facilities for children, extension of social services, family allowances, cheap housing at low rents, the extension of maternity and child welfare clinics to cover women's general gynaecological and psychological problems, and better education for girls in housecraft. They might well have gone on to suggest to capitalism that it was time it abolished itself—but they were obviously concerned to be 'reasonable'.

Change was not a result of the smooth progress of enlightenment with regard to the poor and needy. In fact there was much back-tracking. The chances of more nursery facilities being provided were not much further forward in the 1930s than in the 1900s when it had been felt that pre-school education would follow the expansion in elementary and secondary education. The 1918 Fisher Act allowed local authorities to set up nursery schools or classes. But the Maternity and Child Welfare Act the following year transferred responsibility from the Board of Education to the Ministry of Health. In theory this seemed a sensible measure, but in practice it made standards so high that few nurseries qualified for grants and the separation between public and private nurseries grew worse. By 1932 there were only 52 state nursery schools, by 1938 there were 112. These did not begin to solve the problem, and although the Hadow Report in 1933 came out in favour of more nursery facilities, its recommendations remained largely a dead letter.

Family allowances, along with other welfare measures, seemed impossibly utopian despite Eleanor Rathbone's energetic campaign in the late thirties. They were finally introduced in different circumstances as a result of the war. There was opposition to them from the trade-union movement. It was thought that they would be used like the old poor law as an excuse by employers to keep wages down. In fact because of the strength of the working class in the post-war full employment, this was not to prove the case.

Better education for girls in housecraft was an old refrain. Ever since the industrial revolution laments about the domestic ignorance of working class girls had appeared. Liberal feminist proposals for girls' education tended to be limited to middle class academic teaching, or

222 *ibid*, p 129.

simply demanding better industrial training. They did not question the sexual conditioning of girls of all classes.

The assumption in the 1938 report is that the conditions of motherhood can be improved by asking more from the capitalist state—more clinics, better maternity provision, an extension of welfare. The power relations behind the machinery of welfare are obscured. Nor do they see the poverty, suffering and hardship of the pregnant working-class woman, and the oppressive form which child rearing in capitalism assumes, as the result of the sexual division of labour in the family and the organisation of capitalist production as a whole.

In presenting their 'reasonable' demands and in reacting against the dismissal by the feminist movement earlier of motherhood, these liberal and labour women never fundamentally questioned the society they sought to reform.

22

Birth Control, Abortion and Sexual Self-determination

Before World War I some attempts were made to spread birth control information in working-class areas like Southwark, Bermondsey, and Lambeth. In 1913 there were open air meetings at which women came up and gave harrowing accounts of their gynaecological experiences. The Malthusian League prepared a leaflet giving information about the 'safe' period, douching, soluble pessaries, and the mensinga or check pessary, and the use of a plug of cotton wool, vaseline and boric acid powder. In Rotherhithe a group of women kept together throughout the war and in 1920 were still acting as an informal birth control information service for their area.

Marie Stopes had published her rather flowery *Married Love* in 1918. Three years later she opened a clinic in Islington, and Norman Haire followed a few months after with a clinic in South London, in which birth control advice was combined with maternity care and child welfare. Speakers on birth control went out to Women's Co-operative Guild groups and Labour Party women's sections. In 1925-26 clinics were opened in several towns outside London. During the war the relationship between the feminists, the socialists and the birth control movement had become closer. In 1915 Margaret Sanger came to England and met, amongst others, Dr Alice Vickery, still advocating feminism at birth control meetings, Edith How-Martyn, an LSE graduate who had broken with Mrs Pankhurst's WSPU, and Stella Browne. The Fabians had arranged a meeting for Margaret Sanger and she noticed the contrast between the respectable audience in hats, and the little socialist gatherings she had spoken to in America, where mainly working women came.

'I told them what I had been trying to do through the Woman Rebel and explained my private and personal conception of what Feminism should mean; that is, women should first free themselves from biological slavery, which could best be accomplished through birth control.'[223]

223 Sanger, *Autobiography*, p 166.

She met Marie Stopes after this meeting, who was trying to find a publisher for *Married Love*. It was still risky to publish books and pamphlets on birth control because one could be charged with obscenity.

Rose Witcop published Margaret Sanger's *Family Limitation* in 1922 and was charged with producing an obscene work. The prosecution maintained that 'birth control was a danger to the race and against nature's law'.[224] Rose Witcop lost her case but continued to publish *Family Limitation*. She was not prosecuted again but there was some danger of her being deported as an alien. Guy Aldred wanted her to appeal to the High Court against the verdict, but Rose—still a direct actionist—refused.

The case for *Family Limitation* received support from various working-class organisations, and the growing support for birth control in the labour movement during the twenties probably contributed towards making it more difficult to make the obscenity charge stick. Contraception was slowly ceasing to be a forbidden topic—though many women still remained ignorant of how they could prevent pregnancy. The Women's Co-operative Guild which had already defended the rights of the unsupported mother, passed a resolution at their Congress in 1923, urging upon the Ministry of Health and local authorities 'the advisability of information in regard to Birth Control' being given in maternity and child welfare clinics.[225]

The next year the Labour women's conference said the Ministry should allow local health authorities to provide birth control information for those who wanted it and should not withdraw grants from the places where this was done. Again in 1925 they passed a resolution saying that doctors should be allowed to give birth control advice to married people. Unmarried girls were as yet outside the terms of discussion. But the Labour Party conference in the same year rejected their resolution. Within the Labour Party the Catholic lobby kept up a persistent and well-organised resistance.

It was often said that miners' wives were not interested in contraception but when a temporary birth control clinic was set up in the Cannock Chase pit district near Wolverhampton, 140 miners' wives and 28 other women attended. In 1927 Mrs Lawther, a miner's wife from Blaydon, Durham, appealed at the Labour Party conference for support from the miners for birth control in return for the women's solidarity with the miners in the lock-out. She referred to the maternal death rate which was still very high, and said, 'It is four times as dangerous for a woman to bear a child as it is for you to go down a mine'.[226]

224 Aldred, *No Traitor's Gait*, 1963, Vol 3, no 1, p 447.
225 Quoted in Fryer, *The Birth Controllers*, p 286.
226 *ibid*, p 291.

However the women were again outmanoeuvred by the Roman Catholics in the Labour Party.

Other sources of opposition remained. Although some socialists were active in the birth control movement, including Robert and Nancy Graves who gave out contraceptive information to village women in Harlech in 1919 to the scandal of the Graves family, many of the old anti-Malthusianism ideas remained. Guy Aldred organised a tour for Margaret Sanger when she returned to Britain in 1920. In Glasgow she did a midday Sunday meeting on Glasgow Green and an evening meeting in a hall. Margaret Sanger says in her autobiography that the men came partly out of curiosity to hear an American woman, partly out of interest in the subject and also 'to fight the ancient battle of Marx against Malthus'. She maintained,

'Efforts of the English neo-malthusians to introduce birth control to the masses has been hampered not only by the opposition of the upper classes, but more specially by the persistent hostility of the orthodox socialists.'

The women came along too.

'One old-timer said he had been a party member for eleven years, attending Sunday night lectures regularly, but never before had he been able to induce his wife to come; tonight he could not keep her at home. "Look!" he said, in amazement, "The women have crowded the men out of this hall, I never saw so many wives of comrades before".'[227]

When Margaret, in great trepidation, came to speak off the City Road in London, Rose sat in the chair and told her not to be nervous. But when it came to announce the subject 'Birth Control for the Workers', Rose lost her nerve and could only whisper 'Comrades'. Margaret Sanger fortunately managed to recover hers.

The 'hostility of the orthodox socialists' to malthusianism was not without rational foundation. The pre-war eugenicist arguments for population control were not by any means exhausted. While one group of imperial breeders were prepared to support social reform for efficient and healthy motherhood, another group advocated population control for the poor as a solution to social problems. The undesirables could thus be eliminated by sterilisation. Mosley, who was far from being a militant feminist, for instance, was to advocate population control in the 1930s. In *Fascism: 100 Questions* he stressed the need to,

'secure the production of children by the fit. . . . At present birth control is known and practised by the relatively well-off. It is largely unknown and less practised by the very poor. The result is exactly the reverse of the national interest. . . . The unfit will be offered the alternatives of segregation sufficient to prevent the production of unfit children, or voluntary sterilisation.'[228]

227 Sanger, *Autobiography*, pp 267-268.
228 Semmell, *Imperialism and Social Reform*, p 255.

It was, however, as easy for anti-malthusian arguments to provide merely a 'progressive' excuse for anti-feminist prejudice as it was for eugenicist arguments to defend the existing social order.

Stella Browne, who was a member of the birth control movement and of the Communist Party until 1923, when she left because they would not support abortion on demand, fought on both fronts. In 1917, for instance, she accused the Eugenics Education Society of 'class-bias and sex-bias'. She pointed out that they had,

> 'persistently refused to give any help towards extending the knowledge of contraceptives to the exploited classes. Similarly, though the Eugenics Review, the organ of the society, frequently laments the "selfishness" of the refusal of maternity by healthy and educated women of the professional classes, I have yet to learn that it has made any official pronouncement on the English illegitimacy laws or any organised effort towards defending the unmarried.'[229]

Stella Browne's approach to birth control was part of a wider political perspective in which she argued always for the woman's right to choose.

'We women are out to smash compulsory sterility, with its tragedy of bitterness and disease just as much as compulsory maternity.'[230]

She was one of the few socialists who realised that women's control over reproduction and the means of defining and determining female sexuality were as essential as the creation of a society where the material conditions for child bearing and rearing were not oppressive.

'It is for them to choose whether they will have children or not; and if so, how many, at what intervals and with whom.'[231] She therefore advocated not only birth control but abortion on demand.

In 1922 she became involved in a controversy in the paper *The Communist*—the predecessor of the Communist Party paper *The Weekly Worker*. In March the paper produced a two-page spread under the heading 'Communism for Women. Women for Communism'. Stella Browne wrote about the impossibility of making better conditions for women 'under competitive industrialism and the obsolescent debris of a patriarchal family system which is breaking before our eyes under sheer economic stress.'[232]

She lists several conditions for women's liberation.

> 'The freedom to do any work for which she is fitted. . . . Adequate special protection of the child and the child-bearing mother by the community . . . the entire individual responsibility of women in regard to the acceptance or refusal of motherhood, the fundamental human right of the mother to bear life gladly or not at all and of the unborn to be wanted and welcomed. The human right of refusal, as I pointed out in 1915 and

229 Browne, *Women and Birth Control*, p 251.
230 *ibid*, p 254.
231 *ibid*, p 257.
232 *ibid*, p 257.

again in 1917, is a crucial point of Socialist ethics . . . the freedom of sexual
relationships from legal or economic coercion.'[233]

She contrasted the situation of women in the Soviet Union with
their position in Britain. 'Capitalist "morality" prefers baby farming,
infanticide and the systematic blackmail, the moral and physical septi-
caemia of widespread clandestine abortions, performed under ignorance
and filth.'[234]

Cedar Paul wrote more cautiously on the same page arguing that
the existence of contraceptives meant that 'modern intelligent women'
were unlikely to accept the prospect of household and privatised childcare which was their lot in capitalism. She echoed the eugenicist arguments with a feminist twist.

'. . . Unless men and women are wise enough to establish a communist
society, the intelligent modern woman will "birth control" the race out of
existence, or will "birth control" it back to a pre-human level of mentality
(because only half-idiotic women will consent to become mothers). Full
communism will be forced upon the race—unless we prefer the alternative
of race suicide.'[235]

In August another article appeared under the pseudonym of 'Clete',
which maintained that birth control was in the interests of the capitalists,
if they did but realise it. Clete argued that the capitalists had changed
their attitude towards contraception since 'the unemployed have apparently lost the habit of quietly starving . . . and are beginning dimly to be
class-conscious.' The threat of the organised unemployed made the
employers more sympathetic to population control. 'Clete' criticised
Harold Cox (who appeared as a defence witness for Rose Witcop)
for ignoring the rights of fatherhood and referred sneeringly to 'the
wonderful Birth Control Conference'[236] which had taken place that
year.

Stella Browne was quick to take up the challenge. On 19 August
she accused 'Clete' of expressing an 'exclusively masculine point of
view'. She went on to say,

'As Communism is the only explicit political and economic creed which
advocates complete sex equality and sex solidarity, I trust you will allow
me to point out that birth control for women is no less essential than workshop control and determination of the conditions of labour for men. . . .
Birth control is woman's crucial effort at self-determination and at control
of her own person and her own environment.'

The demand for abortion had appeared in the Soviet Union,
Czechoslovakia, Austria and Germany from socialist and working-class

233 F W Stella Browne, The 'Women's Question', *The Communist*, 11 March
     1922, p 7.
234 *ibid*, p 7.
235 Paul, 'Women and Communism', *ibid*, p 7.
236 'Clete', Birth Control, *The Communist*, 5 August 1922, p 2.

women. The fact that contraceptive methods were 'frequently advocated from an anti-socialist point of view, as a palliative and even soporific' did not mean that workers should refuse to study and make use of them. The Malthusian League (renamed the New Generation League) had always shown 'a conspicuous fairness'[237] in allowing her to put the case for the revolutionary acceptance of birth control. Its new constitution accepted as members everyone who believed the knowledge of birth control should be available to all classes, not just Malthusians who believed there were fixed ratios of food supply and population.

A week later another correspondent attacked Stella Browne and defended 'Clete'. S Francis said they should remember they were 'marxians' first and malthusians afterwards, and pointed out that workers' control affected women as well as men. This was true of course but it obscured Stella Browne's attempt to see control over re-production as part of the total human control over nature. S Francis was adamant.

> 'I do think if women were a little more willing to take their share in the fight against present working class conditions and a little less ready to talk about the evils of child-bearing and the domination of men, we should be nearer to that true equality of the sexes only to be attained when we have established true economic freedom.
>
> 'On the subject of sex equality, the majority of my women comrades are as unsound as their capitalist-minded sisters. It is time that some of our sex-obsessed comrades realised that woman's so-called "slavery" to man is solely owing to her economic dependence on him and can only end when the capitalist regime ends.
>
> 'Meanwhile there are other things in life besides the sex act . . . I think personally, that if our comrades in general were to spend less of their energy on that, and more on the teaching of Marxian ethics, the CPGB would be a more efficient section of the Third International.'[238]

The 'sex-obsessed comrades' would appear to have been defeated. Sadly, S Francis's sledge-hammer moralism prevailed and Stella Browne left the Communist Party the following year although she continued campaigning for women's right to abortion. She did not use the argu-ment that abortion was a necessary evil if women were poor or had large families or were ill. She insisted that the decision to terminate a pregnancy was a woman's right. 'Our bodies are our own.'[239] Abortion was an aspect of birth control, and birth control was politically essential to women if they were to determine their own sexuality.

The debate within the Communist Party would appear to have narrowed in scope. For instance when a working-class woman wrote to *The Woman Worker*, birth control is discussed in terms of poverty and hardship.

237 F W Stella Browne, Reply to Clete, *The Communist*, 19 August 1922, p 2.
238 Letter from S Francis, *The Communist*, 26 August 1922, p 6.
239 Quoted in Keith Hindell, Stella Browne and Janet Chance, *The Listener*, 29 June 1972.

'Now comrade, do let us have some information and discussion in the "Women Worker" soon about birth control, for this is one of the most important things to working women—and their menfolk.

'I have had a terrible struggle between ill-health, too many pregnancies and terrible confinements. Five children is too many on wages as they are at present, and have been ever since I can remember . . . between illness and worry and babies, it's no wonder that lots of women get too tired and dull to bother with politics.'[240]

The paper responded to her request with an article which while attacking the capitalist arguments for contraception—'We breed too many lower class humans . . . the unfits who go on the rates . . . Not a word about the unfit conditions which produce the "unfits" '—also, criticised the right-wing opponents of birth control who said it was 'immoral' and 'not religious' and 'we have the Empire to defend'. Birth control was defended on the grounds that it '. . . becomes necessary that working women should limit the number in the family so as to devote time in this struggle'. When women slaved away with larger families, the desire for freedom was 'stifled'.

This was an advance on 'Clete' because abstract anti-Malthusianism was here being forced to confront the situation of working-class women. But Stella Browne's observation that socialists need not neglect the significance of contraception simply because in capitalism supporters of the status quo are prepared to use the knowledge in their own interests, had not really registered. Even more important, her approach to birth control as an essential aspect of female sexual self-determination had disappeared. Birth control had been reduced to a reform which could help women to do more political work in the party. Valuable as this might have been in immediate practical terms for the Communist Party, it subordinated sexual self-determination as a revolutionary principle to a convenient technique for preventing hardship.

The defeat of sexual politics within the revolutionary movement in the twenties and thirties was the cumulative effect of innumerable tiny and apparently obscure battles such as this, in which the prevailing dogmatic orthodoxy dismissed sexual and personal questions and ignored the political significance of the manner in which human beings experienced and expressed their lives in sexual relations. Because sexual pleasure was seen as a diversion, which had to be tolerated in moderation because of some of the comrades' weaknesses, it was easy to dismiss the demand for control over the reproduction of self through sexuality as well as through economic production.

This reduction of the terms of the argument was not only a tragedy which restricted the development of socialist feminism: it was part of and contributed towards the theoretical and practical stunting of revolutionary politics.

240 Too Many Children give Women No Time for Vital Problems, letter from a woman worker, *The Woman Worker*, June 1926, p 4.

The struggle for abortion law reform met with even more opposition than birth control. Stella Browne was a lonely voice in 1917 when she supported it as a second line of defence, though believing that in 'the finer social order for which some of us are fighting', it would become a 'rare', though 'respected individual right'.[241]

In the early 1930s support began to grow for abortion law reform. This was partly because in the course of investigations of the high maternal mortality rate, it became evident that all the deaths were not caused by malnutrition. Apart from the women who died from back-street abortions, others were permanently disabled. In 1934 the Women's Co-operative Guild passed a resolution overwhelmingly in favour of the legalisation of abortion. It was moved by the Blackhorse Branch and seconded by Elmers End:

> 'In view of the persistently high maternal death rate and the evils arising from the illegal practice of abortion, this Congress calls upon the Government to revise the abortion laws of 1861 by bringing them into harmony with modern conditions and ideas, thereby making of abortion a legal operation that can be carried out under the same conditions as any other surgical operation.
> 'It further asks that women now suffering imprisonment for breaking these antiquated laws be amnestied.'

The Offences Against the Person Act made it an offence to use an 'instrument' or 'poison' or 'other noxious thing' on oneself or on any other woman. The punishment was imprisonment with hard labour. It could be penal servitude for life. There were thus two sides to abortion law reform; the sufferings of the women who had back-street abortions, and the legal penalties which meant that doctors were reluctant to terminate pregnancies under adequate medical conditions.

In the 1930s, Janet Chance, the writer of a book which had an important propaganda effect, called *The Cost of English Morals*, formed the Abortion Law Reform Association. The Association was at first only only a handful of women. Stella Browne was an early member. Although most Abortion Law Reformers presented their case in terms of preventing hardship, Stella Browne was still pursuing some of the questions she had argued during and after the war. She did not demand abortion only for women in cases of rape, incest, overcrowding, and poverty, or only for women who were married, but for all women 'without insolent inquisitions nor ruinous financial charges, nor tangles of red tape'.[242]

When the Association reported to a committee set up to investigate the large numbers of women who died every year from illegal abortions, she refused to restrict her case to preventing death alone. She also insisted that abortion could be safe if it was performed under proper conditions and need have no harmful psychological effects. When the

241 Browne, *Women and Birth Control*, p 255.
242 F W Stella Browne and others, *Abortion*, London 1935, p 31.

Commissioners asked her how she knew, she had the courage to say she spoke from her own experience. It was one thing to campaign for anonymous unfortunates and another to identify personally with women's sexual freedom.

At the end of the decade an important legal precedent was established on the question of punishment. In 1938, a surgeon called Aleck Bourne was acquitted on a charge of illegal abortion, establishing that abortion was legal if it was done to preserve a woman's mental or physical health. This legal loophole was to be the means of widening the terms of legal abortion.

Much of the evidence for and against abortion came from the Soviet Union, where abortion had been made legal after the revolution. Stella Browne pointed out that the evidence used against abortion was taken from a Congress of Gynaecologists and Obstetricians in 1927 which dealt with abortion in the Ukraine. These abortions had been carried out in the midst of repeated invasions, uprising, famines, epidemics and in unsterilized conditions by unskilled abortionists, and the conditions necessarily affected the results. She also questioned the social priorities in capitalism which made research into high explosives and poison gases both lucrative and respectable but neglected to develop a self-administered safe abortificient.

This was in 1935. In 1936 the Soviet Union changed the abortion law, improved state benefits for women with large families and aimed to double nursery provision by 1939. The retreat in the Soviet Union on the sexual question presumably weakened the case for socialists who argued for abortion, though the left hand seems to have continued to do what the right hand conveniently failed to notice. One of Harry Pollitt's less publicised activities was fixing abortions for Communist Party women.

The confusion over contraception and abortion which had troubled radicals in the 1820s was still evident a hundred years later. The creation by capitalist society of more effective contraceptive techniques overtook the revolutionary movement. The technical possibility of controlling procreation was not synonymous with the liberation of women. It could, and indeed would, be used in the manipulative Malthusian sense. But defensive suspicion of bourgeois science meant that the left was unable to distinguish between population control in the interests of the bourgeois state and the human self-determination which contraceptives would make possible for women in a socialist society where child-rearing was not an economic relationship between parents and children in which violence was either explicit or disguised as love, but a whole and communal relationship between people.

It was true that contraception like any other invention of bourgeois technology, did not (and does not) automatically imply greater human freedom in capitalism. But it was also true as Stella Browne realised, that the separation of sexual pleasure from procreation, contained a vital political freedom for women in making differentiation between the 'erotic and the reproductive functions'[243] practicable. Only when women were freed from 'that terror of undesired pregnancy'[244] could they begin to enjoy sex freely. But a technical solution to this fear was only the beginning. Beyond the technical lay the great accumulated weight of patriarchal culture.

'There has grown up a masculine mythology suppressing and distorting all the facts of women's sexual and maternal emotions.'[245] This masculine mythology presumed to declare upon women's consciousness of sexuality, pontificating on the female inability to enjoy sex except as a preliminary to motherhood. This had affected women's own ideas of themselves. '. . . for generations women have been discouraged in any independent thought or action in sexual matters; they have been systematically stultified, kept ignorant and dependent.'[246]

Stella Browne dreamed in 1935 of a new society of sexual 'sympathy and candour', 'economic justice' and 'international peace', 'stretching out from the bodies and beds of human lovers. . . .' The dream remains to be realised. . . .

243   Browne, *Women and Birth Control*, p 255.
244   *ibid*, p 256.
245   *ibid*, p 253.
246   Browne, *Abortion*, p 39.

23

Feminism and Socialism after World War 1

In November 1918, Melvina Walker who had worked with Sylvia Pankhurst in the East London Federation of the Suffragettes, went to the first Labour Women's Conference which was organised by the new Labour Party. She went, not because she agreed with the politics of socialism by gradual reforms, but to hear and meet working women

> '. . . who have the same struggle to live as I to live and who like myself have been chloroformed in the past by parsons and pious ladies who tell poor women that if they want better homes they must wait till they get up above for heaven is their home.'

She was jerked back into nostalgia.

> 'Dear old Caxton Hall; how many times during our fight for the vote have we working women stood up in that hall and declared our desire for emancipation. I sat close to the door and watched the groups of women coming in. I could pick out the Cockney women, the women from East and West London, from Wales and Scotland. I saw comrades who had given me hospitality in the Provinces; it really was a reunion.'

The reunion, however, was a painful one, for though she was close to many of these women personally, politically she was estranged from the great figures who appeared on the platform. She was especially scornful of Beatrice Webb and explained the reformist politics of the Labour Party as a monstrous trick. The educated middle-class people had captured the workers' party. Melvina Walker agreed with a tramwayman's wife who said that more working-class women should speak: '. . . if I was in the chair I wouldn't be guided by no-one but myself, and I wouldn't want to hear so much of the platform but more of the rank and file'.

Melvina Walker felt the middle-class educated women were divided from working women not only by their class but by their dismissal of the need to improve the conditions of women who were mothers. But she still felt the working-class women might take back the leadership of the women's section of the party.

'. . . keep your eyes open', she told them. '. . . organise yourselves, don't be led away by people with "superior brains", we have something more than that; we have practical experience.'[247]

She was still wondering whether these women would support the liberals and conservatives, or set up a socialist state 'like that in Russia'.[248] These seemed to her the only alternatives. It did not occur to her that working-class women in the Labour Party might choose neither.

The war had made the split between the revolutionary socialists, and the right-wing feminists who had supported war, irreparable. Mrs Pankhurst settled into conservatism and was clearly politically on the other side. The *Workers' Dreadnought* had nothing but denunciations for the right-wing 'Women's Party' which was pro-Tory and pro-imperialist. Although women still did not have the vote on equal terms with men, the limited measure of 1918 served to make a single-issue campaign no longer possible. This broke up whatever unity had existed before 1914. It shifted the arguments towards other demands. After World War I several strands of the pre-war feminist movement were also concerned to connect the liberation of women to radical social change. Graves for instance says it was common to hear the phrase 'Feminism is not enough'. The *Workers' Dreadnought* announced themselves as unable 'to assent to the old-fashioned suffragist standpoint that the political activities of women must begin and end with two subjects, Votes for Women and venereal diseases'.[249]

Sylvia Pankhurst and the *Dreadnought* assumed that feminism would simply become part of the revolutionary movement, though this was to be complicated by her dispute with Lenin and with the Communist Party over the relationship to parliament. Sylvia Pankhurst does not seem to have contemplated the possibility of feminism being overpowered and subsumed within a male-dominated revolutionary movement.

There were presumably other feminists who like Rose Witcop and Stella Browne became involved in the birth control movement. Here the opposite problem applied. Impatience with the anarchist and communist movements' lack of interest in birth control could lead to a concentration on this issue above all others, which excluded the connections between control over reproduction and production.

The dilemmas of the pre-war period had not really been solved. The problem particularly of how to struggle against capitalism, within

---

247   Melvina Walker, 'My Impressions of the Women's Conference', *Workers' Dreadnought*, 2 November 1918.
248   *ibid.*
249   *The Workers' Dreadnought*, 2 November 1918.

capitalist society, without losing the total vision of what one opposed, still created confusion among socialist feminists.

It was easy to dissociate socialist feminism from conservatives like Mrs Pankhurst and Christabel. But it was less easy to decide how to relate to Labour women who were still in the tradition of the Second International and social democracy. The Labour Party, despite Melvina Walker's objections to its platform, was after all capable of calling a conference of working-class women to campaign on issues which had the support of socialist feminists. Also many feminists were turning towards the new party which was still making what appear now as startlingly radical pronouncements.

In all fairness too, to the middle-class women in the Labour Party, Melvina Walker's criticisms were not all well founded. The women who contributed to a book called *Women and the Labour Party* edited by Marion Phillips in 1918, did include proposals for improved maternity conditions, higher benefits, better status for midwives, and changes in the position of the unmarried mother. Margaret McMillan on 'The Nursery of Tomorrow' was in fact rosily optimistic, predicting that it would soon become law that every mother should have a nursery for her children.[250]

Furthermore, women like Margaret and Rachel McMillan, Margaret Llewelyn Davies, Katherine Bruce Glasier, had served their time. They had not been sprung upon the Labour Party Women's Section but had been battling away for a long time, about education, nurseries, in the Co-op Guild and the ILP. The problem with their political approach, which had an important effect and absorbed a sizeable strand of the feminist movement, was not that they imposed themselves as a leadership on Labour working-class women, but that the previous experience of both middle-class and working-class women in the ILP and the Labour Party meant that many Fabian arguments seemed quite reasonable to them. Because they saw socialism as an accretion of reforms, and the state as a neutral force which would pass to the working class when they became sufficiently enlightened, they also assumed that improvement in the position of women would come in the same way. Nor was their achievement, in their own terms, negligible. They did use the vote to change the laws; they even, despite the economic conditions of the 1920s and 1930s, accomplished some welfare reforms. But in the process certain qualities of the earlier international feminist movement were lost.

Melvina Walker's suspicions were curiously accurate in the long term, though the charges she made would not have stuck in 1918. When there was in some sense a feminist movement, the struggle for better housing, or pit-head baths, was still part of a wider criticism of the whole position of women in capitalism and expressed the capacity and

250 See Phillips (ed), *Women and the Labour Party*.

power of working class women to break out of the conditioning, or 'chloroforming' which made them doubt themselves both as working class and as women. This consciousness, linked, however imperfectly, different aspects of women's struggles.

However, as the divisions between the women's organisations remained, and as the demarcation lines between gradualist and revolutionary socialists became clearer, the tendency to dissociate from the nostalgic remnants of feminism became stronger, and equally it was easy to slip from a constitutionalism which still stressed the expression of the rank-and-file's ability, to a constitutionalism which defined itself as bringing socialism to a passive and unworthy electorate.

A parallel process can be observed in feminism. The women in the thirties who continued to campaign were not only isolated from the younger generation; they contributed to the erosion of the pre-war feminist consciousness, which, however confused, had still extended uncontrollably beyond the reform of the Vote into an attack on male-dominated culture as a whole.

Out of the confusion they emerged reasonable and liberal, but confining feminism to a series of isolated goals. Feminism meant more reforms, more welfare, equal pay. It did not mean any longer a rejection of a man-made way of living and a man-made way of seeing. It was no longer in opposition to the structure and culture of capitalist male-dominated society.

The early vision may have been partial and utopian, but it had been there. The feminists of the 1930s lost the earlier emphasis on sisterhood, on women doing things for themselves collectively, on the East London Federation's attempts to make a grass-roots organisation. The feminists, like the Labour men and women, were let into parliament and put on committees. Once inside the constitution, they forgot that they had sought admission because they believed the world should be made anew. They became weighed down with the traditional responsibility of the ruling class, keeping things as they are. The liberal feminists, like the Labour people, came to define success as the recognition and approval by the power structure they had opposed. They measured the progress of women in the rise of a minority to competence and the bestowal of honours upon a few.

It is true that objective circumstances were against them. But in narrowing the feminist vision they paralysed their own capacity to fight the new problems capitalism was creating. Reasonable, constitutional, liberal feminism was, like the women in the Labour Party, incapable of understanding the changes in the structure of women's work, the embryonic market of household consumer durables and the cosmetics industry, the duality in welfare which meant every reform came as part of the consolidation and growth of the bourgeois male-dominated state and could be contained within a structure women could not control. They had no political weapons with which they could counter 'The Gifts of Sheba', or even those passionate natural women whom Lawrence moulded out of his fears of feminism. They were wary of thinking in terms of defining their own sexuality, because of their dismissal of sex. They were also too suspicious of working-class men to understand the contradictory pull of class and sex antagonism for working class women. In the 1930s some feminists opposed all industrial protection for women—on the grounds that this was responsible for discrimination. This ignored the position of women in the family and exposed women workers to greater exploitation.

They observed their isolation from younger women and thought they could overcome it by instructing them about their achievements. As Ray Strachey wrote in the introduction to *Our Freedom and its Results* in 1936: 'Modern young women know amazingly little of what life was like before the war, and show a strong hostility to the word "feminism" and all which they imagine it to connote.'

These young women had been taught to despise their own movement by a culture which was anti-feminist. But this was not the whole of it. They inherited a feminism which had lost its glory, and forgotten its power, and thus saw little that could capture their feelings.

The concerns of the older women did not express their predicament. Feminism was a sentimental attachment of older women. 'The women's movement, to them, is out of scale, it bulks larger than its own consequences.'[251]

In the context of the hunger marches, Spain, and anti-fascism young women who inclined towards radicalism had more pressing political choices. They were likely to be dismissive of feminism, because they only knew it as a limited movement and because they felt they no longer needed to be feminists. The women in left political organisations, including the Labour Party, could feel that they worked as individuals and that a specific consciousness as women was a kind of indulgence.

But there were many women who were not touched by either left politics or the remains of the feminist movement. In the 1920s and 1930s masculine complaints about the innate conservatism of women missed the reasons for political passivity. Women's political responses to trade unions and left organisations were not mysterious. On the contrary, they were intelligible in the context of most women's social situation, the home and the nature of female production in the family. They were bound up with the cultural conditioning girls received from childhood, and with the sexual position of women which few left-wing men bothered to either consider or seek to change.

251 Strachey (ed), *Our Freedom and its Results*, pp 9-10.

Nor was the women's indifference unconnected to the indifference of male-dominated organisations to women. Dora Russell's comments on the conservatism of women in the twenties are instructive. She believed that the popular assumption that the 'flappers' were indifferent to left politics and that women did nothing with their vote but support the right-wing was 'insidious propaganda'. She claimed that in fact large numbers of working-class women worked for the Labour Party, and were being joined by 'many of the middle class women who were young enough to be revolted by war politics in 1914'. She pointed out that the Labour Party only produced women candidates in constituencies where Labour hadn't a chance of winning and then people said it showed women wouldn't vote for a woman. In fact, 'had the Labour Party machine been less dominated by masculine perspective', she thought they would not have lost so heavily in 1924.[252]

It would be naive to assume that the masculine perspective was dominant only in the Labour Party—and that other left organisations were immune. Instead of assuming that women were somehow naturally conservative it is more probable that the majority of women could find no focus for their discontent as a sex and so they became apathetic about a notion of politics which did not include them.

By the 1930s, the connection between feminism and revolutionary socialism had become very tenuous. The connections of the past were remote and obscure. Socialists today are apt to be complacent about this divorce. The crimes of bourgeois feminism are seen as an inevitable expression of the class interests of the middle-class suffragettes. This assumes that the course of the feminist movement was completely determined and that the response of socialists at the time had no influence—as if the socialists remained completely impervious to the anti-feminism which prevailed in capitalist society.

A feminist consciousness was still very strong internationally after the First World War, and the need to involve women in revolutionary politics was consequently seriously recognised in the communist movement.

With the collapse of the Second International, war and the outbreak of the Russian revolution, the initiative passed from German Social Democracy to the Russian Communist Party. The Comintern, following Lenin, was committed to special work among women, through special organs of the party, but opposed to the separate organisation of women in the party. However some communists were opposed on principle even to separate work with women workers. It was argued that the Communist Party gave equality to women so there was no need for any differentiation. But it was apparent in reality that women were in a minority both in the national parties and in trade unions. It was in opposition to these communists that the resolution was put and adopted at the Congress of the Comintern in 1921 on propaganda work among women. This resolution stated there were no 'female' questions in the sense that all women's issues also affected the social position of men. This did not mean that there were not specific female demands. Every section of the Communist International should set up a structure for special work among women.[253]

The implementation of this proved to be complicated. In Britain the women's committee does not appear to have been started until March 1922. Its aims were defined in the newspaper *The Communist*. It was to '(a) devise ways and means of attracting working women to the Communist Party; and (b) to watch out for and, wherever necessary, to seize every opportunity of bringing the Communist Party to the aid of the women workers.'[254]

However, this move was not without controversy. Comrade K Serner complained the women were meeting separately and there had been suggestions of special speakers, sewing and music classes—this took time from general branch work. Minnie Birch replied 'There is no intention to create a separate women's organisation'. The women simply felt a need 'to meet together and discuss how we are going to reach the masses of women outside our movement'. She added that the woman's situation at home and the existence of prostitution meant there were forms of oppression that men did not share. As for the sewing classes, they had succeeded in recruiting two young male comrades. She defended speakers classes for women. 'The small proportion of women speakers in the movement make it necessary to concentrate on the training of women propagandists.'[255]

As for taking time from general branch work, the same could be said of any other group in the Communist Party.

Comrade Serner said, in reply, that she believed women should have special groups in trade unions and in guilds, but the branch should have control over its own members. Women should be branch officers, not hived off in special groups, and they should train more men as well as women speakers.

It is important to remember the context of this debate. It was still the case that many trade unions excluded women, who thus often saw their fight merely as one of gaining entry. They feared that any forms of separate organisation would merely strengthen male prejudice and make it easier to ignore women. But it is clear that merely attending the same branch did not mean that most women were equal to men in the organisation.

253 See Waters, 'Feminism and the Marxist Movement', *International Socialist Review*, October 1972.
254 Should a Woman Tell? *The Communist*, 11 March 1922, p 6.
255 Minnie Birch, *The Communist*, 8 April 1922, p 12.

It is not clear whether this debate about organisation had any relationship politically to the struggle Stella Browne was engaged in at the same time to make a theoretical connection between the orthodox marxist emphasis on the control over the means of production, and the particular needs of women for sexual self-determination. Helen Crawfurd who edited what by July had become 'A Page for Women (which Men can read with advantage)' certainly justified the existence of a separate page for women on the grounds of women's specific oppression.

> 'Some of us believe that the Communist message applies to women in a very peculiar way. Did the average woman realise the real meaning of Communism and the liberation from capitalist and sex domination for which it stands, she would be its most ardent advocate. . . .'
> '. . . While it is true that material conditions determine development, it is perfectly evident to anyone who thinks, that in performing the function of the reproduction of the human species, woman is placed at certain periods in a position of utter dependence, very often in humiliation unspeakable. Have we not, time and again, heard women say when asked why they continued to live with a tyrant: "It was very difficult to leave. I was either going to have a child or was nursing one".'
> 'Communism stands for the economic independence of woman and the right of motherhood to care during pregnancy.'[256]

She emphasises the economic aspect of reproduction like Engels, not the question of sexual pleasure and self-determination like Stella Browne. But she *is* committed to an analysis which recognises that the position of women cannot be simply included within the position of men.

These theoretical questions do not seem to have been pursued in an effort to relate communism to the feminist movement. This was due in part to the decline of a mass feminist consciousness, and to the tendency under Stalin to reduce marxism to the immediate problems of scarcity in the Soviet Union.

As the currents of liberal feminism, sexual liberation, gradual socialism and communism became increasingly divergent, the possibility of making a revolutionary feminist movement faded. In the British context the vision of social transformation which the revolutionaries had carried before and after World War I was forced into defensive retreat. After 1926 there was little enough bread; the roses became no more than a distant memory.

256   Helen Crawfurd, A Page for Women, *The Communist*, 15 July 1922.

Postscript

Endings seem to leave me with endless beginnings. The reasons for the fading of the feminist movement and its re-emergence in women's liberation are not discussed in this book; nor are the changes in capitalist society which have brought a new movement into being.

Although it is apparent that our contemporary concerns are not entirely new, it is clear that their present shape is unique. Also the context of argument has shifted considerably, so that, for instance, the questions of the relationship between control over procreation and control over production and the way in which the liberation of women connects to the liberation of children have appeared more clearly.

Certain contradictions have intensified within capitalist society. The need for women's labour both at home and at work, in the modern capitalist economy, has produced tensions which affect the structure of the family, women's bargaining position at work and the ideas women have of themselves. Similarly, the growth of the welfare state has meant a deeper intrusion of the state into family life. The growth of new media and the importance of advertising in maintaining consumption has meant that the values of capitalist society are penetrating the subterranean realms of our consciousness. Within capitalist society there is a conflict over sexuality and attitudes to sex. The old model of orgasmic thrift and sensual abstinence is being assailed by a new morality of permitted release. Now while this in no sense means that our sexual life is part of a human relationship rather than an exchange of services, it nonetheless contains a threat to certain aspects of patriarchal control.

It is quite possible that the capitalist mode of production will contain all these contradictory changes, indeed that they could actually serve to maintain and strengthen it. The action of people who are opposed to both patriarchy and to the wage labour system will therefore be crucial.

Here we suffer from past failures. There has been no working-class revolution in the advanced capitalist countries. Socialist feminism hangs, suspended and fragile, in half forgotten memories. The wrenching apart of the socialist and the feminist movements which occurred from 1914 onwards has meant that the dominant political emphases in the feminist movement became either to seek admission for an elite of middle-class women into the privileges of the male ruling class or to attempt to reform capitalism gradually on behalf of working-class women.

Since World War II these approaches seemed more reasonable than an abstract plea to connect feminism and revolutionary socialism. It seemed to most people that feminist demands were attainable as part of the inherent progress of capitalist society.

Implicit within the feminist movement before 1914 was a much wider challenge—a challenge to masculine control over women and a vision of transforming relations between the sexes. There was, too, a confidence born of being part of an international movement. But the connection of these emphases to how the working class was to gain control over its own production and reproduction remained unresolved.

Changes in the capitalist economy after World War II appeared to satisfy the demands of the liberal and social-democratic feminists. Some reforms, like the increasing number of women in higher education and in new types of work, the improvements in welfare and the spread of contraception did not come as a result of mass feminist struggle. They arose out of changes in the labour market, in the relationship of the state to the organisation of production and through the population explosion. Ironically enough, the actual feminist movement was organisationally weak and theoretically bankrupt when apparent gains were being made. Instead, single issue pressure groups for equal pay, abortion or homosexual law reform were more effective.

Reforms from above or on behalf of the oppressed can actually serve to rationalise capitalist production. It is much harder to contain people's persistent resistance to conditions of production and cultural definition which separate them from their own sense of themselves. We are involved in a continuing struggle to claim our bodies and our labour power which social relationships of domination have removed from our control.

The revolutionary reawakening in advanced capitalism since 1968 has brought in its wake wider movements which are attacking capitalism in new areas. The emphasis in these has not been upon getting more within capitalism for particular groups, but upon how we can create a society in which all human beings can control every aspect of their life.

Women's liberation is part of this reawakening and a socialist feminism is again possible in the world. Such beginnings though are very fragile and the fortunes of the new feminism will depend on our capacity to relate to the working class and the action of working-class women in transforming women's liberation according to their needs.

Bibliography

This bibliography is merely a list of the books, articles etc cited in the footnotes. For a more general, annotated bibliography see *Women's Liberation and Revolution: A Bibliography Compiled by Sheila Rowbotham*, Falling Wall Press, 79 Richmond Road, Montpelier, Bristol 1972. Place of publication of all items listed is London unless otherwise stated.

Aldred, Guy, *No Traitor's Gait*, Glasgow 1955-56.
Aldred, Guy, *The Religion and Economics of Sex Oppression*, Pamphlets for the Proletarian no 2, 1907.

Banks, J A and Olive, *Feminism and Family Planning in Victorian England*, Liverpool 1964.
Bax, E Belfort, *Essays in Socialism*, 1907.
Bell, Lily, 'Matrons and Maidens', *Labour Leader*, 27 June 1896.
Blease, W Lyon, *The Emancipation of English Women*, 1910.
Birch, Minnie, in *The Communist*, 8 April 1922.
Blatchford, Robert, *Britain for the British*, 1902.
Blatchford, Robert, *My Eighty Years*, 1931.
Bennett, Arnold, *Our Women*, 1920.
Blewitt, Neal, 'The Franchise in the United Kingdom', *Past and Present* no 32, Dec 1965.
Bottomore, T B (ed), *Karl Marx: Early Writings*, 1963.
Bourne, Gladys, *The Women's Trade Union League*, New York 1942.
Branson, Noreen and Heinemann, Margot, *Britain in the Nineteen Thirties*, 1971.
Brittain, Vera, *Lady into Woman*, 1953.
Browne, F W Stella and others, *Abortion*, 1935.
Browne, F W Stella, 'Reply to Clete', *The Communist*, 19 Aug 1922.
Browne, F W Stella, 'Women and Birth Control', in M E and Cedar

Paul (eds), *Population and Birth Control*, New York 1917.

Browne, F W Stella, 'The Women's Question', *The Communist*, 11 March 1922.

Buhle, Mary Jo, 'Women and the Socialist Party 1901-1914, *Radical America*, Madison, Feb 1970.

Carpenter, Edward, *Love's Coming of Age*, 10th ed London 1918.

Carpenter Collection, Sheffield Public Library.

'The Case of Four Homeless Families', *The Workers' Dreadnought*, 2 Dec 1922.

'Clete', 'Birth Control', *The Communist*, 5 Aug 1922.

Cohn, N, *The Pursuit of the Millenium*, 1957.

Collins, Henry and Abramsky, Chimen, *Karl Marx and the British Labour Movement*, 1965.

Conference on the Reorganisation of Industry, Ruskin College 1916.

Craig, Alec, *Sex and Revolution*, 1934.

Crawfurd, Helen, 'A Page for Women', *The Communist*, 15 July 1922.

Dangerfield, George, *The Strange Death of Liberal England*, New York 1961.

Davies, Margaret Llewellyn, *Life as We Have Known It*, 1931.

Delaveny, Emile, *D H Lawrence and Edward Carpenter: A Study in Victorian Transition*, 1971.

Delmont, Sara, 'Fallen Engels', *New Edinburgh Review* no 18, 1972.

Drake, Barbara, *Women in Trade Unions*, 1921.

East London Federation of Suffragettes, *Minutes*, Institute of Social History, Amsterdam.

The Education of the Adolescent, Board of Education, HMSO 1926.

Engels, F, *The Origins of the Family, Private Property and the State*, 1940.

Eyles, Leonora, *The Woman in the Little House*, 1922.

Eyles, Leonora, *Women's Problems of Today*, 1926.

Fishman, William, 'Rudolf Rocker' in *This is Whitechapel*, Whitechapel Art Gallery, 1972.

Fitzgerald, Brian, *Daniel Defoe: A Study in Conflict*, 1954.

Ford, Isabella, *Industrial Women and how to help Them*, nd.

Ford, Isabella, letter to Alf Mattison, 1 Feb. 1918, Alf Mattison's letter book.

Ford, Isabella, *Women and Socialism*, 1904.

Ford, Isabella, *Women as Factory Inspectors and Certifying Surgeons*, Women's Co-operative Guild, 1898.

Fourth International Women's Conference, 1931, *Labour and Socialist International Reports and Proceedings*, 1932.

Francis, S, letter in *The Communist*, 26 Aug 1922.

Fryer, Peter, *The Birth Controllers*, 1965.

Gallacher, William, *Revolt on the Clyde*, 1936.
Gallacher, William, and Campbell, J R *Direct Action*, 1972.
Gardiner, Jean, 'The Structure of Women's Work in the 20th Century', unpublished paper.
Glasier, J Bruce, *The Meaning of Socialism*, 6th impression Leicester 1923.
Godelier, Maurice, 'The Origins of Mythical Thought', *New Left Review* 69, Sept-Oct 1971.
Graves, Robert, *Goodbye to all that*, London 1966.
Graves, Robert, and Hodge, Alan, *The Long Weekend*, 1971.

Hannington, Wal, *Never on our Knees*, 1967.
Harrison, J F C, *Robert Owen and the Owenites in Britain and America*, 1969.
Hewitt, Margaret, *Wives and Mothers in Victorian England*, 1958.
Hill, Christopher, 'Clarissa Harlowe and her Times', in *Puritanism and Revolution*, 1962.
Hill, Christopher, *The World Turned Upside Down*, 1972.
Hindell, Keith, 'Stella Browne and Janet Chance', *The Listener*, 29 June 1972.
Holtby, Winifred, *Women in a Changing Civilisation*, 1934.
Horne, Bob, '1915. The Great Rents Victory', *SM, Scottish Marxist* no 2, winter 1972.
Hutchinson, A S M, *This Freedom*, 1922.
Hutt, Allen, *The Condition of the Working Classes in Britain*, 1933.

Iona, 'The Women's Outlook', *Labour Leader*, 5 June 1908.

Kendall, Walter, *The Revolutionary Movement in Britain: 1900-1921*, 1969.
Kilham, John, *Tennyson and the Princess: Reflections of an Age*, 1958.
Kollontai, Alexandra, *Sexual Relations and the Class Struggle*, Bristol 1972.
Kollontai, Alexandra, *Women Workers Struggle for their Rights*, Bristol 1971.

Laver, James, *The Age of Optimism*, 1966.
Lawrence, F W Pethick, *The Bye Election Policy of the Women's Social and Political Union*, 1908.
Layton, Mrs, 'Memories of Seventy Years', in M L Davies (ed), *Life as We Have Known It*, 1931.
Lerner, Shirley W, *Breakaway Unions and the Small Trade Union*, 1961.
Lewis, I M, *Ecstatic Religion: an Anthropological Study of Spirit Possession and Shamanism*, 1971.

Lloyd, A L, *Folk Song in England*, 1967.

MacArthur, Mary, 'The Women Trade Unionists Point of View', in Marion Phillips (ed), *Women and the Labour Party*, 1918.

Mackay, Charles, *Memoirs of Extraordinary Popular Delusions*, 1852.

McMillan, Margaret, *The Life of Rachel McMillan*, 1927.

Mann, Tom, 'How I became a Socialist', in E J Hobsbawm (ed), *Labour's Turning Point*, 1948.

Mann, Tom, 'Leisure for Workmen's Wives', in *Halfpenny Short Cuts*, 28 June 1890.

Marx, Eleanor, and Aveling, Edward, 'The Woman Question from a Socialist Point of View', *Westminster Review*, 1885.

Marx, Karl, *Capital*, I, Moscow 1959.

Marx, Karl, and Engels, Friedrich, *The German Ideology*, 1965.

Meek, Ronald L (ed), *Marx and Engels on Malthus*, 1953.

Miliband, Ralph, *Parliamentary Socialism*, 1961.

Mitchell, David, *Women on the Warpath*, 1966.

Mitchell, Hannah, *The Hard Way Up*, 1968.

Munby, Lionel M (ed), *The Luddites and other Essays*, 1971.

Neff, Wanda F, *Victorian Working Women*, 1966.

O'Brien, Jo, *Women's Liberation in Labour History*, Spokesman Pamphlet, no 24, Nottingham nd.

Osborn, Reuben, *Freud and Marx*, 1937.

Owen, Robert, *Book of the New Moral World*, 1844.

Pankhurst, Richard, *The Saint-Simonians, Mill and Carlyle*, nd.

Pankhurst, Sylvia, Collection, ELFS, Institute of Social History, Amsterdam.

Pankhurst, E Sylvia, *The Suffragette Movement*, 1931.

Paul, Cedar, 'Women and Communism', *The Communist*, 11 March 1922.

Paul, Maurice Eden and Cedar (eds), *Population and Birth Control, a Symposium*, New York 1917.

Paul, Maurice Eden, 'Eugenics, Birth-Control and Socialism' in M E and C Paul (eds), *Population and Birth Control*, New York 1917.

Paul Maurice Eden, *Socialism and Eugenics*, 1911.

Phillips, Marion, *How to do the Work of the League*, nd.

Phillips, Marion, *The Miners' Lockout*, 1927.

Phillips Marion (ed), *Women and the Labour Party*, 1918.

Pinchbeck, Ivy, *Women Workers and the Industrial Revolution*, 1969.

Pinto, V de Sola and Rodway, A E (eds), *The Common Muse*, 1965.

Pollitt, Marjorie, review of Theresa Wolfson, 'The Woman Worker and the Trade Unions', in *The Communist*, January 1928.

Quessel, Ludwig, 'A Spectre Haunts Europe—the Spectre of the Birth Strike', in M E and C Paul (eds), *Population and Birth Control* New York 1917.

Raeburn, Antonia, 'What Emily Did', *Spare Rib*, July 1972.

Ramelson, Marion, *Petticoat Rebellion*, 1972.

Report of the Standing Joint Committee of Industrial Women's Organisations, *The Position of Women after the War*, 1918.

Rice, Margery Spring, *Working Class Wives*, 1938.

Rocker, Rudolf, *The London Years*, 1956.

Rothwell, Peggy, 'Mainly About Women', *The Communist*, 4 March 1922.

Russell, Dora, *Hypatia, or Women and Knowledge*, 1925.

Samuels, H B 'Women's Rights and the State', *The Social Democrat*, October 1909.

Sanger, Margaret, *An Autobiography*, 1939.

Semmel, Bernard, *Imperialism and Social Reform*, 1960.

Smith, W Anderson, *The Universalist*, 1892.

Snowden, Ethel, *The Woman Socialist*, 1907.

Strachey, Ray (ed), *Our Freedom and its Results*, 1936.

Tawney, R H and Power, Eileen (eds), *Tudor Economic Documents*, II, 1963.

Thomas, Keith, 'The Double Standard', *Journal of the History of Ideas*, XX/2, April 1959.

Thomas, Keith, *Religion and the Decline of Magic*, 1971.

Thomas, Keith, 'Women and the Civil War Sects', *Past and Present* no 13, 1958.

Thompson, Dorothy, *The Early Chartists*, 1971.

Thompson, Dorothy, 'La Presse de la Classe Ouvrière Anglaise', in Jacques Godechot (ed), *La Presse Ouvrière*, Paris 1966.

Thompson, Edward P, *The Making of the English Working Class*, 1963.

Thompson, Edward P, 'The Moral Economy of the English Crowd in the Eighteenth Century', *Past and Present* no 50, Feb 1971.

Thompson, William, *Appeal of one half of the human race, women against the pretensions of the other half, men to retain them in political, and thence in civil and domestic slavery*, 1825.

Tsuzuki, C, 'The Impossibilist Revolt in Britain', in *International Review of Social History*, 1/3, 1956.

Turner, Beth, 'Women in the Labour Market, *The Communist*, Nov 1927

Utter, R P, and Needham, G B, *Pamela's Daughters*, 1937.

Walker, Melvina, 'My Impressions of the Women's Conference', *Workers' Dreadnought*, 2 Nov 1918.

Waters, Alice, 'Feminism and the Marxist Movement', *International Socialist Review*, Oct 1972.

Webb, Sidney and Beatrice, *The History of Trade Unionism*, 1919.

Wilkinson, Lily Gair, *Revolutionary Socialism and the Women's Movement*, SLP c 1910.

Wilkinson, Lily Gair, *Women's Freedom*, Freedom Press c 1914.

Workhouses and Women's Work reprinted from the Church of England Monthly Review, 1858.

Women's Trade Union League, *Quarterly Report and Review*, no 4, 18 January 1892.

Wollstonecraft, Mary, *Vindication*, 1972.

Wolfe, Lilian, 'Lifetime Resistance', *Shrew*, 4/4, 1972.

Bibliographical Postscript

The second edition of *Hidden from History* allows me to add a few titles which I would like to have used in this book, including some which have appeared since its first publication.

Anderson, Michael, *Family Structure in Nineteenth Century Lancashire*, Cambridge 1971.

Beard, Mary R, *Women as Force in History: a Study in Tradition and Realities*, New York 1962 (first ed. 1946).

Davidoff, Leonora, *The Best Circles*, Croom Helm 1973.

Davin, Anna, *Imperialism and the Cult of Motherhood*, Ruskin College Oxford, History Workshop pamphlet 1974.

Foster, John, *Class Struggle and the Industrial Revolution*, London 1974.

Harrison, J F C, *The Early Victorians 1832–51*, London 1973.

Henriques, V R Q, 'Bastardy and the New Poor', *Past and Present*, No. 37 July 1967.

Holcombe, Lee, *Victorian Ladies at Work*, Newton Abbot 1973.

Leeson, R A, *Strike: a Live History*, London 1971.
> Includes several accounts by women trade unionists, such as Isobel Brown, Bessie Dickinson and Sarah Wesker.

Neale, R S, *Working Class Women and Women's Suffrage in Class Ideology*, London 1972.

O'Faolain, Julia and Martines, Lauro, *Not in God's Image*, London 1973.

Pierson, Stanley, 'Edward Carpenter, Prophet of a Socialist Millennium', *Victorian Studies*, XII March 1970.

Pierson, Stanley, *Marxism and the Origins of British Socialism: the Struggle for a New Consciousness*, Cornell University Press 1973.
> Brief description of ideas of Margaret McMillan, Katherine St John Conway, Enid Stacey, Carolyn Martyn and Edward Carpenter.

Pinchbeck, Ivy and Hewitt, Margaret, *Children in English Society*, Vol. 2, *From the Eighteenth Century to the Children's Act 1948*, London 1973.

Raeburn, Antonia, *The Militant Suffragettes*, London 1973.

Rose, Michael E, *The Relief of Poverty 1834–1914*, London 1972.

Rover, Constance, *Women's Suffrage and Party Politics*, London 1973.

Rover, Constance, *Love, Morals and the Feminists*, London 1970.

Schneir, Miriam (ed.), *Feminism: the Essential Historical Writings*, New York 1972.

Thompson, Laurence, *The Enthusiasts: a Biography of Bruce and Katherine Glasier*, London 1971.

Vicinus, Martha (ed.), *Suffer and be Still: Women in the Victorian Age*, Indiana University Press 1972.

Wallis, Lena, *Life and Works of Carolyn Martyn*, London 1895.

Index

About the Author

Sheila Rowbotham is a young social historian and was educated at Oxford. She lectures in history for the Workers' Education Association and is the author of *Women, Resistance and Revolution* and *Woman's Consciousness, Man's World.*

VINTAGE POLITICAL SCIENCE
AND SOCIAL CRITICISM